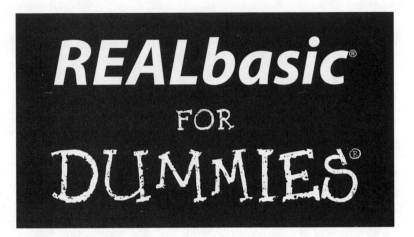

by Erick Tejkowski

Foreword by Geoff Perlman
President, REAL Software, Inc.

Hungry Minds™

HUNGRY MINDS, INC.

New York, NY ◆ Cleveland, OH ◆ Indianapolis, IN

REALbasic® For Dummies®

Published by
Hungry Minds, Inc.
909 Third Avenue
New York, NY 10022
www.hungryminds.com
www.dummies.com

Library of Congress Control Number: 00-108211

ISBN: 0-7645-0793-1

Printed in the United States of America

10 9 8 7 6 5 4 3 2 1

1O/RV/QT/QR/IN

Distributed in the United States by Hungry Minds, Inc.

Distributed by CDG Books Canada Inc. for Canada; by Transworld Publishers Limited in the United Kingdom; by IDG Norge Books for Norway; by IDG Sweden Books for Sweden; by IDG Books Australia Publishing Corporation Pty. Ltd. for Australia and New Zealand; by TransQuest Publishers Pte Ltd. for Singapore, Malaysia, Thailand, Indonesia, and Hong Kong; by Gotop Information Inc. for Taiwan; by ICG Muse, Inc. for Japan; by Intersoft for South Africa; by Eyrolles for France; by International Thomson Publishing for Germany, Austria and Switzerland; by Distribuidora Cuspide for Argentina; by LR International for Brazil; by Galileo Libros for Chile; by Ediciones ZETA S.C.R. Ltda. for Peru; by WS Computer Publishing Corporation, Inc., for the Philippines; by Contemporanea de Ediciones for Venezuela; by Express Computer Distributors for the Caribbean and West Indies; by Micronesia Media Distributor, Inc. for Micronesia; by Chips Computadoras S.A. de C.V. for Mexico; by Editorial Norma de Panama S.A. for Panama; by American Bookshops for Finland.

For general information on Hungry Minds' products and services please contact our Customer Care Department within the U.S. at 800-762-2974, outside the U.S. at 317-572-3993 or fax 317-572-4002.

For sales inquiries and reseller information, including discounts, premium and bulk quantity sales, and foreign-language translations, please contact our Customer Care Department at 800-434-3422, fax 317-572-4002, or write to Hungry Minds, Inc., Attn: Customer Care Department, 10475 Crosspoint Boulevard, Indianapolis, IN 46256.

For information on licensing foreign or domestic rights, please contact our Sub-Rights Customer Care Department at 650-653-7098.

For information on using Hungry Minds' products and services in the classroom or for ordering examination copies, please contact our Educational Sales Department at 800-434-2086 or fax 317-572-4005.

Please contact our Public Relations Department at 212-884-5163 for press review copies or 212-884-5000 for author interviews and other publicity information or fax 212-884-5400.

For authorization to photocopy items for corporate, personal, or educational use, please contact Copyright Clearance Center, 222 Rosewood Drive, Danvers, MA 01923, or fax 978-750-4470.

Hungry Minds™ is a trademark of Hungry Minds, Inc.

About the Author

Erick Tejkowski is an author and programmer from the St. Louis area. When he's not busy with a computer-related project, he and his wife, Lisa, can be found pursuing one of their favorite subjects — linguistics.

You can reach Erick at etejkowski@mac.com.

Dedication

This book is dedicated to the memory of my great-aunt, Agnes Oakes. A Southerner to the bone, her jokes about my Yankee ways will never be forgotten.

Author's Acknowledgments

Books are team projects. I would like to extend my sincerest gratitude to Greg Croy, acquisitions editor; Susan Pink, project editor; and the rest of the Hungry Minds team involved in producing this book.

Special thanks go to my project editor, Susan Pink, who made my journey through the book-writing process painless. Susan offered superb feedback and loads of moral support throughout.

At REAL Software, I want to thank Geoff Perlman, who served as the technical editor. His recommendations and suggestions were invaluable in improving the final manuscript.

A distinguished thank you goes to Steve Wozniak, cofounder of Apple Computer. His technical prowess, humble nature, and dedication to children should be an inspiration to us all.

You can't be a REALbasic programmer without giving a tip of the hat to the REALbasic community. The following people provided me with code examples, assistance, and tips over the past several years: Benjamin Schneider, Colin Faulkingham, Doug Holton, Matthijs van Duin, Michio Ono, James Sentman, James Milne, Matt Neuberg, Joe Huber, and Rodney Dyer. Their friendly help is representative of the REALbasic community as a whole and makes REALbasic all that more enjoyable to use.

Finally, thank you to my family and friends who helped with babysitting, put up with my endless computer chatter, and encouraged me along the way. I am particularly grateful to my wife, Lisa, for her tireless support and boundless patience, and to my daughter, Mercedes. They're the reason I do what I do.

Publisher's Acknowledgments

We're proud of this book; please send us your comments through our Online Registration Form located at www.dummies.com.

Some of the people who helped bring this book to market include the following:

Acquisitions, Editorial, and Media Development

Project Editor: Susan Pink

Acquisitions Editor: Gregory S. Croy

Technical Editor: Geoff Perlman

Permissions Editor: Laura Moss

Senior Permissions Editor:

Media Development Specialist: Jamie Hastings-Smith

Media Development Coordinator: Marisa E. Pearman

Editorial Manager: Constance Carlisle

Media Development Manager: Laura Carpenter

Media Development Supervisor: Richard Graves

Editorial Assistant: Amanda Foxworth

Production

Project Coordinators: Jennifer Bingham, Dale White, Leslie Alvarez

Layout and Graphics: Sean Decker, LeAndra Johnson, Jackie Nicholas, Jacque Schneider, Jeremey Unger

Proofreaders: Angel Perez, Carl Pierce, Nancy Price, Marianne Santy, York Production Services, Inc.

Indexer: York Production Services, Inc.

Special Help
Jean Rogers

General and Administrative

Hungry Minds, Inc.: John Kilcullen, CEO; Bill Barry, President and COO; John Ball, Executive VP, Operations & Administration; John Harris, CFO

Hungry Minds Technology Publishing Group: Richard Swadley, Senior Vice President and Publisher; Mary Bednarek, Vice President and Publisher, Networking and Certification; Walter R. Bruce III, Vice President and Publisher, General User and Design Professional; Joseph Wikert, Vice President and Publisher, Programming; Mary C. Corder, Editorial Director, Branded Technology Editorial; Andy Cummings, Publishing Director, General User and Design Professional; Barry Pruett, Publishing Director, Visual

Hungry Minds Manufacturing: Ivor Parker, Vice President, Manufacturing

Hungry Minds Marketing: John Helmus, Assistant Vice President, Director of Marketing

Hungry Minds Online Management: Brenda McLaughlin, Executive Vice President, Chief Internet Officer

Hungry Minds Production for Branded Press: Debbie Stailey, Production Director

Hungry Minds Sales: Roland Elgey, Senior Vice President, Sales and Marketing; Michael Violano, Vice President, International Sales and Sub Rights

◆

The publisher would like to give special thanks to Patrick J. McGovern, without whom this book would not have been possible.

◆

Contents at a Glance

Cartoons at a Glance

By Rich Tennant

page 293

page 7

page 233

page 43

page 125

Cartoon Information:
Fax: 978-546-7747
E-Mail: richtennant@the5thwave.com
World Wide Web: www.the5thwave.com

Table of Contents

Foreword

●●●

*W*hen Erick told me he was writing a book on REALbasic, I was happy to hear it. I was even happier to hear that it was going to be a *...For Dummies* series book. The title of this series lets you know that this book is going to start from ground zero and work its way up from there. An inviting message to be sure. And that's exactly what you need if you are new to programming and to REALbasic.

With other programming languages, you have much to learn before you see any progress. REALbasic, on the other hand, is perfect for those new to programming. Its visual interface builder and the design of the language make it easy to discover a little and then try it out. You can learn how to develop applications iteratively, building on your knowledge as you go. You will see progress every step of the way.

REALbasic is perfect for experienced programmers as well. With traditional programming languages, quite a bit of the code provides the graphical user interface that makes the program so easy to use. There is also a lot to learn about writing applications for any particular operating system. REALbasic lets you build the graphical user interface visually and takes care of the operating-system-specific stuff for you. This lets you focus on the real problem you are trying to solve. And although new and experienced programmers will save time, REALbasic doesn't sacrifice ease of use for power. You still have access to the operating system APIs and the capability to extend REALbasic with languages such as C++ through REALbasic plugins.

REALbasic For Dummies not only takes you through the basics of programming common to most languages but also teaches you modern object-oriented programming techniques that you can apply to other languages, such as C++ and Java.

Erick is an authority on REALbasic and has been using it from the beginning. He's very active on the REALbasic Network Users Group mailing list, answering other users' questions as well as sharing his valuable insight and knowledge of REALbasic and of programming in general. Erick has also had several of his articles on REALbasic published in *MacTech* magazine. He's also got a small child, so he's used to explaining things to absolute beginners (No, Mercedes. Videocassette recorders don't eat oatmeal.)

Whether you are interested in learning programming out of your own academic interest or have a problem to solve, *REALbasic For Dummies* will help you accomplish your goal faster. You are starting a journey whose destination is limited only by your imagination. There's no better map to help get you going in the right direction than the book you are holding in your hands.

Geoff Perlman

President & CEO

REAL Software, Inc.

geoff@realsoftware.com

Introduction

● ●

Welcome to *REALbasic For Dummies*. This book shows you how to create your very own Macintosh and Windows software, complete with stunning interfaces and sophisticated features. And the best part is that you can do it very quickly and without having to learn a complex computer language.

About This Book

REALbasic For Dummies is a beginner's guide to REALbasic programming for Macintosh and Windows. It takes you through the process of writing computer programs so that you can finally take full advantage of the power that lurks deep within the confines of your computer's circuitry. Why bother waiting for someone else to write software that makes your computer do what you want? You want to control things yourself.

This book will not make you a computing genius, but it will show you how to create fancy software that used to require a rocket scientist to program. You'll be amazed at how quickly you can get up and running. With drag-and-drop ease, you can create beautiful interfaces that rival professional products. Add a few lines of code from the easy-to-read REALbasic language, and you give your interface functionality. In some cases, you don't have to write a single line of code to gain instant functionality.

REALbasic For Dummies covers the basics of REALbasic programming as well as more advanced topics, so it is equally at home with a beginner learning programming as with an IT manager who wants to quickly automate a task. The beauty of REALbasic is that you spend less time fighting with complicated programming languages and arcane operating system requirements, giving you more time to solving the task at hand.

Foolish Assumptions

To begin creating computer software, you need a few essentials. First, you need a Macintosh computer with Mac OS 7.6 or higher installed to build and test your software. The computer should have a minimum of 16MB free RAM, although REALbasic works much better with larger amounts of RAM. If you plan to write software for Windows, you also need a computer with a Windows operating system (Windows 95, 98, NT, or 2000) for testing your completed software.

In addition to having a computer, you should also have a few computer skills under your belt. For starters, you should be comfortable with using a mouse, launching applications, saving files, and restarting your computer. Moreover, you should be familiar with other basic operations such as drag and drop, installing software, and inserting a CD in the computer.

Finally, you need a copy of REALbasic. If you don't have one already, you can install it from the *REALbasic For Dummies* CD that accompanies this book. Although this book is geared towards REALbasic 3, a large portion of the descriptions and examples are equally applicable to REALbasic 2 (and even REALbasic 1).

New to this version of REALbasic is the capability to use it with the Mac OS X operating system. Mac OS X incorporates the new Aqua interface, radically changing the appearance of the Mac OS. The majority of examples in this book retain the Mac OS 9 Platinum appearance. Do not be concerned if your REALbasic interface looks different than the included screenshots. The Mac OS is currently in a state of flux and you happen to be one of the early adopters of Mac OS X. Despite this difference in appearance, REALbasic for Mac OS X works identically to its Mac OS 9 counterpart.

Conventions Used in This Book

This book takes you step-by-step through the process of creating real-world applications with REALbasic. You create interfaces and give them functionality by adding REALbasic code. The code examples sprinkled throughout this book appear in a monospaced font. For example:

```
Window1.Width = 250
```

REALbasic is case insensitive, so you may enter code examples in lowercase, uppercase, or some mixture of both. If you want the examples in the book to match those on your computer screen, follow the mixed case as it appears in each example. The capitalization is there to help make the code easier for you to read.

Occasionally, capitalization does matter. For example, consider the difference between *windows* and *Windows.* The former is a square thing that you drag around your computer screen with the mouse; the latter is the name of an operating system. Distinctions like this are clearly pointed out in the text.

Web site addresses listed in this book also appear in a monospaced font:

```
www.realbasic.com
```

How This Book Is Organized

REALbasic For Dummies is comprised of five main parts. Each part increases in complexity. This is handy for reference purposes. If the topic you need to find is basic, look towards the front of the book. If it's advanced, look towards the back.

Each part is further subdivided into chapters. Most chapters cover a specific topic and provide code examples and a sample project or projects for you to complete. By the end of one of these chapters, you have a functional application that makes use of the topics covered in that chapter.

Part 1, Important REAL Estate: The Lay of the Land

Part I takes you on a tour of the REALbasic application and briefly discusses its features. To get your feet wet, you jump right into creating your first application.

Part II, Understanding the REALbasic Language

In Part II, you get to create cool looking interfaces and add functionality to them using REALbasic code. The code you use in this part gives you a good basis for working in the REALbasic language. In no time, you'll be barking orders at your computer — and the thing will actually respond and carry them out.

Part III, REAL Goodies: Making Your Program Do Something Cool

What good is a computer program without bells and whistles? In Part III, you discover how to add graphics, audio, and movies to your own programs. And if that isn't enough, you also find out how to manipulate files, output information to a printer, use the Internet in your own projects, and even create an arcade game.

Part IV, Getting REAL Fancy with Advanced Topics

Part IV takes you to the level of super programmer. You use databases, AppleScript, and plugins like the pros do, but without all the hassles that the pros endure. The part concludes with a discussion about creating software for Windows and the latest Mac OS, X.

Part V, The Part of Tens

Part V contains timesaving information that you'll find useful in the form of tips, shortcuts, and advice about what to do when things go wrong.

Icons Used in This Book

This icon indicates a useful pointer that you shouldn't pass up.

This icon represents a friendly reminder. It describes a vital point that you should keep in mind while proceeding through a particular section of the chapter.

For the computer geeks out there, this icon signifies that the accompanying explanation might be informative (or, even interesting!), but it is by no means essential to understanding REALbasic programming. Feel free to skip these sections.

This icon alerts you to potential problems you may encounter along the way. Read and heed to avoid loss of life and limb (or maybe just your sanity).

Whenever you see this icon, you can look on the accompanying *REALbasic For Dummies* CD to find valuable source code, plugins, or software. The CD also contains copies of the projects for each chapter, so you don't have to type any code.

Where to Go from Here

It's time to get started programming! If you are nervous about such a daunting task, relax in the knowledge that anyone can program a computer. This book shows you how.

REALbasic comes in two versions: Standard and Professional. If you are using the Standard edition, you will not be able to complete all the examples in this book, particularly those involving databases, Windows, and Carbon compatibility. The remainder of the topics apply to both the Standard and Professional versions.

Part I

Important REAL Estate: The Lay of the Land

The 5th Wave — **By Rich Tennant**

"I'LL BE WITH YOU AS SOON AS I EXECUTE A FEW MORE COMMANDS."

In this part . . .

To get you started in the right direction, Part I begins by introducing you to the REALbasic environment. After you know your way around REALbasic, you're ready to begin making a REALbasic project of your own. In the first project, you create a small but useful Macintosh application of your own. More importantly, you find out about the procedure for creating REALbasic projects, which you can use throughout the book.

Chapter 1

A Brief Tour of the REALbasic Environment

This chapter introduces you to the REALbasic environment and explains the process of creating applications. These skills prepare you for understanding and completing the remainder of the examples and projects in this book.

Those who aren't new to REALbasic might want to skim this chapter. Although you may not discover anything new with regards to using REALbasic, you will find out about the terminology used throughout the book. If you're the impatient type, go ahead to another chapter and reference this chapter whenever you have questions.

To use REALbasic, you follow a sequence of three steps. First, you launch REALbasic. Next, you create a project and write the code for a computer program. Finally, you build an application that anyone can use with any computer. By following these easy steps, you'll be creating your own applications in no time.

Firing Up REALbasic

To begin using REALbasic, launch it by double-clicking the REALbasic icon in the Finder, as shown in Figure 1-1.

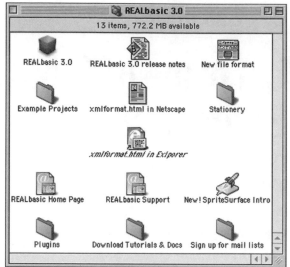

Figure 1-1:
The
REALbasic
icon in the
Finder.

If you're already lost, don't give up. *Opening,* or *running,* an application is what you do each time you begin surfing the web, checking your email, or writing a letter to you grandmother (you do write her, don't you?). REALbasic is an application on your computer just like any other application. The only difference is that REALbasic is an application that lets you create your own applications. So, if you know how to launch any other application, launch REALbasic in a similar manner. Double-click the REALbasic icon and you're ready to go.

After you launch REALbasic, you can follow one of two possible paths:

   ✔ Build a new project.

   ✔ Open an existing project.

Creating a project

By simply launching REALbasic, you're already on the fast track to programming your computer. To begin creating an application, you must first create a project. Upon launching, however, REALbasic automatically provides you with a new project. Believe it or not, that's all there is to it! If you're already working on a project in REALbasic and want to create a new one, choose File⇨New.

A *REALbasic project* is a container for the various items you'll be using to create a completed application. A few of the components you might find in a project include the following:

- ✔ Windows
- ✔ Menus
- ✔ Graphics and sound files
- ✔ AppleScripts

These and other components are located in the appropriately named Project window, described a bit later in this chapter.

Saving a project

After toiling over your REALbasic project, you will undoubtedly want to save your work. Choose File➪Save to save the project. In the event that you forget to save and attempt to close a project, REALbasic asks whether you would like to save the project before sending all your hard work into the great computer unknown.

Opening an existing project

Sometimes, instead of creating a project, you may want to continue working on an existing project. To open an existing project, choose File➪Open. An Open dialog box appears on the screen, so that you may navigate to your project and open it.

If you decide to create a project while working on another project, REALbasic asks you to save the open project before it allows you to create one. REALbasic is always keeping an eye on things for you, so that you don't accidentally close a project before saving all your work.

The Project window

The Project window displays each item in your project. Think of it as your home base. Normally it appears somewhere towards the top of your desktop. Should you lose track of it, however, you can always bring it to the foreground by choosing Window➪Project or by pressing ⌘-0. Figure 1-2 shows a Project window with an assortment of components added to it.

Figure 1-2:
The Project
window
houses
all the
components
in your
project.

All applications begin life as the same type of REALbasic project, regardless of your intended final target platform. In fact, you use the same project to create applications for each target platform.

You can create executable applications for the following platforms:

- ✔ Mac OS 7, 8, and 9
- ✔ Mac OS X (REALbasic Pro only)
- ✔ Windows 95, 98, NT, and 2000 (REALbasic Pro only)

The Editors

Three important editors make up the bulk of REALbasic's programming tools. With these editors, you can create interesting interfaces, add functionality using REALbasic code, and manage the look and feel of your application's menus. The names of the editors are

- ✔ Window Editor
- ✔ Code Editor
- ✔ Menu Editor

The Window Editor

Perhaps the most important item in the Project window is a window object. Windows are the foundation of most interfaces in these days of point-and-click software. Again, REALbasic takes care of matters for you and provides a default window titled *Window1* with each new project you begin.

To modify a window, double-click it in the Project window. This opens the Window Editor for that window. The Window Editor enables you to create and design an interface. With the Window Editor opened, you can

- ✔ Alter the appearance of a window.
- ✔ Add items to the window to build an interface.
- ✔ Delete items from a window interface.

Figure 1-3 shows a project with an open Window Editor.

You can open a Window Editor also by selecting a window in the Project window and pressing Return.

Figure 1-3:
The
Window
Editor is
where you
create the
interface for
your
application.

The Code Editor

Within each REALbasic window is a place to store code. The code is simply a list of instructions, much like a recipe, that tells your program what to do and how to do it. To view or alter this code, however, you must first open the Code Editor for the window that contains the code.

To open the Code Editor for a window, follow these steps:

1. **Bring the Project window to the foreground by choosing Window⇨Project or by pressing ⌘-0.**

2. **Open the Window Editor.**

   To open a Window Editor, either double-click the window in the Project window or select the window in the Project Editor and press Return.

3. **Open the Code Editor for that window.**

   Double-click somewhere within the Window Editor or simply press Return.

Now that the Code Editor is open, note the long list of words on its left side. These words are events. When you select an event from the left side, its corresponding code appears on the right side.

All the events that you see inside a window are containers for code. Thus, a project contains windows, which in turn contain code. Figure 1-4 shows the Code Editor.

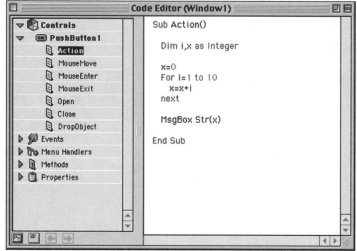

Figure 1-4:
The Code
Editor is
where you
enter your
source
code.

```
Sub Action()

    Dim i,x as Integer

    x=0
    For i=1 to 10
        x=x+i
    next

    MsgBox Str(x)

End Sub
```

The Code Editor has a group of settings that you can access by choosing Edit⇨Preferences, as seen in Figure 1-5. A brief explanation of these settings follows:

- ✔ **Source Editor.** Assign a font and font size for the code that appears in the Code Editor.

- ✔ **Source Printing.** Assign a font and font size for printing the source code.

- ✔ **Default Control Font.** Select a default font and font size for controls. When adding a control to a window, its text defaults to the font and size set here.

- ✔ **Auto Hide When Code Editor Is Frontmost.** Some folks like to have a little elbowroom when programming source code. For those coders, REALbasic automatically hides the Tools, Properties, or Colors window for you when opening the Code Editor.

✔ **Language Reference.** The *REALbasic Language Reference* allows you to search for a keyword as well as go directly to a specific topic. Toggling this setting forces the *Language Reference* to go directly to a topic instead of searching for the keyword within the entire *Reference*. Look for more details later in this chapter.

If you happen to notice the Tools, Properties, or Colors window suddenly disappearing on you and you'd rather have the window stay open while you type your code, change the Auto Hide setting.

Figure 1-5:
Change the
Preferences
to suit your
personal
tastes.

Preferences
Source Editor:
Font: Geneva ⬍ Font Size: 12 ⬍
Source Printing:
Font: Geneva ⬍ Font Size: 10 ⬍
☐ Bold keywords   ☐ Print in color
Default Control Font:
Font: Geneva ⬍ Font Size: 10 ⬍
Auto Hide When Code Editor is Frontmost:
☐ Tools   ☐ Properties   ☐ Colors
Language Reference:
☐ Default to Go rather than Search
Cancel   OK

The Menu Editor

Since the advent of today's visually based computer interfaces, menus have played a vital role in making applications easy to use and consistent. Fortunately, REALbasic has a built-in Menu Editor that makes menu creation a cinch.

Each project that you create comes complete with a Menu Editor that resides in the Project window. To add menus to your application:

1. **In the Project window, double-click the Menu object to open it.**

2. **Select a position in the menu bar where you would like to add a menu.**

   After you choose a menu from the Menu Editor's menu bar, its corresponding menu expands to reveal all menu items within it.

3. **Click the menu item at the end of the menu to add a new menu item.**

4. **Change that menu item's Properties using the Properties window.**

   When you select a menu item, the Properties window automatically updates to display the menu item's characteristics, or *properties* (hence, the Properties window). To change a property of the menu, simply click somewhere within that property.

   If the property is one that you can turn on and off, click the check box for that property. For example, turn on the Bold property by clicking its check box in the Properties window.

   Other properties contain text information. When this is the case, click in the property's field in the Properties window to change its appearance. To change the text that appears in the currently selected menu item, for example, you would click the Text property.

   Similarly, to create a keyboard shortcut for a menu item, click the CommandKey property and enter a letter such as N in the field. A user can then perform the action by pressing ⌘-N instead of clicking the menu item.

   By convention, if your keyboard shortcut will consist of letters, you should use uppercase letters.

5. **When you have finished changing its properties, press Return to make the changes take effect.**

   Figure 1-6 shows a sample Menu Editor.

6. **Move the menu item to its desired location, if necessary.**

   When you add a menu item to a menu, it automatically appears at the end of the menu. To move the menu item to another position within that menu, drag the menu item up or down the list. You can also use this method to change the menu's order later, not just during creation of a menu item.

Figure 1-6:
The Menu
Editor
provides a
preview
of your
application's
menus.

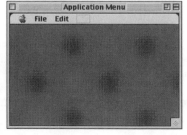

Although adding and changing menus with the Menu Editor is simple, it is only the first step in using menus in your application. The Menu Editor only allows you to design the look of menu items. It does not add functionality to the menus. That task requires code instructions from you, which you examine in Chapter 2.

The Windows

In addition to the three main editors, REALbasic sports some additional windows to assist you in your programming endeavors. These windows provide you with information as well as access to a host of tools for creating projects. The windows include the following:

- **Reference window.** A handy reference to the REALbasic language.

- **Tools window.** A palette of controls you can use to create attractive and functional interfaces.

- **Properties window.** A convenient panel for setting the properties of windows, interface elements, and other project components.

- **Colors window.** A palette of colors that you commonly use when creating interfaces.

The Language Reference window

REALbasic has an amazing number of interface and language features. To keep you from having to memorize dozens of commands and features, REALbasic thoughtfully provides the Language Reference window, from which you can get a comprehensive reference of the commands and controls available to programmers.

To display the Language Reference window, you can do any one of the following:

- Choose Windows⇨Language Reference.

- Press ⌘-1.

- Press the Help key.

The Language Reference window consists of two halves, as shown in Figure 1-7. The left side lists the various methods, controls, and REALbasic language features at your disposal. You can sort the topics alphabetically or thematically by clicking the Alpha or Theme button, respectively, at the top left.

Figure 1-7:
The
Language
Reference
window
provides a
convenient
way to
quickly look
up specific
information
about
REALbasic
features.

Language Reference	**Search**

Alpha **Theme**

▷ **Introduction**
▷ **AppleEvents**
▷ **Arrays**
▷ **Boolean**
▷ **Classes**
▷ **Code Execution**
▽ **Constants**
  DebugBuild ->Bc
  RBVersion ->Do
  RBVersionString
  Target68K ->Bo
  TargetCarbon ->
  TargetMacOS ->)
  TargetPPC ->Boi
  TargetWin32 ->)
▷ **Controls**

TargetCarbon Constant

Used to determine the type of code that is currently running.

Syntax

result=**TargetCarbon**

Part	Type	Description
result	Boolean	Returns True if the application is executing Carbon code under MacOS X, either as a standalone application or within REALbasic.

Notes

The Carbon version or REALbasic compiles as Carbon while running in the IDE.

Target68K, TargetPPC, and **TargetCarbon** are mutually exclusive subsets of TargetMacOS. TargetPPC is True only if PPC code is running on a PowerPC under a 'classic' MacOS.

See Also

TargetWin32, DebugBuild, TargetMacOS, TargetPPC, Target68K, RBVersion, RBVersionString functions; #If statement.

When you select a topic from the list on the left, information about its features and use appear on the right half. The Language Reference window usually provides a full description followed by a code example that you can drag directly into a Code Editor. This is just the first of REALbasic's many timesaving drag-and-drop features. Simply drag the code example from the Language Reference into the Code Editor to gain instant functionality without typing one line of code. In addition to finding information in the hierarchical menu of categories, you can also search for specific terms by entering text in the Search field.

REALbasic 3.0 allows you to either search for a keyword in the entire *REALbasic Language Reference* or go directly to a specific topic that the keyword describes. To go directly to a topic rather than searching the entire *Language Reference,* press the Option key and the *Search* button instantly reads *Go.* You can also change the default behavior of the Search button by changing REALbasic's Preferences, as described previously in this chapter.

The Tools window

A window serves as the foundation of a REALbasic interface. A control serves to give that window function.

A REALbasic *control* is an object contained in an interface that gives the interface functionality. Typically, this functionality includes the following:

✔ Making your interface look nice

✔ Interacting with the user through standard interface devices such as a button

✔ Displaying information as text

✔ Displaying or playing multimedia

✔ Communicating with another computer on a network

✔ Finding or adding information to a database

Wow! That's a lot of power. What's even more amazing is that all of this functionality is within anyone's grasp using drag and drop through the Tools window.

The Tools window is the home of most controls in REALbasic. To use the Tools window and consequently the controls contained within, follow these steps:

1. **Open the Tools window, which is shown in Figure 1-8.**

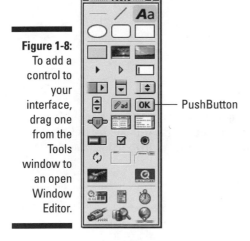

Figure 1-8:
To add a control to your interface, drag one from the Tools window to an open Window Editor.

— PushButton

The Tools window may already be visible, but if it isn't, choose Window➪Tools or press ⌘-Option-1.

2. **Open a Window Editor.**

Double-click a window in the Project window to open its Window Editor.

3. **Drag a control from the Tools window to Window Editor.**

For example, drag a PushButton like the one shown in Figure 1-8 to your open window.

REALbasic 3.0 adds the capability to change the orientation of the toolbar, giving you more elbowroom when you need it. Click the ZoomIcon on the toolbar to toggle between horizontal and vertical orientation, as shown in Figure 1-9.

ZoomIcon

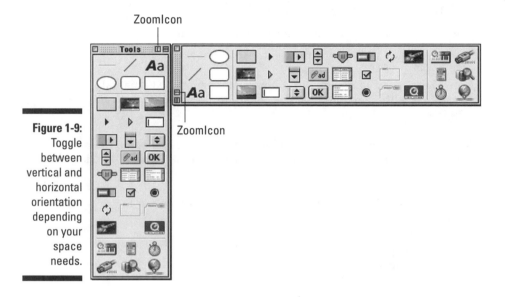

ZoomIcon

Figure 1-9:
Toggle
between
vertical and
horizontal
orientation
depending
on your
space
needs.

The Properties window

Just as you might describe everyday objects using adjectives such as tall, wide, green, and ugly, you can describe objects in REALbasic by defining their *properties*. Windows, for example, have several properties that describe them. Some include

✔ Height and width

✔ Background color

✔ Resizable

The Properties window gives you access to this information by displaying the properties and corresponding values for any window or control. To view or change a property:

1. **Make sure the Properties window is open.**

   If it isn't, choose Windows⇨Show Properties or press ⌘-Option-2.

2. **Open a Window Editor.**

   Double-click a window in the Project window to display its Window Editor.

3. **To view the window's properties, click somewhere in the window. Or, to view a control's properties, click the control in the window.**

   If you select a control, a colored ring appears around it.

4. **View the properties in the Properties window.**

5. **Change the properties, as desired.**

   In addition to viewing the Properties, you have the ability to edit each value. Click the property field you would like to change and alter its value. Figure 1-10 shows a selected PushButton and its associated Properties window.

6. **To make the Property changes take effect, press Return, or click somewhere outside the Properties window.**

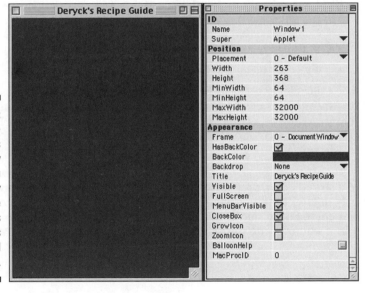

Figure 1-10:
The Properties window allows you to quickly edit the properties of controls and windows.

If you make a mistake editing a property or want to change, you can always go back and change it later.

The Colors window

Amidst the hustle and bustle of the REALbasic environment stands a diminutive, but useful, palette named the Colors window, shown in Figure 1-11. If you don't see it on your screen, choose Windows⇨Show Colors or press ⌘-Option-3.

Figure 1-11:
The Colors
window
stores
frequently
used colors
for easy
access.

The Colors window is a palette of — you guessed it — colors. This palette enables you to store frequently used colors with your project as swatches. *Swatches* are the small squares located in the Colors window. When you first launch REALbasic, the Color window does not have any defined swatches. To add one to the palette:

1. **Click an unused swatch square in the Colors window.**

2. **Choose a color using the ColorPicker.**

   The ColorPicker dialog box is the standard interface for choosing a color on Macintosh computers. (The Windows operating system has a similar feature.) Choose a color palette from the left side of the ColorPicker and then choose a color on the right side.

3. **Click OK.**

To use a stored color, drag it from the Colors window onto an appropriate property in the Properties window. Many different items have a property that involves color. For example, you can open a window and drag a color from the Colors window onto the window's BackColor property in the Properties window.

The Debug Menu

After you build an interface and add code to your project, you will undoubtedly want to see your handiwork in action. REALbasic allows you to test your project before building a final application. To do so, choose Debug➪Run, as shown in Figure 1-12.

Figure 1-12:
Use the
Debug
menu to test
your project.

Your project instantly launches and runs as though it was an application, but it isn't really an application yet. You're just testing it. This is a chance for you to view the operation of your project and catch any errors in your code.

When you are finished testing your project, choose File➪Quit. You return immediately to the REALbasic environment, free to continue working on your project.

The mythical bug

If you program computers for any time at all, you're bound to encounter the term *bug,* describing a malfunction or error in the software's source code. Programmers use the term to describe all types of problems, but the main idea is always the same: Something is wrong. The process of correcting bugs in source code has come to be known as *debugging.*

Why all the insects, you ask? Well, a popular tale purports that Grace Hopper coined the term sometime in the 1940s when a moth was discovered in one of the components of a U. S. Navy computer. Other variations of the story have her coining the term *debugging* as well.

Although there was indeed a date in the 1940s when a naval computer operator logged an incident of finding an insect in a computer (and attaching the moth to the log entry), the words *bug* and *debug* are, in fact, much older. No two dictionaries seem to agree on the subject, but it is generally accepted that the word *bug* was in use as early as the 1870s. Many sources attribute the word to Thomas Edison. *Debug* came later, but it still precedes the Navy story by at least 50 years.

What's so amazing about this tale is its omnipresence. Not only does the REALbasic documentation pass along the tale, but the popular quiz game show *Who Wants to be a Millionaire* used it for the million-dollar question in one episode. If you'd like to read some more about this phenomenon, take a look at these web sites:

✔ www.wilton.net/wordorb.htm (scroll down to the etymology for the word *bug*)

✔ www.maxmon.com/1945ad.htm

✔ www.lewhill.com/ firstcomputerbug.html

Chapter 2

Creating Your First Project

. . . .

In This Chapter

▶ Looking at the process of creating an application

▶ Creating an interface

▶ Checking out some REALbasic code

▶ Taking the code out for a test run

▶ Building an application

▶ Updating an application with improved features

. . . .

*W*orking with REALbasic to create your own applications is one of the most fun, rewarding, and useful computer skills you can acquire. For once, you can tell the computer what to do, instead of relying on someone else to make software to do it. Creating your own software is great also because

- ✔ You can customize it for your needs.
- ✔ You can save time and money.
- ✔ You can sell it to friends.
- ✔ You can use it to cheat on your homework.
- ✔ It can make you rich and famous.

Okay, maybe some of these reasons are dubious, but you get the idea. Being able to create software is a powerful skill indeed!

In the past, creating great software required years of experimenting, a fair amount of genius, and a bit of head scratching. REALbasic reduces the learning curve to the point where you can create a functional application in one sitting. It also takes the rocket science out of programming with the inclusion of a language that's simple to understand. Gone are the cryptic conventions of most modern programming languages. And the only head scratching will be from your family, classmates, or coworkers, wondering how you made such sophisticated and cool software.

To get your feet wet in the REALbasic pond, this chapter describes the process of creating software applications with REALbasic. It takes you through the steps that every programmer uses to create great (and sometimes not-so-great) software. By the end of this chapter, you'll know enough to create a functional application and begin your quest for world — or at least neighborhood — domination.

Five Easy Steps to Creating an Application

To create an application with REALbasic, follow these five steps:

1. **Think of an idea and write it down.**

   You need to have an idea of what you want your computer to do before you can make it do it. Just think of the last time you said, "Boy, I sure wish this computer did. . . ." This method usually yields a good idea — and sometimes even a great one. Writing it down helps you see the big picture while also staying focused. Moreover, it might help you prevent problems.

2. **Create a new project and build an interface.**

   To create a new REALbasic project, either choose File⇨New or launch REALbasic. REALbasic has a variety of tools to aid in the creation of visually pleasing and easy-to-use interfaces. All of this functionality is accessible using only drag and drop. Never before has interface building been so easy.

3. **Use the REALbasic language to add code to the interface.**

   Although an interface is nice, a program still has to do something. Fortunately, REALbasic gives you a powerful set of commands to aid in your pursuit of creating software. The language is simple to learn yet sports features of more complex languages. And if that isn't enough, you can add the code examples provided by REALbasic directly to your interface with a simple drag and drop.

4. **Test the project.**

   With interface and code in hand, it's time to test the project. If you run into any problems here, you need to go back to Step 1 or 2 and correct the errors in your interface or code. REALbasic won't leave you hanging, though. It comes complete with several tools to help you debug your project. After everything is just right, proceed to the last step.

5. **Build the final application.**

   Your project looks good and your code does everything it was designed to do. It's time to build the final application. After this step is complete, you're free to unleash your creation on the world (or, again, your neighborhood).

If you use this process each time you program with REALbasic, you can't go wrong. Now that you have an idea of the REALbasic programming process, fire up REALbasic and get ready to make some software.

An Interface Only a Mother Could Love

After thinking of an idea, the next step in creating software with REALbasic is to build an interface. The *interface* is how a user interacts and uses your application. Suppose, for example, that you would like to create a small calculator. (I mentioned cheating on homework, didn't I?) Think about what type of interface a calculator program should have. Then, answer these questions. Does it always have to look like that? Can you improve it? Does another design benefit you more? All these questions should be on your mind when creating and designing an interface.

The mechanics of building an interface are a cinch, thanks to REALbasic. Simply drag a control from the Tools window onto the Window Editor of your choice. For example, to build a simple calculator interface, follow these steps:

1. **Create a new project.**

   REALbasic launches with a new project by default.

2. **Open a Window Editor.**

   In the Project window is a window titled Window1. Double-click Window1 to open its Window Editor. You should be looking at a blank window. You add interface objects to this window.

3. **Set the properties of the window as shown in Table 2-1 and leave the remaining properties untouched with their default values.**

4. **Drag three StaticText objects to the Window Editor.**

   The Tools window displays the objects you can add to an interface. To use one of these objects, you simply drag it from the Tools window into the Window Editor. Figure 2-1 shows the location of the StaticText object (and other objects) in the Tools window. The new objects will be named StaticText2 and StaticText3, respectively.

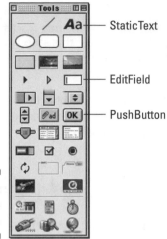

StaticText

EditField

PushButton

Figure 2-1:
The Tools
window.

5. Change the properties of the StaticText objects.

When you add objects to an interface, REALbasic assigns default property settings for each. You'll probably want to change these values. For example, to change the Text property of StaticText1, select the object in the Window Editor; its associated properties appear in the Properties window. Click the property you want to alter and change its value. Finally, press Return to enter the change. Table 2-1 lists the calculator project's StaticText controls and the properties you should use with them.

By now, the interface should look something like Figure 2-2.

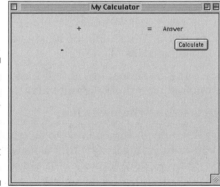

Figure 2-2:
The
calculator
interface
with altered
StaticText
objects.

6. **Drag two EditField controls to the Window Editor.**

   Return to the Tools window and add two EditField objects to the
   Window1 Window Editor. An *EditField object* (labeled in Figure 2-1) is a
   box where a user can enter text. The user enters numbers into these two
   EditFields to perform a computation. In math-speak, they're called
   operands.

7. **Change the properties of the EditField objects.**

   Again, the default properties accompanying the EditField objects need
   some adjustment. Table 2-1 lists the changes you should make.

8. **Drag a PushButton object to the Window Editor.**

   REALbasic automatically names it *PushButton1*. PushButton1 will
   perform a calculation using the numbers that a user enters in the two
   EditFields.

9. **Change the properties of the PushButton.**

   Set the properties of PushButton1 according to Table 2-1.

10. **Complete the interface so that it looks like Figure 2-2.**

    I hope you're beginning to see a pattern here. First, you add a control.
    Then you change the properties of the control. Keep following this
    methodology until your interface is complete.

Table 2-1	Calculator Project Properties	
Object	*Property*	*Value*
Window	Name	Window1
	Width	370
	Height	300
	Title	My Calculator
StaticText	Name	PlusSign1
	Text	+
	Left	106
	Top	26
	Width	30
StaticText	Name	EqualSign1
	Text	=

(continued)

Table 2-1 *(continued)*

Object	Property	Value
	Left	232
	Top	26
	Width	30
StaticText	Name	Answer
	Text	*<Leave blank>*
	Left	271
	Top	26
	Width	80
EditField	Name	Number1
	Left	19
	Top	23
	Width	80
EditField	Name	Number2
	Left	143
	Top	23
	Width	80
PushButton	Name	PushButton1
	Left	291
	Top	267
	Caption	Calculate

You might notice that the window appears sparsely populated. It is. The window is extra large so that you can add more features to it later.

Enter Some Code — But Only a Little

With an interface designed and built for a task, the next step is to add some code to the interface using the REALbasic language. To enter code, the Code Editor for a window must be open.

To open the Code Editor for Window1, select the window in the Project window and press Option-Tab. If you don't like weird keyboard shortcuts, you can follow these steps to open the Code Editor instead:

1. **In the Project window, double-click the window in which you designed the interface.**

   In this example, we're using the Window1 window.

2. **In the Window Editor, double-click anywhere within Window1, as long as you don't click on a control.**

The Code Editor is where you store your code. On the left side of the Code Editor is a hierarchical list of

- ✔ Controls
- ✔ Events
- ✔ Menu handlers
- ✔ Methods
- ✔ Properties

This list represents the contents of Window1 and the default contents of any window. Expand the Controls list by clicking the triangle to its left. Expand one of the controls even further (by clicking its triangle), and REALbasic displays the event structure for the control.

For now, think of the control's *event structure* as a bunch of containers for your source code. Each container is called an *event,* and you store code in that event. Each type of control has its own unique set of events, though many controls have events that share the same name.

To see an event, open the Code Editor. On the left side of the Code Editor is a hierarchical list. Expand the Event item in this list to reveal the events for this window. For example, the window has an Open event that executes each time the window opens.

Events have names that often describe their action. For example, some controls have an event called MouseDown. When a mouse click occurs in a control's boundary, the MouseDown event fires and executes the code within it. The control's boundary is based on the Left, Top, Width, and Height properties. If you want to respond to the MouseDown event, you must put code in it. Confused yet? Don't worry! An example will help clarify.

You should already have the Code Editor for Window1 opened. (If you don't, look back a few paragraphs). In the Window Editor, double-click PushButton1. The Action event of PushButton1 opens, ready for code.

In the PushButton's `Action` event, enter the following code:

```
dim num1 as integer
dim num2 as integer
dim result as integer

num1=val(Number1.text)
num2=val(Number2.text)
result=num1+num2

Answer.text=str(result)
```

If you're unsure about entering code, take a deep breath and proceed slowly. The first three lines of code create *variables,* which are simply temporary containers to hold values, similar to X and Y in algebra. The next three lines assign values to the variables. The final line puts the result into the Text property of the Answer object.

Look at the code in smaller chunks to better understand what is happening:

```
dim num1 as integer
dim num2 as integer
dim result as integer
```

The first question you may have is about the word `dim`. Although dim might describe the author of this book, it certainly does not describe the outlook here. Dim is shorthand for *dimension,* which is just a fancy way for you to tell your computer to prepare space in its memory for a variable. If you are unfamiliar with variables, fear not, friend!

Think of your computer application as a hotel for data. It can house all kinds of data — including numbers, text, graphics, and sounds — in its hotel rooms, which are called *variables.* The problem is that the data hotel, like a regular hotel, is picky and will allow only certain kinds of data in certain rooms. Regular hotels have special types of rooms for families, for honeymooners, for smokers, and more. In the same manner, the computer stores only number data in number variables, only graphic data in graphic variables, and so on.

Furthermore, like regular hotels, reservations are necessary. This is the purpose of the `dim` command. The `dim` command tells the computer, "Hello, I'd like to make reservations to store a variable. Its name is num1 and its type is integer. Please reserve room for it." (An *integer* is a number without a decimal portion. For example, 1 and 2 are integers, but 2.5 is not.) The second and third lines of code repeat the same function, creating space for two more numbers.

The next portion of code looks like this:

```
num1=val(Number1.text)
num2=val(Number2.text)
result=num1+num2
```

The first two lines of code assign values to the num1 and num2 variables. The values assigned to num1 and num2 come from the text that a user has entered into one of two EditFields in the interface. To retrieve the data from the two EditFields (named Number1 and Number2), look at the Text property of each EditField. The Text property of an EditField contains the text a user enters into that EditField.

To get the contents of the Text property, REALbasic relies on a methodology called dot-notation, in which you refer to a control by name, followed by a dot (a period), followed by the name of a property. The result is the value stored in that property.

For example, `Number1.text` refers to the number the user entered in the EditField titled Number1 in the interface. Unfortunately, the Text property of an EditField holds data as a string of text. This kind of data is not allowed in integer rooms at the computer hotel. Therefore, you have to convince the computer into thinking that the text data is a number. To do this, convert the Text property data with the `Val()` command. `Val()` converts all text data that appears between its parentheses into a number. As mentioned, number data type is allowed in the integer rooms, called `num1` and `num2`, but text data isn't. `Val()` solves this problem by converting text to a number. The program adds these numbers and stores the sum in the variable called `result`.

By setting the Text property of the Answer object, the data appears in the interface. Because `result` is a number, the `str()` method converts it to a string:

```
Answer.text=str(result)
```

Because the Text property of the Answer EditField is capable of storing only a string of text, you must convert the `result` variable (an integer) into a string of text. To convert from a number to a string of text, use the `str()` command. Think of `str()` as the evil twin of `val()`. Figure 2-3 shows how the code should appear in the Code Editor.

Congratulations! You've just coded your first program in REALbasic. Although you may not realize it, you've also used several important programming concepts (more on this later!).

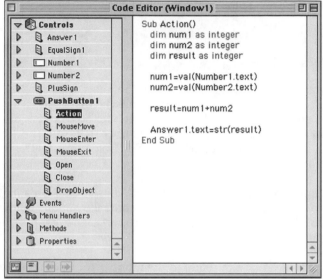

```
Code Editor (Window1)

▽ 🔲 Controls              Sub Action()
  ▷  📄 Answer1                dim num1 as integer
  ▷  📄 EqualSign1             dim num2 as integer
  ▷  🔲 Number1                dim result as integer
  ▷  🔲 Number2
  ▷  📄 PlusSign               num1=val(Number1.text)
  ▽  ⊙ⴲ PushButton1            num2=val(Number2.text)
       📄 Action
       📄 MouseMove            result=num1+num2
       📄 MouseEnter
       📄 MouseExit            Answer1.text=str(result)
       📄 Open               End Sub
       📄 Close
       📄 DropObject
  ▷  🐝 Events
  ▷  🔲 Menu Handlers
  ▷  📄 Methods
  ▷  🔲 Properties
```

Figure 2-3:
The Action
event of
Push-
Button1.

Testing the Project

At this point, I bet you're anxious to see your hard work in action. To test the Calculator project, choose Debug⇨Run. If all goes well, the project runs and displays a window. Enter a number into each of the two EditFields and then click the Calculate button. A StaticText control instantly displays the answer.

If everything doesn't go as planned and an error prevents the program from functioning properly, stay calm. Maybe you typed too quickly and misspelled something. Perhaps in your haste to race through this super exciting example, you managed to leave out some code. Go back through the code and look for typos and missing code. Programmers call this types of mistakes *bugs,* hence the term *debug*.

REALbasic can help you in your plight against software bugs. It recognizes misspellings and sometimes missing code. The REALbasic debugger will even show you the exact location of your mistake in the Code Editor.

When you try to run the project, the Debugger instantly transports you to the location of the error in the Code Editor. Other times, such as when you have the wrong type of code altogether, the bugs are more troubling to find. To illustrate, change the last line of code in the Calculator project to read:

```
Answer.text = str(num1)
```

This code is perfectly acceptable to use in your project. You will see no error, and REALbasic will not show you where the error occurred. The bug rears its ugly head, however, when you test the project. Although the project runs fine, the program produces incorrect results. The code is legitimate code as far as REALbasic is concerned. The error is that this code is not right for this purpose. In cases like these, it's up to you to follow through the logic of the code and discover the error. This is a good time to extol the virtues of planning your program before writing code because the planning phase can help eliminate or reduce these types of errors.

After you have tested the project thoroughly and know that it functions properly, it's time to build the final application.

The Final Frontier — Building an Application

Way to go! You've made it to the last step. The goal in programming your computer is the finished application. An *application* is a computer program that anyone can use. When you use a word processor or a web browser, you are using an application.

A *REALbasic project,* on the other hand, is only a list of instructions and an interface for how an application should behave and look. After you complete the project, the final step is to build or create an application. Your grandmother can use the application on her computer. Unless she's a REALbasic programmer (maybe it's time to get her started?), a REALbasic project file will do her no good.

To build the final application, follow these steps:

1. **Choose File⇨Build Application.**

   The Build Application dialog box appears. This is where you choose settings for your final build.

2. **At the top left of the Build Application dialog box, select the Macintosh target by clicking the Macintosh check box.**

3. **In the Macintosh Application Settings area, enter a name for your application and choose a specific Macintosh platform (68k vs. PPC).**

4. **Choose the 68K and PowerPC settings so that all types of Macintosh computers can use the final application.**

   Figure 2-4 shows the settings for a final build.

5. **Click the Build button.**

   The final application appears on your hard drive in the same folder where you saved the project. If you forgot to save the project before building, the application will appear in the same folder as the REALbasic application.

6. **Throw a party!**

   You've just completed your very own computer program. Wait until you see your friends' faces when you tell them about your new hobby as a computer programmer. The great part is you that never have to tell them just how easy it was!

If you are the proud owner of a REALbasic Professional Edition, you also have other choices for the final build: Carbon/Mac OS X and Windows applications. You can use the same project to build applications that are compatible with Mac OS X and Windows 95, 98, NT, and 2000 operating systems. When you compile applications for Mac OS X or Windows, the application takes on the standard user interface of the respective operating system when you test it. For example, the Calculator project automatically gains all the interesting visuals of the Aqua interface when you build an application for Mac OS X.

To illustrate, try building a Windows version of the Calculator project, by following this path:

1. **Choose File⇨Build Application.**

   The Build Application dialog box appears.

2. **In the upper-left corner of the dialog box, click to deselect the Macintosh check box and then select the Windows check box instead.**

3. **In the Windows Application Settings area, type a name for the executable and a caption, which will be the title displayed in your application's main window.**

   Figure 2-5 shows the Windows build settings.

4. **Click Build to make the final Windows executable application.**

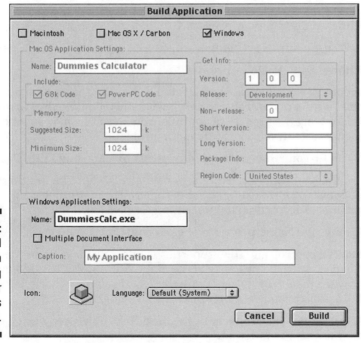

Figure 2-5:
The Build
Application
dialog
box for
Windows
applications.

Now, imagine your friends' faces when you tell them that you're a cross-platform computer programmer.

Going the Extra Mile

Your first project doesn't do much yet, but I promised that you would get a chance to make it better. As Bill Gates will tell you, people want features. So far, your project has one feature: It adds two numbers together. What if your users want to subtract, multiply, or divide instead?

If you want these features in your project, you have to add them. And doing so is a breeze. (Any new properties are summarized in Table 2-2.) Follow these easy steps:

1. **Open the Window Editor.**

2. **Choose Edit⇨Select All or press ⌘-A.**

   All controls in your interface appear highlighted to indicate that they are selected.

3. **Choose Edit⇨Copy or press ⌘-C.**

   All these controls are temporarily stored in the Apple Clipboard.

4. **Choose Edit⇨Paste or press ⌘-V.**

   A copy of each control you selected in Step 2 appears highlighted. Drag this new set of controls further down the window, so they are not obstructing the first set of controls. You'll use this new set of controls to include a subtraction feature in the project.

5. **Paste two more sets of copied controls by choosing Edit⇨Paste again.**

   By now, you should see four sets of controls where before there was only one. You will use each set of to perform an arithmetic operation: addition, subtraction, multiplication, or division.

6. **Change the Name property of each control.**

   Select a control, and the Properties window displays its properties. Change the Name property of the StaticText objects you will use to display the results to Answer1, Answer2, and so on. Similarly, change the EditFields to names from Number1 to Number 8.

7. **Change the Text property of the StaticText objects to designate their new arithmetic function.**

   The Text property of the StaticText objects should read +, -, *, and /, respectively. When you select each control, its Text property appears in the Properties window, ready for you to change it.

8. **Add code to each new PushButton.**

   You can copy the code that appears in the `Action` event of PushButton1. Open the Code Editor and navigate to the `Action` event of PushButton1. Choose Edit⇨Select All and then choose Edit⇨Copy (or press ⌘-C) to

copy the source code. In the `Action` event of each PushButton, choose
Edit⇨Paste to paste the code into the new control.

9. **Change the arithmetic operation for each PushButton.**

   You used the first PushButton for performing addition. Therefore, to get
   added functionality, change the other PushButtons to perform subtraction, multiplication, and division, respectively. REALbasic does the bulk
   of the work for you. You have to change only the addition sign (+) to the
   appropriate sign for the operation you want (- for subtraction, * for
   multiplication, and / for division).

10. **Test the project.**

    Choose Debug⇨Run or press ⌘-R.

11. **If you encounter problems, check for misspellings or missing code.**

12. **When everything is just right, build the final application.**

    Choose File⇨Build Application or press ⌘-M. In the Build dialog box,
    click the Macintosh Target check box and name the application.

Table 2-2	Improved Calculator Project Properties	
Object	*Property*	*Value*
StaticText	Name	Answer1
StaticText	Name	Answer2
StaticText	Name	Answer3
StaticText	Name	Answer4
StaticText	Name	PlusSign1
	Text	+
StaticText	Name	MinusSign
	Text	-
StaticText	Name	MultiplySign
	Text	*
StaticText	Name	DivideSign
	Text	/
EditField	Name	Number1

(continued)

Table 2-2 *(continued)*

Object	Property	Value
EditField	Name	Number2
EditField	Name	Number3
EditField	Name	Number4
EditField	Name	Number5
EditField	Name	Number6
EditField	Name	Number7
EditField	Name	Number8
PushButton	Name	PushButton1
PushButton	Name	PushButton2
PushButton	Name	PushButton3
PushButton	Name	PushButton4

The completed interface for the My Calculator project is shown in Figure 2-6.

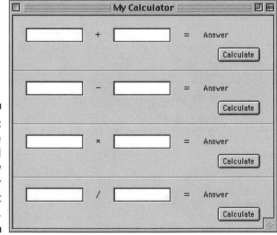

Figure 2-6:
The completed My Calculator project interface.

The final source code for the project follows:

```
Window1.PushButton1.Action:
Sub Action()
  dim num1 as integer
  dim num2 as integer
  dim result as integer

  num1=val(Number1.text)
  num2=val(Number2.text)

  result=num1+num2

  Answer1.text=str(result)
End Sub

Window1.PushButton2.Action:
Sub Action()
  dim num1 as integer
  dim num2 as integer
  dim result as integer

  num1=val(Number3.text)
  num2=val(Number4.text)

  result=num1-num2

  Answer2.text=str(result)
End Sub

Window1.PushButton3.Action:
Sub Action()
  dim num1 as integer
  dim num2 as integer
  dim result as integer

  num1=val(Number5.text)
  num2=val(Number6.text)

  result=num1*num2

  Answer3.text=str(result)
End Sub

Window1.PushButton4.Action:
Sub Action()
  dim num1 as integer
  dim num2 as integer
  dim result as integer
```

```
num1=val(Number7.text)
num2=val(Number8.text)

result=num1/num2

Answer4.text=str(result)
End Sub
```

Part II

Understanding the REALbasic Language

THE GREAT THING ABOUT OBJECT-ORIENTED PROGRAMMING IS, IT'S MADE SOFTWARE DEVELOPMENT AS EASY AS PUTTING ONE FOOT IN FRONT OF THE OTHER.

In this part . . .

REALbasic is both an application and a programming language. REALbasic, the application, is great because it enables you to create sophisticated interfaces and add functionality with only a modest amount of effort. REALbasic, the language, is the means by which you add functionality to the interface.

This part begins by showing you how to use windows to build an interface. To make your interface pretty, REALbasic gives you a large variety of premade components, called controls, that you can add to your project with drag-and-drop ease. Finally, to make the interface actually do something, you issue commands in the REALbasic language. The remainder of Part II shows you how to speak the REALbasic language so that you can control the interface.

Chapter 3

A Window into the Soul

The graphical user interface of the Macintosh and Windows operating systems make extensive use of windows. In fact, windows are the containers for the very controls that make up the user interface.

Because windows are such an important part of the computer experience these days, REALbasic is replete with a variety of window types that you can fashion into a myriad of appearances.

This chapter guides you through the maze of window features by showing you how to create windows as well as change their appearance and functionality. Also included is a discussion about all available window types. The chapter concludes with a look at some common code examples for dealing with windows.

Basic Window Actions

A window serves as the backdrop to an interface; all interface controls reside within a window. In fact, to display any type of control, you need a window. Is it any wonder that a popular operating system would name itself after the window, the root of the interface? This section steps you through the most basic window operations of creating, saving, deleting, and reusing windows.

Creating a window

When you start a new project, REALbasic automatically creates a window. REALbasic names the window Window1 by default, though you are welcome (and encouraged) to change it. To do so, open the Window1 Window Editor by double-clicking Window1 in the Project window. With the Window Editor open, change the Name Property in the Properties window. At some point, you'll want to use more than one window. To create a new window, choose File⇨New Window. A new window appears in the Project window. REALbasic automatically names new windows Dialog1, Dialog2, and so on. Yes, you heard right. The first window is Window1 but subsequent windows are named Dialog1, Dialog2, and so on. This most likely stems from the idea that the first window you create is a document type of window, whereas the remaining windows are dialog boxes that support the application.

It is customary, though not necessary, to immediately change the name of a new window to something more descriptive. That way, other people can look at your project and tell a little bit about what it does just by looking at the window names. Moreover, if your project uses multiple windows, unique names help you keep things straight. SearchWindow, for example, is a much more descriptive window title than Window1.

Saving a window

After you have spent a lot of time creating a fabulous looking window, you may want to use it in other projects. To export, or save, a window, do one of the following:

- ✔ Drag the window from the Project window to the Finder. Your window instantly becomes a file that you can add to other projects.

- ✔ With the window you want to save selected in the Project window, choose File⇨Export.

Deleting a window

Sometimes you may change your mind and decide that you don't need a particular window. To delete it from the project, follow these steps:

1. **Bring the Project window to the foreground by choosing Window⇨Project or by pressing ⌘-0.**

2. **In the Project window, select the window you want to delete.**

3. **Choose Edit⇨Clear or press Delete.**

Should you mistakenly delete a window that you meant to keep, immediately choose Edit⇨Undo or press ⌘-Z. The window magically reappears in the Project window. Thank goodness for small miracles, huh? What's even more miraculous is the fact that you can keep undoing your previous actions. REALbasic has unlimited Undos!

Reusing a window

REALbasic saves all windows automatically within projects for later use each time you choose File⇨Save, but sometimes you may want to use a window from your project in another project. Another scenario might include sharing a window with a friend or a colleague. Luckily, REALbasic allows you to do just that.

To export a window for trading with a friend, for example, do either of the following:

⚗ Choose File⇨Export Window

⚗ Drag the window from the Project Editor to the desktop

To reuse a saved window in a different project, choose File⇨Import or drag the file from the Finder to the Project window. If you import a window with the same name as a window already in the project, the imported window does not appear in the Project window until you change the name of the existing window.

Changing a Window's Properties

When you create a window, it's customary to immediately change its properties. Windows have several important properties that alter various aspects of its appearance or functionality, such as

⚗ Color

⚗ Position

⚗ Size

⚗ Frame

In this section, you get a chance to play with all of these properties. To begin:

1. **Choose Window⇨Project.**

   The Project window moves to the foreground.

2. **In the Project window, double-click a window.**

   The window's Window Editor opens and the Properties window changes to reflect the properties specific to the window.

3. **In the Properties window, change the properties of the window.**

   Because the Properties window is now displaying the properties of the window, it is a simple matter to change any property. Select the property you want to alter and enter a value appropriate for that particular property.

Color

You may change many window properties using code. For example, to change the background color of Window1 to black, enter this code in the Open event of a window:

```
Window1.BackColor=RGB(0,0,0)
```

Use the RGB function to assign colors. The three numeric values represent the amount of red, green, and blue turned on for this color. Values range from 0 (off) to 255 (full on). Colors are particularly important to graphics and are discussed in greater detail in Chapter 8.

Position

To change the position of a window with code, you must set its Left and Top properties. The unit of measure assigned to these properties is the pixel. For example, many people have monitors with widths of 640 or 800 pixels.

The following code, placed in the Open event of Window1, moves the window 100 pixels from the top-left edge of the screen:

```
Window1.Left=100
Window1.Top=100
```

Size

To change the size of a window in code, you must alter its Width and Height settings. Enter this code in the Open event of Window1 to change the dimensions of the window to 300x400:

```
Window1.Width=300
Window1.Height=400
```

Of course, this isn't the only way to change the size of a window. You can always resize the window within REALbasic just as you do in the Finder: by dragging the window's Grow icon or by entering the Width and Height in the Property Window.

Frame

The Frame property of a window describes what type of window it is. Each type of window serves a different purpose. The next section covers the various types of windows that REALbasic offers.

Types of Windows

You may use of a variety of window styles in the Macintosh user interface. To effectively program the Macintosh, however, you need to understand the differences between these window types. Some of the window types REALbasic gives you to play with include the following:

- ✔ A document window
- ✔ A movable modal and a modal dialog box
- ✔ A floating window and a global floating window
- ✔ A plain box and a shadowed box

Table 3-1 lists the types of windows available in REALbasic.

Table 3-1		Comparison of Default Window Types			
Window	*Movable*	*Resizable*	*Title Bar*	*Must Close*	*Primary Use*
Document window	Yes	Yes	Yes	No	Documents
Movable modal	Yes	No	Yes	Yes	Toolbars, options
Modal dialog box	No	No	No	Yes	About window
Floating window	Yes	?	Yes	No	Toolbar
Plain box	No	No	No	No	About window
Shadowed box	No	No	No	No	About window

It's very easy to change the window's type. Simply open the window's Window Editor and select a type for it from the Frame property in the Properties Window. Each window that you create can have its own window type distinct from other windows in the same project.

Document window

A *document window,* shown in Figure 3-1, is the most common type of window you'll encounter. It's the type of window that makes up a word processing document, a web browser window, or a document in a graphics application. Document windows often sport a zoom box, a resize widget, and a close box. When in doubt, this is usually the type of window you want. The default Window1 created as part of a new project is a document window.

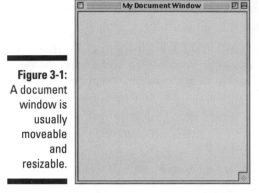

Figure 3-1:
A document window is usually moveable and resizable.

Another window type, called the *rounded window,* is an outdated style that resembles a document window. You'll rarely use it because it can't accommodate a zoom box or a resize box.

Modal

A *modal window* forces you into modes. What's all this talk about modes, you ask? Usually, when people use your computer program, they should be able to move around and do things at will. Sometimes, however, you want to ask users a question before allowing them to do anything else. This is where the modal dialog box comes in.

Movable modal

The *movable modal,* as its names implies, can be moved. That means you can move it to see windows behind it. Figure 3-2 shows an example of a movable modal window.

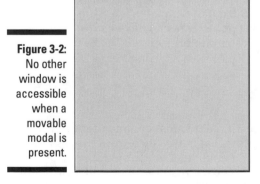

Figure 3-2:
No other window is accessible when a movable modal is present.

When this type of window is displayed, all menus dim and the user can perform no other action until you dismiss the window.

When you create a new window, REALbasic gives it a default Frame property value of Movable Modal. If you do not add a button to the window to close itself, your user will be stuck. Unlike a document window, modal and movable modal windows have no included close box to close them. No menus will be enabled and the window will not allow any other windows to come to the foreground. If this happens to you while testing, simply click outside the window to bring REALbasic to the foreground. Then choose Debug⇨Kill or press ⌘-K.

To avoid being stuck in a predicament where the user can't close a movable modal dialog box, you need to add some code it. Type the following within the Action event of a PushButton:

```
Self.close
```

Another way to avoid being stuck with a window that won't go away is to change the Frame property of the window to something like Document Window.

Modal dialog box

A close cousin to the movable modal is the *modal dialog box,* shown in Figure 3-3. It too dims the menu bar and forces you to close it before you can perform any other actions. To dismiss the window, you must add code. Unlike the movable modal, however, a modal dialog box is incapable of movement.

Figure 3-3:
A modal dialog box forces you into the mode of making a decision.

Floating window

You use a *floating window* primarily for a toolbar. Shown in Figure 3-4, a floating window has a narrow title bar and the capability to hover above all other windows in your application.

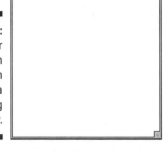

A *global floating window* looks and acts like a floating window, with one exception. A global floating window can float above the windows of all running applications; a floating window can float above only windows within that application.

Plain box and shadowed box

The plain box and shadowed box type of windows act like modal dialog boxes. They are immovable and have no title bars or accessory widgets. The only real difference between a modal dialog box, plain box, and shadowed box is appearance. A plain box has no shadow, a modal dialog box has a slight shadow, and a shadowed box (as the name implies) has the deepest shadow. You should use them primarily for About box windows. Figure 3-5 shows an example of the shadowed box style.

Customized windows

The Macintosh operating system has several other window types stored in memory that the Frame property cannot access. To access these secret styles, change the MacProcID property of the window. There are dozens of values that the MacProcID property can have. Some values produce interesting window styles like that shown in Figure 3-6.

Figure 3-6:
A window with alternate MacProcID values.

The *REALbasic Language Reference* has a comprehensive list of MacProcID values. A copy of the *REALbasic Language Reference* is on the *REALbasic For Dummies* CD.

Even higher on the cool scale is the capability to create custom window shapes. You can accomplish this through the use of a component called a WDEF. WDEF, which is shorthand for window definition, is a special file that defines the shape and properties of a custom window.

Several custom WDEFs are on the *REALbasic For Dummies* CD. Included with these window definitions are example projects that demonstrate their use.

Use a custom window definition to make windows of any shape. Figure 3-7 shows an example of what a WDEF can do for your project.

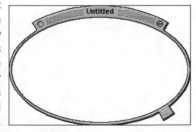

Figure 3-7:
Custom window definitions can change your windows into wild shapes.

Custom window definitions often use a large amount of memory and do not always follow standard interface rules. Therefore, although custom windows are fun to play around with, use standard windows whenever possible.

Window Tricks

It's helpful to have a few tricks up your sleeve when working with windows. This section explains how to make windows appear and disappear, center them on the screen, and make them fill the screen. Moreover, it shows you how to display alternate windows by default as well as count the number of currently open windows. These skills are good to know because you'll use them in nearly every REALbasic project you create.

Making a window appear and disappear

The REALbasic language gives you two ways to make a window appear, depending on how many copies of the window you need. To display only one copy of a window, the `show` command works beautifully. To use it, refer to the window by name, followed by a dot (period) and the `show` command. For example, to display Window1, use code like this:

```
Window1.show
```

To use the `show` command with another window name, simply change *Window1* to the name of the window you want to show (for example, `Window2.Show`).

The problem with code like this, however, is that you can display only one copy of the window. If Window1 is already displayed, the `show` command brings the window to the foreground. To get around this limitation, declare the window as an object and create a copy of that object. That way, each time you want a copy of the window, you simply create a new object.

For example, you might use the following code in the `Action` event of a PushButton:

```
// This creates a Window1 type variable named w
dim w as Window1
// This creates a new copy of Window1
w = new Window1
```

When you create windows in this manner, you may display an unlimited number of them. The `dim` statement begins the code by reserving a space in memory for a Window1 object. Keep in mind that Window1 as it appears on the Project window is a class. A class is merely a template for how to create a Window1 type of window. Because it is a template, you can use it to create as many window objects (each with a type of Window1) as you want. The new command does the actual act of creating the new window:

```
w = new Window1
```

When you have finished displaying a window, you may want to make it vanish. You can accomplish this disappearing act just as easily as you made the window appear. REALbasic gives you two ways to make a window disappear:

- **Hide the window.** The window is hidden from view but still exists in the computer's memory. To see it again, simply send it the show command.
- **Close the window.** The window is gone. To see another window like it, you have to create a new one.

If you want a window to hide itself, use this code, say, in a PushButton's Action event:

```
Hide
```

If you want a window to close itself and clear itself from memory, use this code:

```
Close
```

When you want to single out a particular window for vanishing, refer to the window by name and send it the Hide or Close command. For example, to hide a window called Window1, use this code:

```
Window1.Hide
```

Similarly, to close Window1 permanently, use

```
Window1.Close
```

The mother of all window disappearing is the Quit command. Quitting an application will close all of its windows.

Changing the default window

Most REALbasic projects use a default window as the main interface of the program. The *default window* is the main window of your application. It is the first window to open when your application launches. To set the default window, follow these steps:

1. **Choose Edit⇨Project Settings.**

   The Project Settings dialog box appears, as shown in Figure 3-8.

2. **Select a default window from the list.**

   All windows in your project should appear in the list. If you set the Default window to None, an Application subclass will be responsible for opening windows, as covered in Chapter 6.

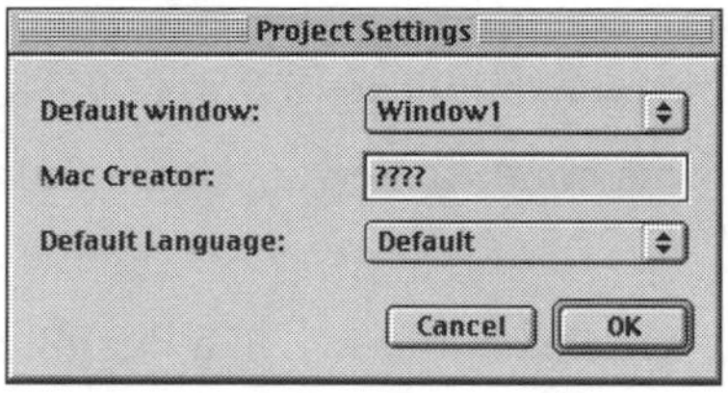

Figure 3-8:
Select a
default
window
from the
Default
window
popup list.

Centering a window

One task that newcomers ask for a lot is to center a window on the screen. The act of centering a window must occur the instant the window opens, or in REALbasic-speak, the instant its Open event executes.

To center a window, enter the following code in its Open event (which you can find in the window's Code Editor menu):

```
Self.Left = Screen(0).Width/2 - self.Width/2
self.Top = Screen(0).Height/2 - self.Height/2
```

This code snippet centers a window on the screen. It works by looking at the width of the screen and dividing it in 2. Next, half the width of the window is subtracted from half the screen width to locate the left edge of the window. The same principle is applied to the height to calculate the Top property of the window.

Filling the screen with a window

To make a window span the entire width and height of the screen, put the following code in the Open event of the window:

```
Self.Top=0
Self.Left=0
Self.Width=Screen(0).Width
Self.Height=Screen(0).Height
```

REALbasic 3 also introduces the FullScreen property to windows. Simply click the FullScreen property check box in the Properties window and — presto — your window covers the entire screen.

Counting open windows

To count the number of open windows, use code like this:

```
Dim WinCount as integer
WinCount=WindowCount
```

This is useful for tasks such as closing all open windows in your application. The WindowCount method tells you how many windows are open. Then, it's a routine procedure to loop through each window and issue it the close command:

```
Dim I as integer

If WindowCount>=1 then
    For I=0 to WindowCount-1
    //Use Window(I).hide if you
    //only want to hide all windows
        Window(I).close
    Next
End If
```

This code uses an index number in parentheses to identify each window. Make sure to note that the foremost window has an index number of 0, not 1. Because of this, the last window has an index number of WindowCount-1.

Chapter 4

Building an Interface

*P*erhaps the single most important feature of a modern operating system might be its visual interface, because it makes the cold and harsh world of computing warm and fuzzy for the average Joe.

Ease for users, however, comes at a price for programmers. Now programmers must be ready for any action that a user might take. Moreover, they often must write hundreds of lines of code to produce the simplest interface.

REALbasic changes all this by using the superb graphical interface of the Macintosh to build interfaces. Now you can create interfaces in minutes rather than weeks — with drag-and-drop ease. This chapter takes you through the process of creating an interface by introducing each of the controls available to you.

Creating an Interface

After you think of an idea for a program, building the interface for the program is the next step for creating applications with REALbasic. The interface is how your user will interact with and use your program.

Because the interface is usually the first means by which a user will judge your program, it's a good idea to take this step seriously. With a copy of REALbasic and a bit of caution, though, you can whip up a great interface in no time.

The planning phase

A critical, but often overlooked, step when constructing an interface is the planning phase. You might find that going low tech for this stage is best. Many programmers push away their computers and sit down with a pencil and paper to sketch out an interface. This gives them the ability to think things out without being distracted by the pretty pictures on their computer screens. It also helps them make some programming goals before they work with the computer.

Whether you find yourself away from the computer or not, a central interface design issue to think about is ease of use. In a good interface design, a user can accomplish tasks easily. Users want maximum results from minimum effort. A carefully constructed interface should

- **Be easy to use.** No one wants to spend an eternity learning how to use your software. Are the buttons clearly labeled? Does the program have a logical layout? Is there a flow to the application?

- **Offer lots of functionality, but not too much.** Look at the nightmarish interface pictured in Figure 4-1, and you'll see that maintaining simplicity is usually a good idea.

- **Look nice.** Is your interface appealing? Have you decided on a ferocious red background when you could have opted for the standard-colored window background? If users can't stand looking at your interface, they certainly won't be able to use it effectively.

Keep this list in mind while building your interface. You'll create a great interface if you successfully meld ease, functionality, and aesthetics.

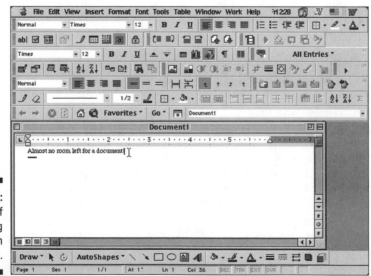

Figure 4-1:
Too much of
a good thing
can spoil an
interface.

Don't fret if your first interface is a real stinker. Interface design is not simple (indeed, some people spend a lifetime perfecting their interface design skills), but your skills will improve with each interface you design and use.

It never hurts to look at how the professionals do it. Launch your favorite application and look at its interface. Check out the location and style of toolbars, windows, and palettes. How are the menus arranged? What steps are required to accomplish a task?

The building process

After you design an interface, it's time to bring the idea to life. To build an interface, follow these four easy steps:

1. **Open a Window Editor.**

   If you haven't made a window yet, do so by choosing File⇨New Window. Next, double-click it in the Project window to open its Window Editor.

2. **Add a control.**

   Drag a control from the Tools window to the open Window Editor.

3. **Change the properties of the control.**

   Select a property in the Properties window and edit its value. You can continue changing any other property of the control as long as it remains selected. If you forget what a particular property of a control does, open the Reference window by choosing Window⇨Reference.

4. **Repeat steps 1 through 3 until you are finished.**

The number of windows you'll use in a project varies. Some applications can get away with only one window; others may require many windows to fulfill their tasks. The number of windows you need largely dictates the amount of time it requires to complete the interface building process — but REALbasic drag-and-drop construction is there to speed up the process.

Working with Controls

A typical interface consists of a window with an assortment of objects that allow the user to input data, change settings, or even color a picture. These objects are known as *controls* in REALbasic, and they form the basis by which a user interacts with your interface.

Some controls make the interface look nice; others provide valuable functionality. REALbasic ships with several types of preinstalled controls.

The Tools window gives you instant access to all built-in and user-installed controls. If you can't see the Tools window, choose Window⇨Show Tools or press ⌘-Option-1.

Adding a control

To begin creating an interface, drag a control from the Tools window to an open window where you would like it positioned. Figure 4-2 shows a sample interface built with controls from the Tools window.

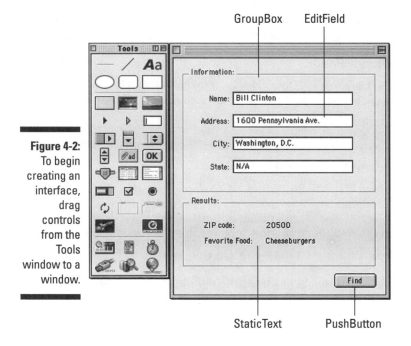

Figure 4-2:
To begin creating an interface, drag controls from the Tools window to a window.

Deleting a control

Interface building might not always go as expected. To remove a control from a window, first click the control to select it. Next, delete it by doing one of the following:

- ✔ Press Delete.
- ✔ Press Del (Forward delete).
- ✔ Choose Edit⇨Clear.

Should you accidentally delete a control that you wanted to keep, choose Edit➪Undo and the missing control magically reappears.

Changing the properties of a control

Every control in the Tools window has a list of associated properties that describe aspects of the control. Just as your automobile has a list of properties such as color and size, so do controls.

When you drag a control to a window, the properties pertaining to that control automatically appear in the Properties window. To edit a property, you simply click it, type a value, and press Return. If you aren't sure what kind of value to enter in a particular property, you can always check the online reference by choosing Window➪Reference.

To continue editing the various properties of a control, press Tab. This causes the cursor to jump from the currently selected property to the next property in the Properties window.

Using the Properties window is not the only way to edit control properties. For example, if you drag a PushButton to a window and then move the PushButton around the window, some properties of the control change automatically. Similarly, when you resize a PushButton by stretching its corner tabs, other properties of the control change.

Thus, you can change a control's position and size in two ways: through the Properties window or by simply moving the control with the mouse. Dragging a control around a window is great for getting it to its general location. This is usually followed up with a manual tweak of the control's properties in the Properties window, which allows you to fine-tune the setting.

Types of Controls

REALbasic controls can be divided into four categories:

- ✔ **Controls that beautify.** This type of control normally doesn't play a part in interaction. Its purpose in life is to make your interface look nice.

- ✔ **Controls that do something.** If a user clicks this type of control, it performs a task. These controls consist of buttons, sliders, check boxes, and more.

✔ **Controls that do something and look cool.** This kind of control not only looks good but also performs a valuable function such as drawing a picture, showing a movie, or playing a tune.

✔ **Controls that perform communications.** As if controls weren't cool enough, some can even talk to computers on the other side of the world.

As you can see, controls are capable of an array of behaviors. REALbasic provides a complete set of controls that represent each of these categories. You may also use controls that other programmers have created.

Controls that just sit there

Some REALbasic controls are designed primarily for aesthetic use. The sole reason for their existence is to make your applications look nice, neat, organized, and professional. Table 4-1 lists these lazy controls.

Table 4-1	Passive Controls
Control Name	*Description*
Line	Line for dividing the interface
Oval	Oval
Placard	Placard for giving your interface a 3D appearance
Rectangle	Rectangle
Round Rectangle	Rectangle with rounded corners
Separator	3D line for dividing the interface
StaticText	Text

Despite their passive nature, lazy controls set you on a good course for building an interface:

✔ The Line and Separator controls divide your interface into sections to make it more pleasing to the eye, as well as easier to navigate.

✔ StaticText controls label the elements of the interface or provide a place to output text data.

✔ Oval, Rectangle, and RoundRectangle spice up an interface by giving you options when you need buttons with a custom shape.

Figure 4-3 shows an interface made of lazy controls.

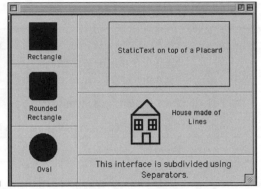

Figure 4-3:
Passive
controls do
have a
function:
beautifying
your
interface.

Now, don't be fooled by the moniker *lazy*. Although these controls spend most of their lives just sitting around, they perform two important functions. First, they can improve the appearance and overall flow of your application. Second, this improved look and flow makes the application easier to use.

Controls that do something for a living

To make things a bit more exciting, not to mention more useful, some REALbasic controls are interactive. For example, a PushButton is a type of control that performs an action. When a user clicks a PushButton control, something happens. Table 4-2 lists the different types of interactive controls.

Table 4-2	Active Controls
Control Name	*Description*
BevelButton	3D button
ChasingArrows	Object showing that a process is underway
CheckBox	Check box
ContextualMenu	Context-sensitive menu
DisclosureTriangle	Triangle-shaped control for changing the size of a window on the fly
EditField	Field in which users can enter text
GroupBox	Box that groups controls
Listbox	A list of items

(continued)

Table 4-2 *(continued)*

Control Name	Description
LittleArrows	Arrow control for incrementing or decrementing a numerical setting
PopupMenu	A list of items in a menu
ProgressBar	Bar that indicates the progress of a task
PushButton	Button
RadioButton	Radio button
Scrollbar	Scroll bar
Slider	Slider
TabPanel	Tab (panel)
Timer	Timer

PushButton, BevelButton, and LittleArrows

Buttons are one of the hallmarks of visual interface elements, providing an easy visual cue for users — heck, even a monkey can push a button. Users can pretty much assume that if they push a button labeled Save, for example, something will be saved.

REALbasic provides three button-like controls:

- ✔ **PushButton.** This is the traditional looking button in most Macintosh and Windows interfaces. You'll use this one a lot. And the properties you'll use most are those that control the size, position, enabled state, and caption of the PushButton.

- ✔ **BevelButton.** In today's race for 3D everything, REALbasic doesn't disappoint. A BevelButton is a three-dimensional looking button. It works similarly to a PushButton, but looks a bit different and is more diverse because of its enormous list of appearance settings. For example, you can change a BevelButton's bevel size and add an icon, among other cool features.

  When you need a button quickly, a PushButton will do. But when you need fine control over appearance, go with the BevelButton.

- ✔ **LittleArrows.** Two controls for the price of one! Add a LittleArrows control and it acts like two buttons. The two buttons usually complement each other, such as the LittleArrows control used to increase or decrease a number.

Figure 4-4 shows what each one of these buttons looks like.

Figure 4-4:
PushButton,
BevelButton,
and
LittleArrows.

RadioButton and CheckBox

When you need to make a choice or a selection, the RadioButton and Checkbox are good controls for the job.

RadioButtons never stand alone. Instead, they are part of a list of choices. From this list, only one selection is allowed. When you have one RadioButton, you should always have at least one other RadioButton (and usually more). For example, in a computer program to sell automobiles, you might have the user choose from a list of available car colors. This interface task is perfectly suited to a RadioButton, as shown in Figure 4-5.

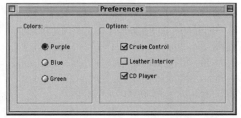

Figure 4-5:
Use the
RadioButton
and
CheckBox
controls
when you
want a user
to make a
choice.

You use CheckBoxes when you want the user to make an on-or-off, yes-or-no, or plus-or-minus type of setting. For example, continuing with the automobile program, a user might need to make decisions like the following:

✔ Do I want cruise control?

✔ Leather interior?

✔ CD player?

You can easily incorporate this list of questions into an interface using CheckBoxes, as shown in Figure 4-5.

Programmers call an on-or-off, yes-or-no, or plus-or-minus type of decision *binary* because it has two possible values.

GroupBox

The GroupBox is a special type of so-called active control. As its name implies, the *GroupBox* groups the controls in your interface within a box. This feature comes into play when you use RadioButtons.

If you need two sets of RadioButtons, for example, but you don't want them to influence each other, use a GroupBox control for each set. All RadioButtons put within a GroupBox function as a set of choices. Again, only one RadioButton control can be selected at a time. When a user clicks one RadioButton, all other RadioButtons within that GroupBox turn off. Meanwhile, another GroupBox in the same window can have a set of RadioButtons that don't interfere with the first set. Figure 4-6 shows an example of the GroupBox in action.

Although the GroupBox has this unique capability of automatically updating the appearance of RadioButtons, you can also use it merely to clean up the appearance of your interface.

Figure 4-6:
Use a
GroupBox
to separate
groups
of Radio-
Buttons or
just to
improve the
look of your
interface.

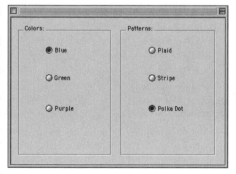

EditField and Listbox

Another essential control is *EditField*, which you use when you want a user to enter data. Some EditFields are small and are used to obtain one piece of data, such as a name. You can also resize an EditField to the size of a window and allow multiple lines of text. Word processing documents are common uses for this type of EditField. Another use for EditFields is to display text that you want a user to be able to copy and paste elsewhere.

When you want a user to have access to text, either for entering some information or for cutting and pasting, use an EditField control. For text that should not be accessed or changed, use a StaticText control.

When you use an EditField with multiple lines of text, REALbasic tacks on ScrollBars for free if you want. Figure 4-7 shows a multiline EditField.

Figure 4-7:
Use
EditFields
for text
entry; use
Listboxes to
display a list
of choices.

The *Listbox* control is used, not surprisingly, to present a list of information. A Listbox is similar to RadioButtons and Checkboxes, except it excels at displaying a long list of choices. Imagine forcing a user to use RadioButtons to make a decision based on one hundred choices! With a Listbox, it's a cinch. Listboxes are scrollable, so you can store a large amount of information in a small space. What's more, a user can select, sort, and rearrange its items, something that's impossible to do with RadioButtons or Checkboxes.

The Listbox also supports the display of multiple columns, hierarchical arrangements, and inline graphics. The Listbox is unique in that it occupies two positions in the Tools window. You can choose between the plain, single-column Listbox control or the fancier multicolumn Listbox control. Nothing prevents you from changing the properties of the Listbox later. Both Listbox controls are equal in that they are Listboxes. They simply represent different default setups for the Listbox control. This setup also mimics the behavior of Microsoft Visual Basic, making your transition smooth if you are new to REALbasic but already a pro with Visual Basic.

PopupMenu

The *PopupMenu* control serves a similar function as a Listbox in that it displays a list of data. The differences are that a PopupMenu displays only the currently selected item until the users selects and, therefore, expands the menu, and it can display only one column of text. The PopupMenu is an excellent choice for presenting lists in cramped quarters, while not cluttering the interface with other information (see Figure 4-8).

Timer

A *Timer* is special kind of control, the likes of which you haven't seen yet. One big difference between the Timer and most other controls is that it's invisible. That's because a Timer control is not really an interface element like a PushButton or a Listbox. Instead, it's more like a container for code. The code in the Timer is executed at regular intervals that you can control.

Figure 4-8: A PopupMenu provides a list of choices when space is at a premium.

When you drag a Timer control into a Window Editor, you can see the control. It isn't until you test or run the application that the Timer becomes invisible. Because the control is invisible during operation, it doesn't really matter where you place it in a window, as long as it is somewhere *in* the window. Figure 4-9 shows a window with a Timer control.

Figure 4-9: The Window Editor is the only place where you'll be able to see the Timer control because it's invisible in an application.

Timers have only two properties worth noting, but they pack a lot of punch:

- ✔ **Period.** The Period property tells the Timer how frequently to fire. The number is in milliseconds, so to figure out the equivalent time in seconds, multiply by 1000. For example, if you want a Timer that fires every 5 seconds, set the Period property to 5000.

- ✔ **Mode.** The Mode property of the Timer control can have one of three values: 0, 1, or 2. A setting of 0 turns the Timer off. A value of 1 causes the Timer to fire once after a length of time equal to the Period property. A value of 2 causes the Timer to fire repeatedly according to the Period, until you set the Mode to 0 or close the window containing the Timer.

Scrollbar and Slider

A Scrollbar can represent a range of numbers that the user can slide between. However, the Scrollbar control has lost popularity to the Slider as a way to enter numbers. You will more commonly use Scrollbars for scrolling graphics within a Canvas control. Figure 4-10 shows the Scrollbar in a variety of interface roles.

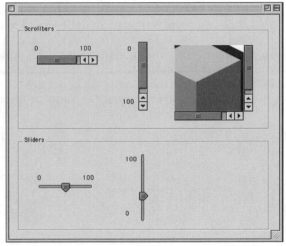

Figure 4-10: The Scrollbar and Slider controls share many features, but the Scrollbar can still do more.

The Tools window gives you access to Scrollbars in horizontal and vertical orientations. These Scrollbar controls are not different types of controls. Instead, they're both Scrollbars but with different default values. (You orient scrollbars horizontally or vertically by resizing the control in the orientation you desire.)

The standard width or height (depending on the control's orientation) of a Macintosh Scrollbar is 16 pixels. Although you can fashion a scrollbar that is 200 pixels wide, avoid the urge. Users are picky about how interface elements appear. They like the status quo, so don't disappoint them.

The *Slider* has taken over as the control du jour for selecting a number from a predefined range of values. Figure 4-10 shows two popular examples of Slider controls and their Scrollbar counterparts.

The Slider control was introduced with Mac OS 8, so earlier versions of the Mac OS display Sliders as Scrollbars both in your projects and in built applications.

ProgressBar and ChasingArrows

Like it or not, sometimes you have to wait when using a computer. This usually happens when the computer is working on a particularly intensive task, such as searching for a file or rendering a 3D masterpiece. When a wait is mandatory, it's common courtesy to let the user know.

Your courtesy tools in REALbasic are the ProgressBar and ChasingArrows controls. They provide the user with feedback about how long the wait will be. The *ProgressBar* can display feedback about the length of the wait incrementally or barber-pole style when the wait is of an undetermined length.

For example, suppose you want your computer to create 500 identical copies of a graphics file of your favorite hamster. Because you know that the computer has to repeat this task five hundred times, simply set the Maximum property of the ProgressBar to 500 and increment the Value property from 0 to 500, like this:

```
Dim i as integer

ProgressBar1.Maximum=500
ProgressBar1.Value=0

//Look at a photograph here
//and increase the Value Property each time
//through the loop
for i=1 to 500
    ProgressBar1.Value=ProgressBar1.Value+1
Next
```

This code causes the ProgressBar to visually indicate the progress of the loop.

Now, suppose you need the computer to search for viruses on your hard drive. Neither you nor the computer knows how long this process will take. It depends on how many files are on the hard drive, how many files contain a virus, and so on. When the length of the process is indeterminate, it's customary to display a barber-pole style ProgressBar. This is accomplished by setting the Maximum property to 0. When you're finished with the process of virus hunting, reset the Maximum property to another positive number and the barber-pole will stop turning.

```
//Set the ProgressBar to a barber pole style
ProgressBar1.Maximum=0

//Start the process here
//Loop
//Until finished searching

//Restore ProgressBar
ProgressBar1.Maximum=100
```

The *ChasingArrows* control works like an indeterminate ProgressBar. The ChasingArrows rotate whenever they're visible. To give them a whirl, simply change the Visible property to TRUE:

```
ChasingArrows1.Visible=TRUE
```

To turn them off again, do the opposite:

```
ChasingArrows1.Visible=FALSE
```

Figure 4-11 demonstrates the various ways to help your users endure the waiting process. Note that ChasingArrows come in only one size: tiny.

Figure 4-11:
Users love it when they can watch a process take place. The ProgressBar and Chasing-Arrows controls do the job nicely.

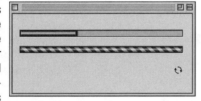

TabPanel

When you need to present a lot of information within a limited area, the *TabPanel* is the perfect choice. The TabPanel is a set of panels stacked on top of each other. You select one of the tabs to bring a particular panel to the foreground.

You can add as many tabs to the TabPanel as space permits. Each of these panels can hold its own set of controls. The effect is similar to a GroupBox, wherein controls are grouped together. But with a TabPanel, each click of a tab brings the controls contained within that tab to the foreground. Figure 4-12 demonstrates the use of TabPanels.

ContextualMenu

Perhaps Windows users understand the ContextualMenu control better than Mac users, because the Mac OS has had this capability only since Mac OS 8. A *ContextualMenu* is a hidden menu attached to a specific part of the interface. This menu has various commands that pertain to (or are *in the context of*) the object to which the menu is attached.

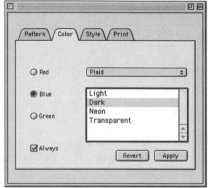

Figure 4-12:
TabPanels organize your interface and increase the available usable space for the interface.

To access the contextual menu, Window's users right-click the object and Mac users press Control while clicking the object. Figure 4-13 shows a ContextualMenu in action.

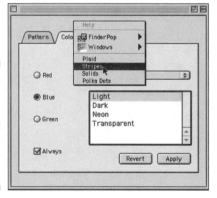

Figure 4-13:
Contextual menus offer you a great way to hide interface features.

Controls that do something cool

So far you have heard about REALbasic controls that make your interface look nice or provide standard elements for a user to interact with. REALbasic also provides a complete set of controls that not only do something, but do something cool.

These controls might be best termed the multimedia controls because they cover a range of multimedia needs. Table 4-3 lists the multimedia controls available in REALbasic.

Table 4-3	Attractive and Functional Controls
Control Name	*Description*
Canvas	Draws graphics
ImageWell	Draws graphics
MoviePlayer	Plays movies
NotePlayer	Plays musical notes
SpriteSurface	Draws sprites for animation and games

To use many of these controls, it's a good idea to have QuickTime installed on your computer. *QuickTime* is a multimedia engine that helps your program display graphics and video, as well as produce sound. Most versions of the Mac OS install it by default, but you can also get it online at the following:

```
www.apple.com/quicktime/
```

To see if you have QuickTime installed, check for the presence of a control panel named *QuickTime™ Settings*.

The REALbasic multimedia controls combined with the powerful import, export, content creation, and playback features of QuickTime offer REALbasic programmers a number of ways to present and create multimedia. Furthermore, as QuickTime adds features, they are automatically available to your REALbasic programs.

Talking to the outside world

The final group of REALbasic controls to consider provides communication functions. REALbasic has three controls that you can use for communication, as shown in Table 4-4.

Table 4-4	Communications Controls
Control Name	*Description*
DatabaseQuery	Automatically talks to databases
Serial	Adds serial communication capabilities
Socket	Provides TCP networking capabilities

The *Socket* control adds TCP/IP capabilities to your applications. With this control, you can perform common Web functions such as email and ftp. You can also create your own networking protocol and communicate that way too. Chapter 14 discusses the Socket control in greater detail.

The *Serial* control offers serial communication. This is useful for talking to hardware and home automation projects.

The *DatabaseQuery* control excels at talking to databases. With little or no code, DatabaseQuery can look up information in a database and automatically update the display of that data. Chapter 16 shows you how to use the DatabaseQuery control.

Events — Where All the Code Hangs Out

An *event* — in the real world and in REALbasic — is a special occurrence at some point in time. Controls have the capability to respond to a variety of events, such as a user clicking a mouse, pressing a key, or shutting down the computer. Each control has a list of events to which it can respond.

You attach code to these events so that when the event occurs (or *fires,* in programmer's jargon), the code is executed. You could think of events as code containers.

To view a particular control's events, follow these steps:

1. **Open a Window Editor.**

   In the Project window, double-click a window.

2. **Double-click a control.**

   The Code Editor opens with the control expanded to reveal its events. Within each of these events is a place to put code.

Figure 4-14 shows the expanded event structure of a PushButton control that contains code to display a message.

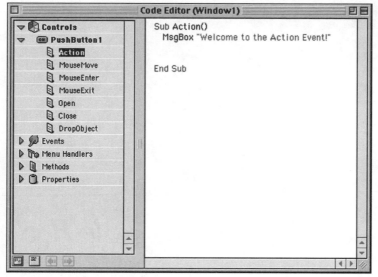

Figure 4-14:
An event is
a container
of code for
a control.

Chapter 5

OOP!

- -

In This Chapter

▶ Object-oriented programming demystified

▶ Creating objects and custom classes

- -

*1*f you're around computer programming for any length of time at all, you are bound to hear something about object-oriented programming. Object-oriented programming, also known as *OOP*, gets its share of hype, and for good reason. It strives to make programming easier and vastly more efficient for the programmer.

To get you started, this chapter explores some of the essential ideas behind object-oriented programming. You can apply most of the principles from this chapter to many different available programming languages. Once you have these basic ideas mastered, you can use them in REALbasic. The remainder of the chapter demonstrates how to take advantage of object-oriented principles in your own REALbasic projects.

Objects

The principal concept behind object-oriented programming is the object (no kidding, huh?). *Objects* are receptacles for information. They allow you to store related data together in one place. Furthermore, objects enable you to store instructions for manipulating that data.

Data? Manipulate? If all this sounds a tad confusing, you'll be glad to know that this type of setup more closely resembles the way things work in the real world. For example, consider an everyday object such as an automobile. An automobile has several unique properties, such as the following:

- ↙ Color: Black
- ↙ Model: Porsche
- ↙ Velocity: 190 Km/hr.
- ↙ Direction: 0 degrees (due North)

You can consider these characteristics to be kinds of data. In REALbasic OOP, you store each piece of information in a property that belongs to the object. Later, you can retrieve the data from the object by simply accessing the appropriate property.

This description of an automobile is nice, but objects in the real world also have functionality. To continue with the automobile analogy, cars can perform many functions. Some include:

- Accelerate
- Slow down
- Turn
- Honk the horn

Object-oriented programming lets you store instructions for performing each of these feats right along with the properties that describe the automobile. You access each of these functions by using the methods of the object. In other words, the *properties* of a REALbasic object represent the various characteristics of the object; the *methods* of the object describe the functionality of the object.

Encapsulation

One of the most important ideas behind object-oriented programming is the idea of encapsulation. *Encapsulation* is the capability of an object to store information about itself as well as the instructions for manipulating that information. Encapsulation permits the object to be self-reliant. No one else needs to worry about how the object works; it just works on its own.

Continuing once more with the automobile analogy, you don't necessarily need to know how an automobile engine works to use it. That's because the functionality is part of the automobile. You need to know only how to tell the car to go, stop, and turn. You don't have to know that gasoline ignites, pistons move, and wheels torque. Because encapsulation takes away the need for knowing about the inner-workings of an object, other people can use the use the object as easily as you can.

All these automobile analogies are nice, you say, but what about REALbasic classes? You've probably already used a REALbasic class. Windows, for example, are objects based on a Window class. When you test a project by choosing Debug➪Run and a window appears, you are looking at a Window object. The window, like the automobile, has some characteristics, or properties, that describe it:

  ✔ Width

  ✔ Height

  ✔ Title

  ✔ BackColor

Likewise, each Window object has built-in functionality in the form of methods. Some of these methods include

  ✔ Close

  ✔ Show

  ✔ Hide

Getting objects to do something

As mentioned, objects are good because they contain their own data and functionality. Nevertheless, how do you get at the data contained in their walls? Easy! You can communicate with the object through its methods. The object responds by carrying out a specific task, maybe even replying with resulting data from the task.

To communicate with an object, you use dot-notation, which begins with the name of the object, followed by the name of the method you would like to execute. For example, to tell an automobile object to slow down, you might use code like this:

```
automobile.slowdown
```

You can use the same dot-notation to retrieve information from one of the object's properties. For example, to find out an automobile's velocity, simply access the appropriate property:

```
Dim i as integer
i = automobile.velocity
```

Creating a Class

Now that you have an idea of what an object is, you're probably itching to create one. To create an object, you must first design a template that describes how the object should behave. This template is a class. After you have designed a class, you can create an object based on that class. Not only that, you can create as many objects as you want this way. Furthermore, you can export this class from your project and reuse it in other projects.

The mechanics of creating a class are simple enough. Choose File⇨New Class. When you do this, a Code Editor for the new class opens. In the Properties window, change the name of the class. To follow along with the example in this chapter, name the class Automobile, as shown in Figure 5-1.

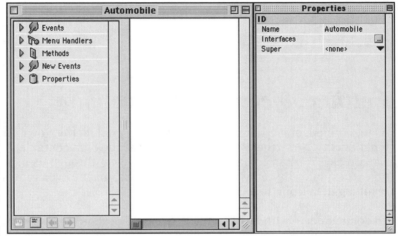

Figure 5-1:
Name new
classes
through the
Properties
window.

Now that you have a blank class staring you in the face, it's time to add some features to it. This is a good time to sit down with pen and paper and write down what you want the class to do. What characteristics will the class have? What functionality will the class perform? Think these questions through before diving headfirst into creating the class. Because you already looked at an imaginary class for automobiles previously in this chapter, you can extend this to a real class in REALbasic.

Adding properties

The first step in designing a class is to add some properties to it. These proper-ties describe the object that this class will produce. As mentioned, an automo-bile might have any number of properties that describe it, and objects do, too.

To add a property to a Class, choose Edit⇨New Property or press @⌘-Option-P. In the dialog box that appears, enter the declaration shown in Figure 15-2. This declaration adds a Velocity property to the Automobile class.

Declaration:	velocity as integer
☐ Private	
☐ Visible	

Delete   Cancel   OK

Continue adding properties to the class, following the same process. As discussed earlier, an automobile also has a make (such as Porsche, Audi, or Volkswagen), a color, and a direction. Table 5-1 shows all the properties and their associated data types. Add each one to the class by choosing Edit⇨New Property as before.

Table 5-1	Automobile Class Properties	
Property	*Type*	*New Property Dialog Box Entry*
Velocity	Integer	Velocity as Integer
Hue	Color	Hue as Color
Model	String	Model as String
Direction	Double	Direction as Integer

If you are unfamiliar with the data types in Table 5-1, suffice it to say that

- ✔ An integer is a number.
- ✔ A color stores color information.
- ✔ A string stores text.

Chapter 6 covers data types more thoroughly. For now, this is all you need to know about data types. And just remember that properties store information that describes an object.

Adding methods

The Automobile class you are creating should have four methods, one for each action the object can perform:

> ✔ Accelerate
>
> ✔ Decelerate
>
> ✔ Honk
>
> ✔ Turn (degrees as integer)

Three of the four methods require no additional information. The Turn method must be told how many degrees you want it to turn.

Adding methods to a class is a nearly identical process to adding properties. Choose Edit⇨New Method and add each method to the Automobile object, as shown in Figure 5-3.

Figure 5-3:
Add new methods to classes by choosing Edit⇨New Method.

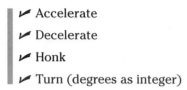

Method name:	Turn
Parameters:	Degrees as Integer
Return Type:	
☐ Private	
	Cancel OK

After you create the four methods for the Automobile class, enter the appropriate code for each method:

```
Sub Accelerate()
   Velocity = Velocity+10
   if Velocity>100 then
     Velocity=100
   end if
End Sub

Sub Decelerate()
   Velocity = Velocity-10
   if Velocity < 0 then
     Velocity = 0
   end if
End Sub

Sub Honk()
   //Honk three times
   Beep
   Beep
   Beep
End Sub
```

```
Sub Turn(degrees as integer))
   Direction = Direction + Degrees
   //only allow a direction in the range 0-360
   //otherwise wrap around
   if Direction > 360 then
     Direction = Direction-360
   end if
   if Direction < 0 then
     Direction = Direction + 360
   end if
End Sub
```

As you can see, the `Accelerate` and `Decelerate` methods increment and decrement the speed, respectively. The code for each also imposes limits on `Velocity`. `Velocity` may not exceed 100 on the top end, nor go below a value of 0 on the bottom end of the range (for this example, the code assumes that an automobile can't go slower than 0). The `Honk` method simply sounds the auto's horn three times. Finally, the `Turn` method either increments or decrements the Direction property. The additional code constrains the Direction to a range of 0 to 360.

Constructors and deconstructors

By manipulating only the properties of the class with methods of the same class, you can assure yourself that you are writing the best possible object-oriented code. So far, you have succeeded in pursuing this goal. What happens, though, when you create the object and you want to set default values for some or all properties of the class? Fortunately, the OOP gods are with you. To overcome this obstacle and prevent you from manipulating the object's properties from outside the object, REALbasic offers constructors and deconstructors for you to use.

A *constructor* is a method that executes the instant you create an object from a class. Because a constructor executes only once when you create the object, it's a convenient place to make initial settings for properties.

By convention, a constructor method shares the same name as the class. To create a constructor method for the Automobile class, choose Edit⇨New Method and enter the constructor's name, as shown in Figure 5-4.

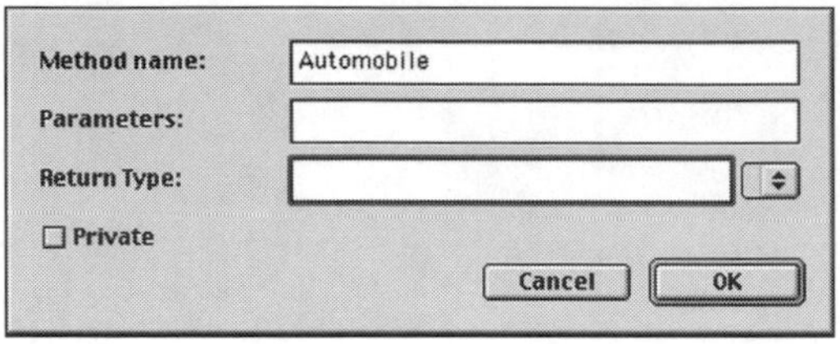

Figure 5-4:
The constructor method has the same name as the class where it resides.

Method name:	Automobile
Parameters:	
Return Type:	⬍
☐ Private	
	Cancel OK

Having defined the constructor method, add code to the method like this:

```
Sub Automobile()
   Velocity = 0
   Model = "Porsche"
   Hue = RGB(0,0,0)
   Direction = 0
End Sub
```

Thus, when your code creates a new Automobile object, it automatically has the values listed in the constructor method. In other words, this class now initializes itself as a black Porsche sitting at a dead stop and pointing due north.

Because the constructor method is part of the class, every Automobile object you create will begin life as a black Porsche. If you want your Automobile class to be a bit more generic and allow a variety of models and colors (blue Volkswagens, for example), you must change the code. For now, leave your Automobile class set to create black Porsches.

You can create a deconstructor method in a similar fashion. A *deconstructor method* executes the instant your program eliminates it from memory. To create a deconstructor method, name the method by placing a tilde character (~) before the name of the object. Figure 5-5 shows a deconstructor method definition for the Automobile class.

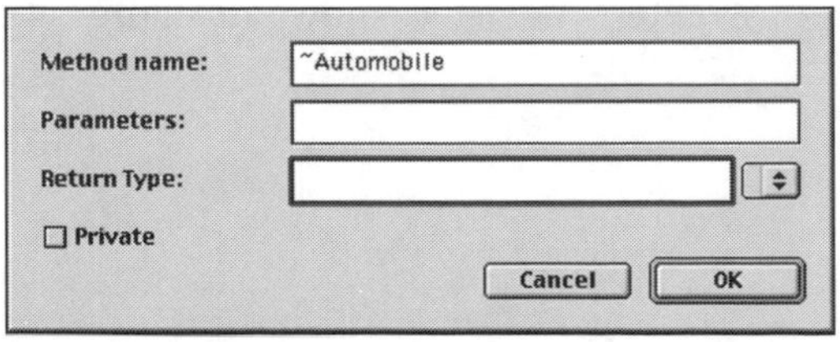

Figure 5-5:
The deconstructor method of a class shares the name of its class preceded by a tilde.

Method name:	~Automobile
Parameters:	
Return Type:	⬍
☐ Private	
	Cancel OK

Creating an Object

Having tediously created a new class called Automobile, it's time to cash in on your hard work. The reason you made a class was so you would have a template for creating an object. Object-oriented programmers call the act of creating a copy of an object *instantiation*. This stems from the fact that you are creating an *instance* of the object. If you created another object, you would be creating another instance of the same type of object. The two new objects have the same type, but are different instances of the same kind of object.

You can carry the analogy over to automobiles. When the factory spits out an automobile, it is instantiating the object. They have created an instance of a car object. When they create a second car, they instantiate another object. It is still a car (and possibly the same model and color), but it is a separate entity.

Using a class you created

With your sample class sitting contentedly in your Project window, it's a trivial matter to use it for creating an object. To create objects in REALbasic, you use the New command.

Before you use the New command, however, you need a place in memory to store the object. Therefore, you must define the name of the object, giving it a type equal to your class. The Automobile class produces objects with a type of Automobile. The code for creating a new Automobile type of object might look like this:

```
Dim myAutomobile as Automobile

myAutomobile = New Automobile
```

This code creates a new object named myAutomobile based on the Automobile class. The instant your code creates the myAutomobile object, the Automobile constructor method executes and initializes the properties of the object.

Now, when you want to send messages to this object, use the familiar dot-notation followed by the name of the method. For example, to create a new Automobile object and honk its horn three times, use the following:

```
Dim myAutomobile as Automobile

myAutomobile = New Automobile
myAutomobile.Honk
```

Because the Automobile class is just a template for an object, you can use it to create multiple objects:

```
Dim myAutomobile as Automobile
Dim myOtherAutomobile as Automobile

myAutomobile = New Automobile
myAutomobile.Honk
myOtherAutomobile = New Automobile
myAutomobile.Honk
```

As you can see, this code creates two independent Automobile objects. The Automobile class simply served as a stencil for creating each of the objects.

Using a class provided by REALbasic

You've seen how you can create objects using classes that you design yourself. In addition, REALbasic provides a wealth of classes that you can use to create all sorts of objects. Table 5-2 lists a few of the classes that REALbasic provides.

Table 5-2	Some REALbasic Classes
Class	*Description*
Clipboard	Transfers data to and from the Clipboard
Color	Stores color information
Picture	Stores a picture
PrinterSetup	Sets or retrieves the settings of the Page Setup dialog box
Date	Reports information about a date and time

You have many more classes than the ones listed in Table 5-2. To get a feel for just how many there are, open the *Language Reference* by choosing Window⇨ Reference or by pressing @⌘-1. Sort the list by Theme and expand the Class submenu as shown in Figure 5-6.

REALbasic classes come in a variety of shapes and with different functions. Because of this, several different methods are available for creating objects from a class. In many cases, you can use the New method to create the object. For instance, the Date class works this way:

```
Dim theDate as Date
theDate = New Date
```

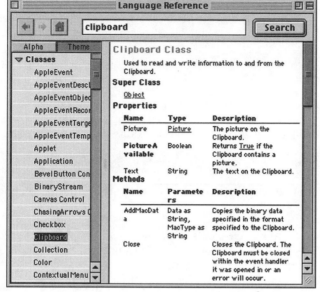

Figure 5-6:
Built-in
classes
provide a
wealth of
functionality.

To explore the use of built-in classes, create a new project in REALbasic by choosing File⇨New. To the project's default window (Window1), add a PushButton. By clicking PushButton, this code copies today's date to the Clipboard for easy access in your other applications.

Double-click PushButton to open its `Action` event in the Code Editor. In the event, enter this code:

```
Sub Action
  Dim theDate as Date
  Dim theClip as Clipboard

  theDate = New Date
  theClip = New Clipboard

  theClip.Text = theDate.LongDate
  theClip.Close
End Sub
```

The first two lines of code create a space in memory to hold a Date and a Clipboard object named theDate and theClip, respectively. The next two lines create the objects:

```
theDate = New Date
theClip = New Clipboard
```

Finally, the code places the LongDate property of theDate into the Text property of theClip. Clipboard objects also have a necessary additional step. You must always close the Clipboard project by sending it the Close message:

```
theClip.Text = theDate.LongDate
theClip.Close
```

Feel free to go ahead and test this project by choosing Debug⇔Run. When you click PushButton, you won't see much happening. Behind the scenes, however, the Clipboard should now sport today's date in a format like this:

```
Saturday, September 2, 2000
```

To see the results of your handiwork, switch to the Finder and choose Edit⇔Show Clipboard.

Although you create some objects with the New command, you create other objects by different means. Another good example is the FolderItem class from the last example. A FolderItem object represents some file on a disk. To create the FolderItem object, you have a couple possibilities:

```
Dim f as FolderItem
f = GetFolderItem("MyFile")

// OR

Dim f as FolderItem
f = PreferencesFolder

// OR

Dim f as FolderItem
f = GetOpenFolderItem("text")
```

Whew! Three different ways to create a FolderItem object? Yep, and that's not even all of them! Again, the specifics of each method are not important here. Just keep in mind that each kind of class may have its own peculiarities when it comes to instantiating an object with it. The New command is perhaps the most generic means of creating an object, but it is certainly not the only way.

The *Language Reference* has a detailed listing of the built-in classes available in REALbasic. The listings demonstrate how to create objects using each type of class. Again, to open the *Language Reference* in REALbasic, choose Window⇔Reference or press ⌘-1.

Chapter 6

Variables and Their Operators

● ●

In This Chapter

▶ Looking at the types of variables

▶ Creating variables

▶ Assigning values to variables and arrays

▶ Manipulating variables with operators

▶ Discovering more tricks with variables

● ●

Computers are great at handling information. They can perform complex mathematical computations, sort lists of text, or search through enormous amounts of data with ease. All these tasks have one thing in common: data manipulation. This might sound scary to a newcomer, but it isn't really so bad. You do data manipulation all the time. Add the value of the two quarters in your pocket. There! You've manipulated data without even knowing it. You combined the value of one quarter (25 cents) with the value of another quarter (another 25 cents) to come up with a total value of 50 cents. To arrive at the answer, you stored two numbers in your short-term memory and then added them.

Computers, too, have a type of short-term memory. To store values in the computer's memory, you use compartments called *variables*. This chapter takes a look at the various types of variables, how to create them, and ultimately how to use them.

Examining Variables

Computers, the finicky beasts, are particular about how you store data in their memory. They will let you use their memory, but only if you play by their rules. That sounds fair enough.

You must follow three basic rules when working with data in REALbasic (and most any other programming language):

- ✔ To manipulate data, you must first store it in a container called a variable.
- ✔ Before using a variable, you must declare it by giving it a name and a type.
- ✔ A variable can contain data of only the defined type.

Variables hold data. You put data into a variable so you can access it later, much like you store the telephone number in your brain for your favorite pizza joint. You give the pizza restaurant variable a name, such as Pizza Joint Around The Corner, and a type, in this case, a telephone number. Later, when you need to use the information again (when you're hungry for a pizza), you can quickly go to the variable and request the data that it holds (you recall the phone number).

And for the last rule, you put only a telephone number type of data in your Pizza Joint Around The Corner variable. That way, you get what you need. What good would it do, say, to put the color of the tablecloths in the variable?

Naming variables

To create a variable, you must give it a name and a type. The name is a string of letters and numbers that uniquely identifies the variable. It can't be the same name as any other variable around it. For example, most parents do not give two of their children the same name. Imagine the chaos of growing up in a house like that. Even when a child inherits a parent's first name, it's usually altered slightly to make it unique (think Junior versus Senior here).

Under special circumstances, variables within the same program can have the same name. However, take the easy route for now and simply name all your variables differently. If you do that, you can be sure to avoid any naming problems.

To come up with a name for a variable, combine any number of alphanumeric characters. *Alphanumeric* is a fancy way of saying "letters and numbers." Keep in mind, however, that

- ✔ A variable name must begin with a letter.
- ✔ Letters can be uppercase or lowercase — REALbasic treats them equally. For example, PizzaJoint is the same as PIZZAjoint.
- ✔ You may use letters and numbers, as well as the tilde (~) and the underscore (_).

Here are some valid variable names:

- ✔ x
- ✔ house23
- ✔ my_phone_number
- ✔ MyDearAuntSally (Note the absence of spaces between words.)

The following are examples of variables that are *not* allowed:

- ✔ 123 (The name does not begin with a letter.)
- ✔ house23*/& (This name contains mathematic characters.)
- ✔ Width (This is a REALbasic keyword.)
- ✔ My Dear Aunt Sally (This name has spaces.)

Get in the habit of naming your variables with explanatory names. A good name might describe the function or feature of the variable. For instance, if you're planning to store someone's age in a variable, why not name the variable something like theAge? This would surely be easier to remember than a more generic name such as abc2.

Types of variables

In addition to a name, a variable has a type. Remember that a variable is a container for information — but only a certain type of information. REALbasic has many types of variables for storing different types of data, as this section describes.

Numbers

One of the most common forms of data is a number. You can store several types of numbers in a variable, depending on your needs. If you are frightened of math, fear not! You're already familiar with these types of numbers: integers and precision numbers.

Integers are numbers with no decimal value. You use them all the time. When you count to ten, do the New Year's countdown, or chant "We're number one!" you're using integers. Integers also include negative numbers. If someone owes you five bucks, you can be said to have -5 (negative five) dollars. Any number less than zero is a negative number.

That wasn't so bad, was it? Integers are good for storing information such as

- ✔ The number of iMacs or G4 Cubes at your school
- ✔ The number of children in your home (unless you have the typical 2.5 kids)
- ✔ The number of speeding tickets you received last year

You typically store values as integers when you want to perform some type of calculation with the value.

The second type of number you can store in a variable is a *precision number,* which comes in two varieties, singles and doubles. No, I'm not talking about tennis, folks. *Singles* and *doubles* are numbers that have a decimal point in their value. Just look at your last grocery store receipt and you'll see an example of precision numbers. A double type allows you to store dollars and cents, but an integer allows you to store the dollar amount only.

Following are some examples of numbers that lend themselves well to a single or double data type:

- ✔ 98.6 degrees Fahrenheit, or 37.3 degrees Celsius
- ✔ 0.1222 (an interest rate, in this case 12.2%)
- ✔ 34.6 miles, or 55.68 kilometers

Like integers, you can use singles and doubles for storing numbers to be used in a calculation.

So, when do you use a single versus a double? The difference between them is beyond the scope of this book. For now, just forget about the singles altogether and simply use a double. A double can handle any task that a single can — and more.

Strings

What do you do when you want to store some information that isn't a number? Suppose you want to store a person's name, the color of a pair of shoes, or a description of your favorite movie. This is where the string type comes into play.

A *string* is a series of characters stuck together — in other words, text. Any text that you might enter into a word processor, including all letters, numbers, and punctuation marks, can be a string.

Wait a second! Did I just say numbers? Yes. In this case, however, the numbers have no mathematical significance. For example, although telephone numbers consist of numbers, you don't do any calculations with telephone numbers, such as adding them. Therefore, telephone numbers belong in a string variable, not a number variable.

Now, back to our regularly scheduled program. Some examples of strings follow:

- ✔ John Doe (a name)
- ✔ 123 Nowhere Street (an address)
- ✔ (555) 555-1212 (a telephone number)
- ✔ Q (a single letter)
- ✔ @^#A%$! (censored comic strip language)
- ✔ An entire e-mail message

Booleans

Boolean (rhymes with *Julian*) variables can store one of two values: TRUE or FALSE. You can extend this metaphor to any other situation in which a variable can hold one of two values. Some common Boolean values in your life include the following:

- ✔ Yes or no
- ✔ On or off
- ✔ Employed or unemployed
- ✔ Legal or illegal

These are opposites and, as such, have no other possible values. What about, say, the color white? You might consider its opposite to be black. But a Boolean is a poor choice for storing a color because the color could also be red, green, blue, or many others. However, if your program gave only two choices for a color (such as black and white), a Boolean might suffice.

Variants

What happens if you're a person who doesn't like to make decisions? You aren't sure whether you want the variable to store numbers or text. Enter the variant type.

A *variant* is capable of storing different types of variables. It can store data in the form of an integer, a double, a string, or a Boolean. It's like a chameleon, adapting itself to its environment. One minute you might store a numeric value in a variant; the next minute you might store some text. REALbasic programmers often use variants for database applications when they don't know what type of information a user will enter.

Now that you know what's great about variants, you should know also that you shouldn't use them unless you have to. When the computer can work with a specific variable type, it performs its task more efficiently (and faster). Thus, if you know what type of variable you will need, use it and not the catchall variant type.

Arrays

When you want to store a list of numbers or names in a variable, you use an array. An *array* is a group of variables that share the same name and type. The only thing that distinguishes each individual item of an array is its index number. It might help to think of a game show in which the contestants are named Contestant 1, Contestant 2, and Contestant 3. A number preceded by the same name identifies each contestant.

The days of the week make a nice array:

> Day(1)=Sunday
>
> Day(2)=Monday
>
> Day(3)=Tuesday
>
> Day(4)=Wednesday
>
> Day(5)=Thursday
>
> Day(6)=Friday
>
> Day(7)=Saturday

Note that the preceding example is not syntactically correct REALbasic code. It's only a generic representation of how arrays work. The next section explains how to write the real code for arrays.

The naming strategy for arrays is identical to the one for variables. In particular, you may name an array with any combination of alphanumeric characters. When using the array, simply refer to it by name. When using a particular element in the array, an index number enclosed within parentheses must follow the name of the array.

Arrays are versatile creatures and can be of any type, such as string, integer, or Booleans. However, you can store only one type of data in an array. If you make an array to hold integers, for example, you may not store any other type of data in the array. The sole exception here is the variant type, which can store many different types of data within the same array.

Declaring Variables

Armed with your knowledge about variable types and their naming conventions, you can finally tackle the tasks at hand: creating and using a variable. Before using a variable, you must tell your program to create it, providing the name and the type. You can do this with the Dim statement, which has the following form:

```
Dim theVariableName as theType
```

This code tells the computer to create a variable with the given name (theVariableName) and type (theType). Dim is shorthand for the word *dimension*.

To try your hand at creating each of the common variable types, enter the following code in the Action event of a PushButton:

```
Dim firstName as String
Dim lastName as String
Dim theAge as Integer
Dim theShoeSize as Integer
Dim theAccountBalance as Double
Dim isTheLightOn as Boolean
Dim NumberOrText as Variant
```

You can combine variable declarations into one statement. The following, for example, is legal:

```
Dim firstName, lastName as String
Dim theAge, theShoeSize as Integer
```

Used with discretion, this shortcut saves you time and space. Putting too many variable names on the same line, however, can make your code difficult to read and maintain.

You can use the variables that you declared with the Dim statement for as long as the code within the event is executing, or *firing*. When the event has finished firing, REALbasic disposes of all variables you created. Don't worry, though. Your program will create them again the next time this event fires. In this way, you can see that variables are like pieces of short-term memory. After you are finished using them, there is no reason for keeping them around.

The Dim statement must come before all other code in an event or a method — with a few exceptions, one of which is shown in Chapter 18. If you put code before the Dim statement, REALbasic quickly displays an error message when you try to test the code:

```
Dim statement must come before code
```

In this case, REALbasic helps you out and tells you the exact problem with your code.

The Dim statement for creating arrays looks a bit different than the one for creating variables. Instead of creating a variable that holds only one value, the Dim statement creates an *array variable*. These variables are easy to spot because they're accompanied by an index number, such as Pizza(3).

When using the `Dim` statement to create an array, you must include a size that indicates how many different values you would like to store. For example:

```
Dim Names(10) as String
```

This creates an array called `Names` that will hold 11 strings of text. Hold on! The statement says `10`! Arrays are zero-based, which means that the index number of the elements in the array starts at 0, not 1. The preceding example creates this array of elements:

```
Name(0)
Name(1)
Name(2)
.
.
.
Name(10)
```

If you want to create an array of 10 strings, you could write the following:

```
Dim Names(9) as String
```

All this zero-element stuff can get a tad confusing. Thus, many programmers use `Names(10)`, for example, and simply ignore the first element of the array (element 0). That is, they begin using the array with element 1 instead of element 0. This makes the code behave a little more as it looks and removes some of the confusion of accounting for the `zero` (0) element.

Assigning Values to Variables

After you declare the variables and arrays you need, it's time to put them to use by assigning them values. To do so, you use an equal sign (=).

The following code continues with the example in the preceding section. First you declare the variables and then you assign them values:

```
Dim firstName, lastName as String
Dim theAge, ShoeSize as Integer
Dim theAccountBalance as Double
Dim isTheLightOn as Boolean
Dim NumberOrText as Variant

firstName = "John"
lastName = "Doe"
theAge = 29
ShoeSize = 10
```

```
theAccountBalance = 120.59
isTheLightOn = TRUE

//the variant can be assigned one type
//of value now and another later
//first, it's an integer
NumberOrText = 5
//now it's a string
NumberOrText = "hello"
```

The equal sign (=) in each statement is not exactly the same as a traditional equal sign. ShoeSize is not *equal* to 10. Instead, ShoeSize gets the value of 10.

Here are a few other things to note about this code:

- ✔ When assigning a value to a string, place double quotes around its value, such as "John" or "123-456-789".

- ✔ Numbers must not have quotes.

- ✔ Booleans don't require quotes because they don't represent the string "TRUE" or "FALSE". Instead, they're a numeric on/off switch.

- ✔ The rule-breaking variant types (they sound mischievous by name, don't they?) can assign variables however they want, though they must follow the rule of quotes around strings.

After you store a value in a variable, you can access its value by simply referring to the variable by name. For example, to quickly display the firstName variable, use the MsgBox command:

```
MsgBox firstName
```

To retrieve the value from a variable and simultaneously assign it to another variable, use code like this:

```
Dim myFirstName, myFriendsName as string
myFirstName = "Erick"
myFriendsName = myFirstName
```

Assigning Values to Arrays

When you need to store a group of related data, using multiple variables can become a bit messy. Fortunately, REALbasic, like most programming languages, has a tool for such a situation. This tool is called an array.

An *array* works much like a variable or a property, but it has the special capability to store a list of values, rather than only one value. An array can store as many values as you like, as long as each element in the array holds the same type of data.

Array elements have a zero-based index number that identifies each item in the array. To use an item in the array, you refer to it by the array's name and its index number. For example, you might name an array of integers `MyNumbers`. The first element of the array has the name `MyNumbers(0)`, the second `MyNumbers(1)`, and so on.

To assign values to arrays, you follow all the usual variable rules for assignment. The main difference is that array elements must also feature an index number.

Again, to continue with the preceding example, add this code:

```
Dim Names(10) as String

Names(0) = "Alan"
Names(1) = "Amanda"
Names(2) = "Conner"
Names(3) = "Gretchen"
Names(4) = "James"
Names(5) = "Kendra"
Names(6) = "Luke"
Names(7) = "Maria"
Names(8) = "McKenna"
Names(9) = "Melanie"
Names(10) = "Mercedes"
```

To retrieve any element of an array, you refer to the element by name and index number. For example, to get the content of element five from the `Names` array and display it quickly in a small window, use the `MsgBox` command:

```
MsgBox Names(4)
```

To assign the value to another value, use the equal sign, as before:

```
Dim SomePerson as String
.
.//"Names" array assignment goes here
.
SomePerson = Names(3)
```

Arrays lend themselves nicely to loops. For example, if you were to store ten names as separate variables, you would have to specify each one individually by name. This tedious task requires ten lines of code. By looping through the array, you reduce the amount of code to a few lines:

```
Dim j as Integer

For j=1 to 10
    MsgBox Names(j)
Next
```

Mathematical Operators Connect Numbers

The real power of using variables comes with the capability to manipulate them. To manipulate a variable, you must perform an operation. You don't have to perform any medical procedure for this operation, but your variables might not look the same again.

An *operator* is a special one-character command that involves one or two variables. Some operators change a variable; other operators connect two variables in some fashion.

You use many operators every day. For example, when you add a tip to your restaurant bill, you're using an operator (actually, maybe more than one). Table 6-1 shows the operators available in REALbasic.

Table 6-1	REALbasic Operators	
Operator	*Function*	*Use It With*
+	Addition	Integers, doubles, strings
-	Subtraction	Integers, doubles
*	Multiplication	Integers, doubles
/	Division	Doubles
\	Division	Integers

Common mathematics is easy with variables and operators. To convert a Fahrenheit temperature to a Celsius temperature:

```
Dim FahrenheitTemp,CelsiusTemp as Double

FahrenheitTemp = 98.6
CelsiusTemp = (5/9)*(Fahrenheit-32)
```

All standard algebra rules apply when using operators. REALbasic evaluates numbers within parentheses first, followed by operations in this order:

- ✔ Multiplication
- ✔ Division
- ✔ Addition
- ✔ Subtraction

A useful mnemonic is the phrase "My Dear Aunt Sally." The first letter of each word in this phrase corresponds to the first letter of each operation.

Of the operators listed in Table 6-1, notice that the + operator is capable of manipulating string variables. Rather than call this addition, programmers like to call it *concatenation.* Normal people might call it "sticking two things together." The + operator takes two strings and merges them into one string.

For example, to concatenate two names:

```
Dim firstName,lastName,wholeName as String

firstName = "Erick"
lastName = "Tejkowski"

wholeName = firstName + lastName
MsgBox wholeName
```

If you run this code, you will see the firstName and lastName variables stuck together in a MsgBox window: ErickTejkowski. REALbasic joins the two names with nothing between them. But this isn't how you usually want to present data. Adding a space between the firstName and lastName, however, is easy:

```
Dim firstName,lastName,wholeName as String

firstName = "Erick"
lastName = "Tejkowski

wholeName = firstName
//a space between the names
wholeName = wholeName + " "
wholeName = wholeName + lastName
//note the leading space
wholeName = wholeName + " likes to read Dummies books."

MsgBox wholeName
```

There's no limit to the amount of string you can add together. When strings get too unwieldy, simplify matters by appending a string to itself, as I did here.

Figure 6-1 shows the difference a little string concatenation can make.

Figure 6-1:
Impress you
friends with
string
concaten-
ation.

If you need to erase the contents of a string, set it to an empty string:

```
wholeName = ""
```

This might be useful, for example, when you want to clear a StaticText display:

```
wholeName=""
StaticText1.text = wholeName
```

REALbasic has a different set of operators for manipulating Boolean variables, as shown in Table 6-2. Mathematicians sometimes call this type of math *logic*.

Table 6-2		Boolean Operators
Operator	*Action*	*Values*
AND	Performs a logical AND operation	TRUE AND TRUE = TRUE
		TRUE AND FALSE = FALSE
		FALSE AND TRUE = FALSE
		FALSE AND FALSE = FALSE
OR	Performs a logical OR operation	TRUE OR TRUE = TRUE
		TRUE OR FALSE = TRUE
		FALSE OR TRUE = TRUE
		FALSE OR FALSE = FALSE
NOT	Negates a variable	NOT TRUE = FALSE
		NOT FALSE = TRUE

The AND operator is useful when you want to make a decision based on several criteria. For example:

```
if (theLightIsOn=TRUE) AND (myAge>=21) then
    MsgBox "The light is on and you are more than 21."
end if
```

Although it appears that the AND operator is comparing two unlike variables (a Boolean and an integer), it is actually comparing two Boolean values. REALbasic evaluates everything that appears within a set of parentheses as either a TRUE or FALSE value. If the myAge variable holds a value greater than 21, that part of the expression evaluates as TRUE. REALbasic checks both expressions for a TRUE value. If both are TRUE, the MsgBox command executes. If one or both expressions evaluate as FALSE, the MsgBox command does not execute.

The OR operator checks to see whether one of the two expressions evaluates to TRUE. Only one of the expressions must evaluate to TRUE for the code to proceed:

```
if (theLightIsOn=TRUE) OR (myAge>=21) then
    MsgBox "Either the light's on, or you are more than 21, or
            both facts are true."
end if
```

The NOT operator simply flips the value of a Boolean variable to its opposite. If the value is currently TRUE, the NOT operator sets it to FALSE and vice versa.

```
theLightIsOn=NOT(theLightIsOn) //turns light on and off
```

More Fun with Variables

REALbasic offers many other ways to manipulate variables. Sometimes you might want to convert a variable from one data type to another. Other times, you might want to squeeze vital information from a string. REALbasic can do all this — and more.

Math lovers will rejoice in the standard mathematics routines. And if all this weren't enough, REALbasic can also take care of making variables look nice for output.

Data conversion

Because variables can hold only a specific type of data, the time may come when you find this inflexible. For example, suppose you want to place the value from an integer variable into a string variable:

```
Dim i as Integer
Dim s as String

i = 7
s= "There are " + i + "days in a week."
MsgBox s
```

This code produces an error:

```
Expecting a numeric operand
```

The code attempted to place an integer variable in a string variable, which is a strict no-no. To get around this problem, you can convert the integer to a string and then place it in the string using the Str command:

```
Dim i as Integer
Dim s,ss as String

i = 7
ss = Str(i)
s = "There are " +ss + "days in a week."
MsgBox s
```

The code returns the following message on the screen: There are 7 days in a week.

Alternatively, to simplify matters and preclude the need for a new string variable, just place the Str command inline:

```
Dim i as Integer
Dim s as String

i = 7
s = "There are " + Str(i) + "days in a week."
MsgBox s
```

If you need to go in the opposite direction, from a string to a number, the Val command comes to the rescue. The Val command returns a double:

```
Dim i as Double
Dim s as String

s = "7.35"
i = Val(s)
```

Because a double and an integer are both numbers, REALbasic gladly converts between the two. Thus, code like the following is also acceptable (although you must strip all decimal values):

```
Dim i as Double
Dim s as String

s = "7"
i = Val(s)
```

The variable conversion commands mentioned so far have all assumed that the numbers would contain a decimal point. To give your REALbasic applications an international flair, use the `CDbl` and `CStr` commands. They work the same as the `Val` and `Str` commands, respectively, but do not assume a decimal point as the numeric separator. Instead, the commands use the current separator from the Numbers control panel of the Mac OS. Thus, the commands tailor themselves to any currency a user desires. Table 6-3 summarizes the four variable conversion commands.

Table 6-3	Commands for Converting Variables	
Command	*Converts*	*To*
Val	String	Double
Str	Double or integer	String
CDbl	String	Double (internationally aware)
CStr	Double	Integer (internationally aware)

Math fun

For the mathematically fearless, REALbasic hosts a fair amount of math routines for your number-crunching needs.

Rounding

REALbasic has three commands for rounding numbers. The standard mathematical `Round` command rounds down if the decimal portion of a number is less than 0.5. If the decimal portion of a number is 0.5 or greater, REALbasic rounds the number up. Here's an example:

```
Dim myTaxes as Double

myTaxes = Round(25.23)
// rounds down to 25 because .23<.5
MsgBox str(myTaxes)

myTaxes = Round(25.62)
// rounds up to 26, because .62>.5
MsgBox str(myTaxes)
```

If you want to control the direction in which the rounding occurs, use the Ceil and Floor functions. The Ceil function rounds up (to the *ceil*ing), and Floor rounds down:

```
Dim myReturn, myTaxes as Double

myReturn = Ceil(25.23)
// force-rounds up to 26
MsgBox str(myReturn)

myTaxes = Floor(25.62)
// rounds down to 25
// and who wouldn't like their taxes rounded down!?
MsgBox str(myTaxes)
```

Trigonometry

REALbasic is a pro at doing trigonometry homework too! It can compute all the typical trigonometry functions, as shown in Table 6-4.

Table 6-4	REALbasic Trigonometric Functions	
Function	*Takes*	*Gives*
Sin	Angle in radians	Sine of the angle
Cos	Angle in radians	Cosine of the angle
Tan	Angle in radians	Tangent of an angle
Asin	Sine of an angle	Angle in radians
Acos	Cosine of an angle	Angle in radians
Atan	Tangent of an angle	Angle in radians

As you can see, each trigonometric function talks about angles in radians. This might make math phobics everywhere run screaming. Fear not! It's a simple matter to convert from degrees (which almost everyone understands) to radians (which only math wizards understand). Suppose you want to find the sine of 90 degrees. Convert degrees to radians like this:

```
Dim myAngle,mySine as Double

myAngle = 90 //degrees
//now convert to radians
myAngle = myAngle * 0.01745
//now find the Sin of the angle
mySine = Sin(myAngle)
MsgBox str(mySine)
```

This code displays a MsgBox containing a number 1.

If you want to go in reverse order and convert radians to degrees, just divide by 0.01745:

```
Dim myAngle,mySine as Double

mySine = 1 //the Sine of an angle
//get the angle in radians
myAngle = Asin(mySine)
//convert to degrees
myAngle = myAngle / 0.01745
MsgBox str(myAngle)
```

This code displays a MsgBox with a value of 90.

Other useful math functions

Math mavens around the world will be glad to know that REALbasic supports most other mathematical functions. Some of the most important are pictured in Figure 6-2 and include

✔ Square root

✔ Exponents

✔ Logarithms

Figure 6-2: Calculating other important mathematical functions is a snap with REALbasic.

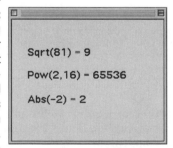

```
Sqrt(81) = 9

Pow(2,16) = 65536

Abs(-2) = 2
```

To find the square root of a number, use the Sqrt function:

```
Dim myNumber as Double
myNumber = 81
myNumber = Sqrt(myNumber)
MsgBox "Sqrt="+str(myNumber)
```

Comic book fans will love the Pow function. Just kidding. The Pow command is really for raising a number to a power. To multiply the number 2 sixteen times, for example, use code like this:

```
Dim myNumber as Double
myNumber = Pow(2,16)
MsgBox str(myNumber)
```

To get the absolute value of a number, use the Abs function:

```
Dim myNumber as Double
myNumber = -2
MsgBox "Abs value of "+myNumber+"="+Str(Abs(myNumber))
```

REALbasic also has a Log function, but it behaves differently than you might expect. That's because it's a natural log function. To get the Log function to act like the Log button on a calculator, simply divide by Log(10):

```
Dim myNumber,myLog as Double
myNumber = 100
myLog = Log(myNumber) / Log(10)
MsgBox "Log(" + myNumber + ")=" + str(myLog)
```

String manipulation

If all this math talk is making your head spin, relax. The math is gone for now. It's time to look at strings. REALbasic offers many nifty functions for manipulating strings of text. It slices; it dices; it turns your strings inside out.

Finding the length of a string

Finding the length of a string in REALbasic is a cinch. The Len command takes a string as its parameter and returns the length:

```
Dim s as String
Dim i as Integer

s = "REALbasic"
i = Len(s)

MsgBox "Length of string = " + Str(i)
```

This code displays the following in a MsgBox window:

```
Length of string = 9
```

Getting parts of a string

You can use REALbasic to look at any part of a string. To pull characters off the beginning or end of a string, use the Left and Right methods. For example:

```
Dim s as string

s="REALbasic is simple to use"

//To get the first 9 characters from s, use Left
MsgBox Left(s,9)
//To get the last 13 characters from s, use Right
MsgBox Right(s,13)
```

The first MsgBox command produces REALbasic. And the second MsgBox command produces simple to use.

If you want to extract some part of a string from anywhere within that string, use the Mid function. It takes three parameters: a string, the starting position for extraction, and an optional length parameter.

Parameters are pieces of data that a method needs to execute properly. To relate parameters to spoken English, you can't use the word *put* in a sentence without including:

- A location for where the *put* should occur
- An object that you want to *put*

In this case, the location and object are parameters of the English verb *put*. Without them, the word *put* doesn't make sense. Don't believe me? Try to make a sentence with the word *put* that doesn't have a location and an object. I bet you can't!

If you choose to leave out the last parameter, REALbasic returns all characters from the starting point.

```
Dim s as String

s = "REALbasic is fun."
//get two characters starting at position 11
MsgBox Mid(s,11,2)
//get all characters starting at position 11
MsgBox Mid(s,11)
```

The first example displays a MessageBox window with

```
is
```

The second example displays

```
is fun.
```

Making variables look nice

Some functions in REALbasic are strictly for making your string variables look nice.

Changing case

It's a trivial matter to change any string to uppercase or lowercase. Use the Uppercase or Lowercase method, which seems fairly obvious. REALbasic also has a special case-changing command called Titlecase. This method converts all text to lowercase and then makes the first letter of each word uppercase. Here's an example of all three:

```
Dim s as String

s="tHiS EXamplE shOwS oFf REalBasIC cAsE mETHods"

s=Uppercase(s)
MsgBox s

s=Lowercase(s)
MsgBox s

s=Titlecase(s)
MsgBox s
```

Figure 6-3 shows the various results of changing the case.

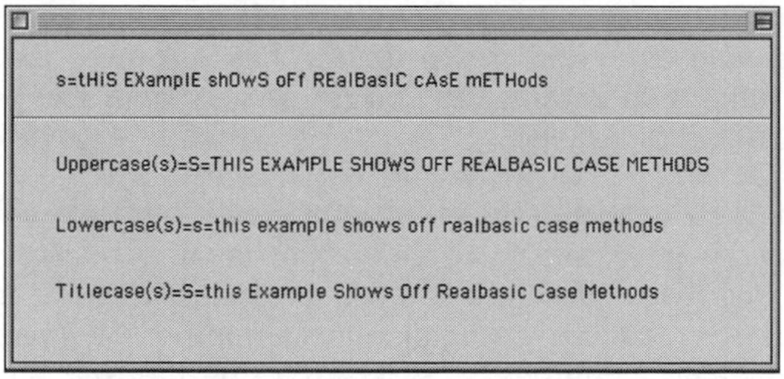

Figure 6-3:
REALbasic
is adept at
changing
the case of
text.

s=tHiS EXamplE shOwS oFf REalBasIC cAsE mETHods

Uppercase(s)=S=THIS EXAMPLE SHOWS OFF REALBASIC CASE METHODS

Lowercase(s)=s=this example shows off realbasic case methods

Titlecase(s)=S=this Example Shows Off Realbasic Case Methods

Trimming extra spaces

To remove extra white space (tabs and spaces) from strings, REALbasic offers three methods. LTrim removes white space from the beginning of a string, RTrim removes from the end, and Trim removes from the beginning and end.

```
Dim s1,s2,s3 as string

s1 = "      REALbasic is good."
s1 = LTrim(s1)
MsgBox s1

s2 = "REALbasic is great.        "
s2 = RTrim(s2)
MsgBox s2

s3 = "      Extra spaces are a terrible fate.      "
s3 = Trim(s3)
MsgBox s3
```

This example displays three different windows with spaces removed. The first window displays

```
REALbasic is good.
```

with the leading spaces removed. The second window displays

```
REALbasic is great.
```

without spaces at the end of the string. The final MsgBox window displays a string with spaces removed from the beginning and end of the string:

```
Extra spaces are a terrible fate.
```

Formatting numbers

The `Double` variable type is a number with a whole bunch of decimal points in it. To tame this wild beast and create strings that look nice, use the `Format` method. `Format` takes two parameters and returns a string. The parameters are the number and a formatSpec.

The *formatSpec* is a string of symbols that represent the format you want your `Double` in and works similarly to the formatting in spreadsheet programs such as Excel. The characters you will use most often in a formatSpec are 0 and #. A # in a formatSpec string displays a number if it exists. A 0 in the formatSpec displays a number if it exists; if it doesn't exist, a 0 appears in its absence. For example:

```
Dim myNumber as Double
Dim myFormattedString as String

myNumber = 3.1415927
myFormattedString = Format(myNumber,"#.####")
MsgBox myFormattedString

myNumber = 3.14
myFormattedString = Format(myNumber, "#.##00")
MsgBox myFormattedString
```

Figure 6-4 displays the results of the Format command.

Figure 6-4:
Use the
Format
command
anytime you
want to
precisely
control the
display of
numbers.

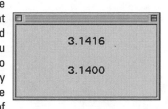

You can add several other characters to the formatSpec for the Format command. Check the *REALbasic Language Reference* included on the *REALbasic For Dummies* CD for a more thorough explanation of this method.

Chapter 7

Bossing Your Program Around

. . . .

In This Chapter

▶ Making decisions with the REALbasic language

▶ Doing things repeatedly

▶ Adding reminders to your code

. . . .

*I*nterfaces and pretty pictures are nice, but you want to make things happen. Controls and windows just sit there. You need the computer to listen to your commands, make some decisions along the way, and perform functions a few thousand times if necessary.

Luckily, the REALbasic language can do all this and more. Its decision-making commands will make your program look like it's a living being capable of thought. Add some commands to perform actions repeatedly, and your program looks like a tireless worker. This chapter takes you through the basics of code control by showing you how to repeat code and make decisions. The chapter ends with a discussion of REALbasic comments, which help you notate your code so that you can make sense of it later.

You Make the Decisions around Here!

Sometimes pretty pictures need to take a back seat to functionality. Besides, what good is an interface if it doesn't do anything? REALbasic gives you full control over making decisions in your code. These code decisions are much like the decisions you make every day. For example:

✔ If your car's speed exceeds 65 mph, you press the brake; otherwise, you press the accelerator.

✔ When you sort through your mail, you hold onto bills, magazines, and letters from your mother but discard junk mail.

When you program computers, you might need to make decisions like these:

- ✔ If the user's name is "Brian" and his password is 321, load the "Brian" address book for the user.
- ✔ If the day of the week is Saturday or Sunday, display the message "Have a nice weekend!"

If-Then statements

The primary decision-making method in REALbasic is the If-Then statement. You can use If-Then statements in a few different ways.

If-Then

The basic If-Then statement works as follows. Note, however, that this example uses *pseduo-code,* which is code that's not syntactically correct but roughly displays the idea behind the programming logic in common language:

```
if some_condition_is_True then
   Execute this code
end if
```

If a particular condition is TRUE, the code that follows then is executed. If the condition evaluates to FALSE, no code is executed. For example, if you wanted to greet your friend, Katie, you could use code (not pseudo this time) such as:

```
if name="Katie" then
   MsgBox "Hello Katie"
   // Other code can execute here too
end if
```

REALbasic evaluates the code like this:

- ✔ Look at the contents of the variable called name and see whether it contains the Katie string. If it does, display the Hello Katie! message.
- ✔ If the contents of name do not equal to the contents of Katie, skip to the code that follows end if, which marks the end of the If statement.

Here's another example:

```
if name="Jerry" AND age<30 then
   MsgBox "Hello Jerry Jr."
end if
```

Here's how REALbasic executes this code:

✔ Look at the contents of the `name` and `age` variables. If `name` contains the `Jerry` string and `age` holds a number less than 30, display the message `Hello Jerry Jr`. Both statements have to be `TRUE` because the word `AND` appears between the conditions.

✔ If both these conditions are not `TRUE`, skip to the code following the `end if` statement.

If-Then-Else

Sometimes you want to do something if a condition is not met. For example:

```
if some_condition_is_True then
   Execute this first code
otherwise
   Execute this second code
end if
```

If some condition is `TRUE`, the first bit of code is executed. If the condition is not `TRUE`, the second bit of code is executed. This is the perfect place to make a decision using the If-Then-Else statement. The basic form of this statement is

```
if some_condition_is_True then
   ExecuteThisCode
else
   ExecuteSomeOtherCode
end if
```

Here's a real code example:

```
if age<30 then
   MsgBox "You are younger than 30"
else
   MsgBox "You are older than 30"
end if
```

This code executes as follows:

✔ Is the age less than 30? If it is, display the `You are younger than 30` message.

✔ Otherwise, display the `You are older than thirty` message.

If you thought that example was fancy, wait until you see the next one, in which REALbasic offers an even fancier way to use If-Then statements.

If-Then-ElseIf-Else

The next version of the If-Then statement adds the `ElseIf` command. The `ElseIf` command allows you to test other conditions within an If-Then statement. Suppose you want to test the conditions in this pseudo-code:

```
if money>1000 then
   //Buy a computer.
if money is not>1000 then check to see whether it is >100
            then
   //Buy a video game.
if money is not >100 then check to see whether it is >10 then
   //Go see a movie.
Otherwise
   //Stay home.
end if
```

It's easy to accomplish something like this:

```
if money>1000 then
   //money=money-1000
elseif money>100 then
   //money=money-100
elseif money>10 then
   //money=money-10
else
     //money amount does not change
end if
```

REALbasic evaluates the code as follows:

- If the amount of money is more than 1000, subtract 1000 from the money to buy a computer.

- If the amount of money is not more than 1000, check to see whether it is more than 100. If it is, subtract 100 from the money for a video game console.

- If the amount of money is not more than 100, check to see whether it is it more than 10. If it is, subtract 10 from the money for a movie ticket.

- If the money is not greater than 10, no change takes place.

Select Case statements

If-Then statements are useful for controlling how your code works, but as you can see from the last example, things can start to get pretty hairy when a lot of decisions are being made. Rather than string together a list of ElseIf statements, it's usually a lot simpler to use a Select Case statement. This type of statement is particularly good at making decisions from a long list of values.

Suppose that you want a program to display a price for each of the 100 types of pizza your restaurant makes. The price varies depending on the topping. Using the traditional If-Then statement, your code begins to look nightmarish:

```
If pizza="mushroom" then
   price=10
elseif pizza="pepperoni" then
   price=11
elseif pizza="sausage" then
   price=12
   .
   .
   .
end if
```

The Select Case statement cleans this mess up quite a bit. The statement starts with `Select Case` followed by a variable name. Next is a list of values that variable might have. Finally, the decision ends with the `End Select` statement. So, the same pizza example using Select Case is much more readable and a lot easier to follow:

```
Select Case pizza
Case "mushroom"
   price=10
Case "pepperoni"
   price=11
Case "sausage"
   price=12
   .
   .
   .
Case "peanut butter"
   price=19
End Select
```

Here's what happens:

- ✔ Look at the variable named `pizza`.
- ✔ If `pizza` is mushroom, the price is 10.
- ✔ If `pizza` if pepperoni, the price is 11.
- ✔ And so on, until every item in the list has been looked at. Then stop looking at the `pizza` variable.

Feeling Loopy?

Another great capability of computers is their willingness to do mundane tasks as many times as you want. They chug along doing some task for 24 hours just as effortlessly as they do for only 1 hour. To get a computer to do a task repeatedly, programmers came up with the idea of a loop.

A *loop* is a block of code that repeats in any of the following ways:

- ✔ A certain number of times
- ✔ Until a condition is met
- ✔ Forever

The REALbasic language has a host of commands to fill each of these looping needs.

Looping a fixed number of times

To repeat a block of code a certain number of times, use the For-Next loop. This type of loop uses an integer variable to keep track of the number of times the loop occurs. (Don't forget that an integer is a number without a decimal point.) You must define the variable with the Dim statement before all other code. For example:

```
Dim i as integer

For i=1 to 10
   Beep
Next
```

This code first defines an integer named i. Then a loop begins. The first time through the loop, the i variable is set to 1 and the computer beeps. At the end of the loop, signaled by the Next statement, the i variable is increased by 1 and the loop repeats. This continues until the variable is assigned the value of 10 for the last run through the loop.

By default, a For-Next loop increases its counting variable by 1. To increase the variable by another amount, you use the Step statement. The next example uses the Step statement to add the even numbers between 2 and 10, inclusive:

```
Dim I as integer
Dim sum as integer

sum=0
```

```
For I=2 to 10 step 2
   sum=sum+i
Next
MsgBox str(sum)
```

The last line of code displays the sum number in a window. The MsgBox command is a simple way to quickly display data in a window without actually having to create a window.

You can also count backwards. Instead of increasing a variable each time through a loop, you can decrease it with the downto keyword. Here's an updated version of the beep example:

```
Dim I as integer

for I=10 downto 1
   Beep
   MsgBox Str(I)
Next
```

This loop starts by giving I a value of 10. When the loop is ready to repeat, the value of I is decreased by 1. The loop continues to execute until the variable reaches 1.

The Step statement enables you to go backwards more than 1 at a time. For example, to add all the numbers divisible by 5 between 1 and 1000, do this:

```
Dim I as integer
dim sum as integer

sum=0
for I=1000 downto 1 step 5
    sum=sum+I
Next
```

This code executes as follows:

- Create two integer variables named I and sum.
- At the beginning of the For loop, set sum to 0 and set I to 1000.
- Add the I variable to sum.
- Decrease the i variable by a factor of 5.
- Add the I variable to sum.
- Repeat the loop until the i variable holds 1 or less.

Looping until a condition is met

Sometimes you don't know how many times to repeat a block of code. Instead, you want to loop until a condition is met. You may not realize it, but you do this type of looping every day. For instance, when you follow directions, you might think through the process like this:

✔ Drive south on Main Street.

✔ Keep driving until you see Oak Street.

In this example, you continue to do some action (drive) until a condition is met (you find the street). A few different commands in the REALbasic language help you accomplish this type of looping.

Do-Loop

Use the Do-Loop to repeatedly perform a set of tasks while a condition is FALSE. As soon as the condition is TRUE, the loop stops. You use the Until keyword to check the condition. The Until statement can come at the beginning or end of the loop, depending on whether you want the loop to execute once before checking the condition or not.

An example of the Do-Loop statement follows:

```
Dim s as integer
s=0
Do
   s=s+2
Loop Until s>10000
```

Here's how REALbasic executes this code:

✔ Define the s variable and initialize it to 0.

✔ Begin the loop. First, increment the value of s by 2.

✔ The Until statement checks whether or not s is greater than 10000. If it is, the loop ends. If it isn't, the loop continues to execute.

Here's a similar example, but this time it checks the condition before the loop begins:

```
Dim s as integer
s=10001
Do Until s>10000
   s=s+2
Loop
```

In this example, the Do-Loop never executes because the condition s>10000 is met and REALbasic skips over the remainder of the loop.

While-Wend

The While-Wend statement is almost identical to the Do-Loop. For example, here's the preceding Do-Loop example reworked with While-Wend:

```
dim s as integer
s=0
While s>10000
    s=s+2
Wend
```

The big difference between the two is that the While-Wend statement can check the condition only at the beginning of the loop, whereas the Do-Loop can check at the beginning or end of the loop.

Looping forever

Loops are a powerful feature for any programming language, and REALbasic is no exception. With this power, however, comes a danger of introducing bugs into your code.

If your loop contains a mistake, it might run without crashing but still produce errors in the results. For example, what would happen in a situation like the following:

```
dim I as integer
I=99
Do
    s=s-1
Loop Until s>100
```

The condition `s>100` never occurs, so the code repeats forever — or until you exit from the project. Computer geeks call this phenomenon an *infinite loop* because it runs on into infinity. To exit gracefully from an infinite loop, press @cmd-Shift-. (period). This will get you out of the loop and return you to REALbasic. After you return to REALbasic, you still must stop the execution of the project. To do so, choose Debug⇨Kill or press ⌘-K.

No Comment

Although the REALbasic is not difficult to read, it's no substitute for your own native language. By adding notes to your code in your own language, you make your code much more readable for you as well as for others.

Imagine trying to remember weeks, months, or even years later what a particular section of code does. Why bother? Instead, add comments in your code to remind you. These comments don't give you the ability to directly command your program, but they do make you a better programmer and sometimes even save your skin.

REALbasic enables you to add comments in three ways:

- ✔ The ' character (the apostrophe)
- ✔ The // characters (two forward slashes)
- ✔ The REM statement

If you're a VisualBasic fanatic, you'll recognize the first comment character because it's the same one used in VisualBasic. C++ programmers comment their code with the second choice, the // characters. The last one, REM, is a throwback to the old days of BASIC. It stands for *remark* and is seldom used by most REALbasic programmers. When in doubt, use the ' character because then you have to press only one key.

Here are comments on their own line:

```
' This is a comment
' Increase x by 1
x=x+1
```

You can also put a comment at the end of a line of code:

```
x=x+1 'increase x by 1
```

Keep in mind that adding comments at the end of line is legal only when using the apostrophe or two forward slashes. The preceding would not work with the REM statement.

When REALbasic sees a comment character or keyword, it ignores everything else that follows it for that line of code. You can add a comment also by pressing ⌘-' (apostrophe) or by choosing Edit⇨Comment Lines. These methods differ from simply typing a comment character because the menu command and keyboard shortcut allow you to comment multiple lines of code at one time.

Another use for comments is when testing your code. Simply add the ' mark to the beginning of any line or lines you want to disable. Being able to disable a line of code is a handy trick because you can use it to track down errors in your code. Later, if you want the functionality back, you have only to uncomment the line to reenable it.

Part III

REAL Goodies: Making Your Program Do Something Cool

The 5th Wave   By Rich Tennant

"Come here, quick! I've got a new iMac trick!"

In this part . . .

Attractive interfaces are nice, but not very useful if they don't do anything. This part shows you how to add all kinds of great functionality to your applications.

Graphics, sound, and video are important additions to any application. REALbasic gives you a full set of tools for incorporating any kind of multimedia into your own project. From beeps to symphonies and from pictures to full-motion movies, REALbasic can give your applications pizzazz. For the ultimate in multimedia experience, you can even build games with REALbasic. This part gives you the background you need for adding all of these exciting features to your own masterpiece.

Not all features, however, are flashy and glamorous. Computers are good at storing information in files as well as providing hard copies of that information using a printer. Although less glitzy, these functions are extremely useful. REALbasic provides you with powerful tools for giving your project these necessary workhorse computer functions. The part closes by demonstrating how to use REALbasic's myriad of Internet capabilities in your own applications.

Chapter 8

When Do We Get to the Pretty Pictures?

In This Chapter

▶ Discovering how graphics are displayed

▶ Selecting colors and drawing shapes

▶ Creating and manipulating images

*N*umber crunching and commandeering your computer is fun and all, but it sure isn't flashy. To liven things up, REALbasic offers an array of techniques for using graphics.

Graphics can have multiple uses in your projects. Perhaps your application will work with graphics directly, allowing users to create and manipulate images. Or maybe your application has nothing to do with graphics, but you'd like to spruce up the interface. This chapter takes a look at how to add both types of graphics capabilities to your REALbasic projects.

Graphics Basics

Displaying graphics on your monitor is a sophisticated choreography of light and computations that your computer performs with ease. It will help you as a programmer if you understand a little about how the process works.

Your computer monitor is somewhat like a big piece of lighted graph paper. Hundreds of tiny little squares called *pixels* compose the screen of a typical computer monitor. Each of these pixels can produce light using three-color components:

- ✔ Red
- ✔ Green
- ✔ Blue

By mixing these color components in different proportions, the computer can produce all colors on the screen. You create graphics on the screen by filling the pixels with different colored light.

To describe a distinct location on the screen, you must use a convention called a coordinate. A *coordinate* consists of two numbers that describe the exact location of a pixel on the screen, in the form (x,y). The x-coordinate describes the left-to-right position of the pixel; the y-coordinate describes the top-to-bottom position of the pixel, with coordinates separated by a comma.

Imagine that a grid appears on your computer screen. In the top-left corner of the screen is coordinate (0,0). As you move across the screen, the first number of the coordinate grows larger. Therefore, a coordinate representing the top-right corner of your screen might be (640,0). Similarly, as you progress down the screen, the second number of the coordinate increases. Starting from the top-left corner again and traveling down to the bottom-left corner, the coordinate might read (0,480).

An Artist Needs a Canvas

Artists who paint use canvases as the backdrop for their creation and paint as the medium. To paint in REALbasic, you follow a process similar to a traditional painter. First, you take out a canvas, and then you paint on it. With REALbasic, however, you use a virtual canvas that you paint with light.

To begin creating graphics with REALbasic, you'll need a REALbasic canvas. Figure 8-1 shows the location of the canvas in the Tools window. A *Canvas* is a special type of control for displaying and creating graphics. Unlike with traditional art canvases, however, you can create and use as many REALbasic Canvases as you like. Your paint supply is also unlimited. (You can almost hear Picasso rolling in his grave, can't you?) And if that weren't enough, you can also use Canvases to display photographs, create custom controls, and even create simple games.

To begin creating your own graphics masterpiece, follow these steps:

1. **Create a new project.**

   As usual, choose File⇨New.

2. **Open a Window Editor.**

   Double-click Window1 in the Project window to open its Window Editor.

3. **Drag a Canvas control from the Tools window to the Window Editor.**

   Place the Canvas anywhere you want in Window1.

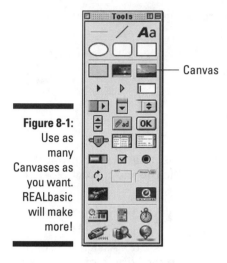
— Canvas

Figure 8-1:
Use as
many
Canvases as
you want.
REALbasic
will make
more!

If you try to test your project now, you'll be less than impressed. Choose Debug⇨Run to test see for yourself. If all goes well, you shouldn't see anything more than a plain old window. The Canvas is there, but it is invisible until you paint on it. Choose File⇨Quit to finish your testing. Save the project, because you can use it to test the code throughout this chapter.

To get the Canvas to display something, drag a picture file into the Project window and select it as the BackDrop property of the Canvas. Now, choose Debug⇨Run. Presto! Graphics without one line of code!

The brain behind the Canvas is its Graphics object, which takes care of storing and manipulating graphics for the Canvas. Then, when the time is right, you or REALbasic displays the graphics from the Graphics object on the Canvas.

To do any graphics work, you must speak directly to the Graphics object of the Canvas using a *method,* or command. To speak to a Graphics object, you use dot-notation. This involves appending a command and its parameters to the Graphics object with a period. A command to the Graphics object of Canvas1 might look like this:

```
Canvas1.Graphics.FillRect 0,0,me.Width,me.Height
```

In this example, you are telling the Graphics object of Canvas1 to fill the canvas with color. In some special cases, you may shorten this long notation to

```
G.FillRect 0,0,me.Width,me.Height
```

You find shorthand code like this only in the `Paint` event of the Canvas. `G.FillRect` is synonymous to `Graphics.FillRect`, but because the code resides in Canvas1, you do not need to specify Canvas1. The `Paint` event of a Canvas is the central location for code to draw on the Canvas. The `Paint` event takes care of redrawing the Canvas at the appropriate times.

To see the `Paint` event in action, add the preceding code example to the `Paint` event of Canvas1:

```
Sub Paint(g as Graphics)
   g.FillRect 0,0,me.Width,me.Height
End Sub
```

Choose Debug⇨Run to see your Canvas filled with color (yes, black is a color too).

In addition to executing methods, the Graphics object has several properties that you can change. Code for setting a property (in this case, ForeColor) of the Graphics object looks like this:

```
Canvas1.Graphics.ForeColor=RGB(255,0,0)
```

This behaves the same way all properties in REALbasic do. Assign the color value `RGB(255,0,0)` (which is red, incidentally) to the ForeColor property of the Graphics object of Canvas1.

The remainder of this chapter takes a closer look at the methods (the commands) and properties (the settings) of a Graphics object.

Color basics

Before you begin painting, you need to choose a color with which to work. The most common way to select a color is to use the global `RGB` method. The `RGB` method has three parameters, which correspond to red, green, and blue values. Each of these color components is an integer in the range 0 to 255. A setting of 255 means that the intensity of a color component is fully on; a setting of 0 represents an intensity that is completely off. By mixing different combinations of red, green, and blue, you can create any color imaginable. Table 8-1 shows some common RGB combinations and the colors they yield.

Table 8-1		Common Color Values		
Color	*Red*	*Green*	*Blue*	*RGB Method*
Red	255	0	0	RGB(255,0,0)
Green	0	255	0	RGB(0,255,0)
Blue	0	0	255	RGB(0,0,255)
Yellow	255	255	0	RGB(255,0,0)

Color	Red	Green	Blue	RGB Method
Purple	255	0	255	RGB(255,0,255)
Black	0	0	0	RGB(0,0,0)
White	255	255	255	RGB(255,255,255)

The RGB method returns a Color object, so you can store the color for later use like so:

```
Dim myColor as Color
myColor = RGB(255,0,0)
```

The RGB color model corresponds nicely to graphics displayed on a monitor because all pixels contain red, green, and blue elements. If you are more accustomed to the CMYK color space common in color printing, you might prefer REALbasic's CMY method. Like the RGB method, CMY takes three parameters but in this case the parameters are cyan, magenta, and yellow. Another important difference is that the components of the CMY method are numbers between 0 and 1. In other words, they are percentages, with 0 equal to 0% and 1 equal to 100%. To set a component to half on, use 0.5 for 50%. For example, to set a Color object to yellow with the CMY method:

```
Dim myColor as Color
myColor = CMY(0,0,1)
```

If all this CMY talk is making your head spin, you can safely ignore it for now. RGB is the preferred method for displaying graphics with a monitor, and that's the focus of this chapter.

Of course, you may not want to choose a color at all. Instead, you may want your users to choose a color for themselves. Most applications make use of the standardized ColorPicker provided by the Macintosh operating system (see Figure 8-2).

Figure 8-2:
The standard ColorPicker lets you choose any color you desire.

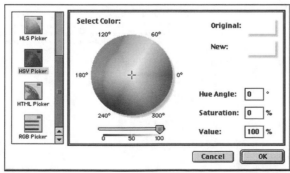

The `SelectColor` method displays the standard ColorPicker. `SelectColor` takes two parameters:

- ✔ Color
- ✔ Prompt

The Color object that you pass to the `SelectColor` method is special because it serves two functions. First, it provides the ColorPicker dialog box with a default color of your choosing that appears in the top-right corner. The second job of the Color object is to take care of storing the color that a user chooses while in the ColorPicker. After the user dismisses the ColorPicker dialog box after choosing a color, the Color object holds the chosen color.

Passing by reference is indeed special. Normally, when you pass parameters to a method, the method makes use of the parameters in its own calculations but doesn't do anything to alter the parameter itself.

When you pass a parameter *by reference,* however, the method is capable of altering the parameter, such that when the method has completed execution, the parameter might be different than when it entered the method. See Figure 8-3. For example, the `SelectColor` method passes a color object as a default color for display in the ColorPicker dialog box. When a user chooses a color from the ColorPicker dialog box and presses OK, the new color now resides in the Color object you originally passed to the `SelectColor` method.

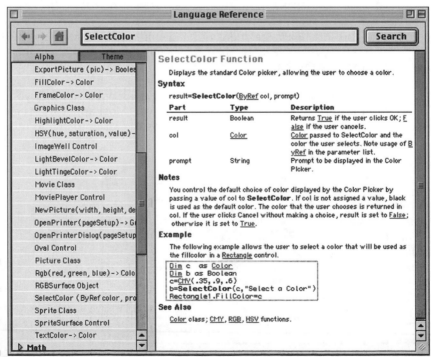

Figure 8-3: ByRef means to pass by reference.

The other parameter of the SelectColor method is a string called Prompt that displays a text message in the ColorPicker dialog box. You normally set this to something like *Select Color:*.

After your user chooses a color and presses OK in the ColorPicker dialog box, the SelectColor method returns a TRUE Boolean value. If the user decides to not choose a color, SelectColor instead returns FALSE. To put all this color information together into an example, enter the following code into the Action event of a PushButton:

```
Sub Action()
  Dim myColor as Color
  Dim ColorWasChosen as Boolean

  //set the ColorPicker to "red" for its default
  myColor = RGB(255,0,0)
  ColorWasChosen=SelectColor(myColor, "Choose a color:")

  if ColorWasChosen then
    MsgBox "Red=" + str(myColor.Red)
    MsgBox "Green=" + str(myColor.Green)
    MsgBox "Blue=" + str(myColor.Blue)
  else
    MsgBox "No color chosen."
  end if
End Sub()
```

This example first sets a Color object (myColor) to the color red. This color appears by default in the ColorPicker dialog box. Then the code calls the SelectColor method, passing to it by reference the myColor Color object as well as the Choose a color: string as a prompt. When the user dismisses the ColorPicker after having chosen a color, the ColorWasChosen Boolean variable holds a value of TRUE. This causes three windows to appear displaying each value of the Color object's red, green, and blue components. Red, Green, and Blue arc all inherent properties of the Color object.

Drawing in a Canvas

Now that you have a color in mind, you probably want to use it to actually draw something. Fortunately, REALbasic affords you a variety of ways to draw graphics involving one of the following:

- Points
- Lines
- Geometric shapes

To draw each type of item, you must either send messages to the Graphics object of the Canvas where you want the items to appear or alter the properties of the Canvas. The Graphics object takes care of storing the picture until you (or REALbasic) transfer it to the Canvas for display. When you place your code in the Paint event of a Canvas, REALbasic automatically takes care of refreshing the display for you.

Points

To draw a point in a Canvas, you must set its Pixel property, designating where you want to draw the point. The point location lies on an imaginary X- and Y-axis of the Graphics object. If a Canvas has a width of 320 and a height of 240, its corresponding Graphics object is 320 pixels wide and 240 pixels high. The origin of the Graphics object is the top-left corner, with coordinates labeled (0,0). As you move in a rightward direction along the Graphics object, the first value of the point increases. This is the X value of the point. As you progress down the Canvas, the second half of the point increases. This is the Y value of the point. Figure 8-4 shows a point at coordinates (2,4).

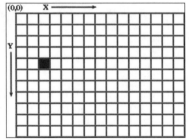

Figure 8-4:
Points are described by a pair of numbers representing its X and Y coordinates.

To plot a point at any location, simply set the Pixel property of a Graphics object equal to a Color object. For example, drag a Canvas into an open window and place the following code in its Paint event:

```
Sub Paint(g as Graphics)
g.Pixel(9,9) = RGB(255,0,0)
End Sub
```

This line of code sets the point (9,9) to red. Test the code by choosing Debug➪Run. If you get out your magnifying lens, you should be able to see a red dot somewhere in the window.

Notice that REALbasic passes the Graphics object as a parameter to the Paint event of the Canvas, so you can refer to it simply as g.

Granted, this is not a very interesting example, but you can exploit its effects with a few simple loops to produce something a bit more exciting. For example:

```
Sub Paint(g as Graphics)
  Dim i as integer
  Dim j as Integer

  for i = 0 to Canvas1.Width
    for j= 0 to Canvas1.Height
      if i=j then
        //set this point to black
        g.pixel(i,j)=rgb(0,0,0)
      else
        //set this point to yellow
        g.pixel(i,j)=rgb(255,255,0)
      end if
    next
  next
End Sub
```

This example loops through every pixel in a Canvas, setting each pixel in the line between the top left and bottom right to black. Otherwise, the pixel is yellow. Figure 8-5 shows the effects.

Figure 8-5:
Use the
Pixel
property to
draw more
than just a
point.

Although you can use brute force methods like this to change each pixel in a Canvas, usually there are much simpler ways to accomplish the same results. Read on to find out how.

Lines

REALbasic is good at drawing much more than simple dots on a Canvas. For example, it's adept at drawing lines. The Graphics object has a method named, appropriately enough, DrawLine that takes care of plotting lines for you. You have to supply only the beginning and ending coordinates of the line:

```
Sub Paint(g as Graphics)
g.DrawLine 0,0,me.width, me.height
End Sub
```

When you create graphics this way, you must imagine that you are in control of an imaginary pen. You can change the color and width of the pen to alter the way the drawing occurs. To change the width of the pen, set the PenWidth property of the Graphics object. By default, the pen's width is equal to 1.

```
g.PenWidth = 10
```

To change the color of the pen, set the ForeColor property with a Color object:

```
g.ForeColor = RGB(255,0,0)
```

When you change the PenWidth and ForeColor properties, they retain their settings until you set them to something else. You set the properties of the pen and then draw the line:

```
Sub Paint(g as Graphics)
g.PenWidth = 10
g.ForeColor = RGB(255,0,0)
g.DrawLine 0,0,me.width, me.height
End Sub
```

This code results in a thick red line (trust me, it's red), as shown in Figure 8-6.

Figure 8-6:
Use the PenWidth and ForeColor properties to change the appearance of lines.

You can use simple line drawings to create nice effects. For example, a *gradient* is a subtle transition from one color to another. You can create a simple gradient by drawing only lines. Start at the top of the Canvas and draw a horizontal line in the starting color. Then continue drawing horizontal lines as you travel down the Canvas, changing the color subtly for each line until you reach the bottom. The next example creates a black-and-white horizontal gradient in a Canvas:

```
Sub Paint(g as Graphics)
  Dim i as integer

  for i=0 to me.Height
    g.ForeColor = RGB(i,i,i)
    g.DrawLine 0,i,me.Width,i
  next
End Sub
```

Figure 8-7 demonstrates your handiwork.

Figure 8-7:
Create
simple
gradients by
using only
lines.

Geometric shapes

Graphics with only lines and points are useful, but they can also get boring after awhile. REALbasic alleviates your boredom by supplying a bounty of methods for drawing all sorts of shapes. Using the methods of the Graphics object, you can easily draw these shapes:

- ✔ Squares and rectangles
- ✔ Circles and ovals
- ✔ Polygons

Squares and rectangles are the same shape as far as REALbasic is concerned. To draw them, use the DrawRect method of the Graphics class. DrawRect draws a rectangle based on the top-left coordinates and the width and height of the rectangle. To draw a rectangle and fill it in with a solid color, use the FillRect method. FillRect takes the same four parameters as DrawRect.

FillRect is a convenient means for covering the background of a Canvas with a solid color.

To fill the background of a Canvas with a solid color using only two lines of code, do the following:

1. **Create a new project.**

   Open the Window Editor of the default window from the Project window and resize it. Make the window 400 pixels wide and 300 pixels high.

2. **Add a Canvas to the Window Editor.**

   Change the Top and Left properties of the new Canvas to 0 and resize the Canvas to a width of 400 and a height of 300. The Canvas should now be covering the entire area of the window.

3. **Enter some code.**

   It takes only two lines of code in the Paint event to fill in the Canvas with a solid color. First, set ForeColor, and then draw using the FillRect method. This example fills the background in with a light blue color:

   ```
   g.ForeColor = RGB(239,253,255)
   g.FillRect 0,0,me.Width,me.Height
   ```

You need not use the FillRect method solely for filling in backgrounds. Draw another rectangle in yellow like this:

```
g.ForeColor = RGB(255,255,0)
g.FillRect 40,40,50,50
```

As long as you place this code following the code for filling in the Canvas in light blue, you will see a 50x50 yellow rectangle at the coordinates (40,40). If you draw the light blue rectangle after the yellow rectangle, it obscures the yellow one. Drawing always goes right over the top of whatever is already there. Thus, you must build your pictures from the bottom up.

If you'd like the yellow rectangle to have a border, draw another rectangle, but this time use the DrawRect method. Like DrawLine, the DrawRect method's pen has a PenWidth property. Rectangles, however, also have a PenHeight property. PenWidth changes the width of vertical lines; PenHeight changes the pen width of horizontal lines. To create an even border, you must set both properties. To draw a red border around the yellow rectangle, use this code:

```
g.ForeColor = RGB(255,0,0)
g.FillRect 40,40,50,50
```

Test the code by choosing Debug⇨Run. For all of your hard work, you should have something that looks like Figure 8-8. (Again, because ...*For Dummies* books are colorblind, the figure will not match the yellow and red colors on your screen.)

Figure 8-8:
`DrawRect`
and
`FillRect`
are great for
filling in the
background
as well as
for drawing
rectangular
buttons and
borders.

Drawing circles and ovals works much like drawing rectangles. Instead of `DrawRect` and `FillRect`, however, use `DrawOval` and `FillOval` (original, huh?). Like their rectangle counterparts, `DrawOval` and `FillOval` take four parameters to do their dirty work:

- ✔ The top-left coordinates of the oval
- ✔ The width and height of the oval

Just as squares are rectangles with equal sides, circles are really only ovals with an equal width and height. For example, to draw an eyeball, first fill a white oval and then draw a smaller colored circle over the oval. Finally, top off the whole thing by outlining the oval in black with `DrawOval`:

```
Sub Paint(g as Graphics)
    g.ForeColor = RGB(255,255,255)
    g.FillOval 150,50,100,50

    g.ForeColor = RGB(0,0,255)
    g.FillOval 185,60,30,30

    g.ForeColor = RGB(0,0,0)
    g.DrawOval 150,50,100,50
End Sub
```

Choose Debug⇨Run to see the results, which are shown in Figure 8-9. Try fiddling with the numbers in each of the preceding `FillOval` and `DrawOval` methods to see what happens.

The final stop on your whirlwind tour of REALbasic's geometric shapes is the polygon. In case you're rusty on your geometry, a *polygon* is a shape with multiple sides. The `DrawPolygon` and `FillPolygon` methods do the job of drawing polygons in REALbasic. Unlike rectangles and ovals, however, polygons can be any shape and, consequently, have any number of points. To get past this problem, the DrawPolygon and FillPolygon methods take an array of points as their sole parameter. This array is a list of x- and y-coordinates in the polygon.

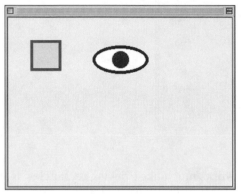

Figure 8-9:
Combine the
FillOval
and
DrawOval
methods for
interesting
effects.

The array you use to store the points in a polygon is one-based. This means that the first element of the array has an index of 1. This is contrary to the way arrays normally work, so watch for this when creating polygons.

To draw a polygon, first define all the points in the polygon, and then draw it using the DrawPolygon or FillPolygon method. The following example draws a red octagon similar to a stop sign:

```
Sub Paint(g as Graphics)
  Dim PolygonPoints(18) as Integer

  PolygonPoints(1)=300   //X1
  PolygonPoints(2)=50    //Y1
  PolygonPoints(3)=325   //X2
  PolygonPoints(4)=50    //Y2
  PolygonPoints(5)=350   //X3
  PolygonPoints(6)=75    //Y3
  PolygonPoints(7)=350   //X4
  PolygonPoints(8)=100   //Y4
  PolygonPoints(9)=325   //X5
  PolygonPoints(10)=125  //Y5
  PolygonPoints(11)=300  //X6
  PolygonPoints(12)=125  //Y6
  PolygonPoints(13)=275  //X7
  PolygonPoints(14)=100  //Y7
  PolygonPoints(15)=275  //X8
  PolygonPoints(16)=75   //Y8

  // Now back to the starting point
  PolygonPoints(17)=300  //X9
```

```
   PolygonPoints(18)=50 //Y9

   g.ForeColor=RGB(255,0,0)
   g.FillPolygon PolygonPoints
End Sub()
```

Look at the results in Figure 8-10.

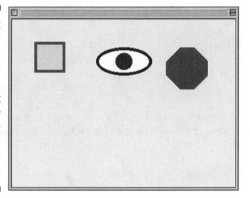

Figure 8-10:
The Draw-
Polygon
and Fill-
Polygon
methods let
you draw
almost any
other shape
you can
imagine.

Text

You can draw not only all kinds of lines and shapes with the Graphics class but also text. This may seem contrary to how you normally think about text. After you draw text in a Graphics object, the text is no longer accessible the way it is in EditField. Rather, drawing text as graphics has the effect of colorizing pixels in the shape of letters.

To draw text as graphics, use the `DrawString` method of the Graphics object. `DrawString` takes three parameters:

- ✔ String to draw
- ✔ X-coordinate of the string
- ✔ Y-coordinate of the string

Two properties of the Graphics object that go hand-in-hand with the `DrawString` method are

- ✔ TextFont
- ✔ TextSize

Setting the TextFont and TextSize properties of the Graphics object alters the appearance of any text you display with the `DrawString` method. To add some text to the red stop sign you created previously as well as a fun message, enter the following code into the `Paint` event of the Canvas:

```
Sub Paint(g as Graphics)
    g.ForeColor = RGB(255,255,255)
    g.TextFont = "Helvetica"
    g.TextSize = 18
    g.DrawString "Stop",295,90

    g.ForeColor = RGB(0,0,0)
    g.TextFont = "Helvetica"
    g.TextSize = 36
    g.DrawString "Graphics are fun!",60,250
End Sub
```

The TextFont and TextSize settings remain until you change them to something else. Figure 8-11 shows what the text looks like when displayed.

Figure 8-11:
A Canvas can not only display shapes but also do text!

Pictures Aplenty

Drawing simple shapes and text is fun, but you may want to display sophisticated graphics. The Graphics object has picture-drawing features that will have you displaying existing colorful photographs and graphics with very little effort.

Displaying a picture the easy way

If you have a graphics file that you would like to display in your own project, simple drag-and-drop methods will have you up and running in no time. For example, to add a PICT file to your project, simply drag it into your Project window from the Finder. See Figure 8-12.

Figure 8-12:
Adding a
picture file
to your
project is
easy with
drag-and-
drop.

REALbasic natively supports files in the PICT format. If you have QuickTime installed on your computer, REALbasic automatically includes any graphics file types that QuickTime supports (such as JPEG or GIF, to name a few).

After you add a picture file to your project, it's very easy to make use of it. Any controls in REALbasic that have a BackDrop property can use the picture. For example, begin by opening a Window Editor. In the Properties window, select the BackDrop property; a small popup menu appears with the names of all the picture files in your project. Select the picture you want, and the picture should instantly appear in the background of the window — all without one line of code! Figure 8-13 shows the BackDrop property in action.

Figure 8-13:
Set the
BackDrop
property of
a window or
control to
use a
picture
without any
code.

This trick works also for the following controls:

- ✔ Canvas control and the BackDrop property
- ✔ SpriteSurface control and the BackDrop property
- ✔ ImageWell control and the Image property

Loading a picture from a file

Adding a graphics file to your project is convenient, but sometimes you may not want the same picture around for the life of the program. In these instances, you load the graphics from a file and then display it.

Before you go loading a picture from a file, you need to store the picture somewhere out of view. This is the job of the Picture object. Then, when you want to see the picture, simply draw the Picture object using the `DrawPicture` method of a Canvas. To illustrate, follow these steps:

1. **Create a new project.**

   Open the Window Editor for the default window that accompanies a new project (Window1) by double-clicking it from the Project window.

2. **Drag a Canvas and a PushButton to Window1.**

   You'll use the PushButton to open the file and the Canvas to display the picture from the file.

3. **Create a new Picture property.**

   You need a Picture property to store the picture a user chooses from a file. This allows your Canvas to properly refresh when necessary (such as when the user moves the window across the screen). Choose Edit➪New Property to create a new property of Window1. Enter the information as shown in Figure 8-14.

Figure 8-14:
Create a
new
property for
storing a
Picture
object.

New Property
Declaration: `myPicture as Picture`
☐ **Private**
☐ **Visible**
Cancel   OK

Before you open picture files, you have to tell REALbasic about the types of files you want to open. To do so, use the File Types dialog box by choosing Edit➪File Types. Add an entry for each type of file you want to use.

REALbasic comes preloaded with settings for many types of image files. Figure 8-15 shows how your File Types dialog box might look after adding PICT, JPEG, GIF, and TIFF file types.

Figure 8-15:
Add a file
type for
each type of
image you
want to
open.

Back in the interface of Window1, double-click PushButton to open the Code Editor and enter the following code:

```
Sub Action()
  Dim f as FolderItem

  f = GetOpenFolderItem("image/x-pict;image/jpeg")
  if f<>nil then
    myPicture = f.OpenAsPicture
    if Canvas1.Width<>myPicture.Width OR
          Canvas1.Height<>myPicture.Height then
      //resize the canvas to fit the picture
      Canvas1.Width = myPicture.Width
      Canvas1.Height = myPicture.Height
      //resize the window to fit the canvas
      self.Width = Canvas1.Left + Canvas1.Width + 13
      self.Height = Canvas1.Top + Canvas1.Height + 45
    end if
  end if

  Canvas1.Refresh
End Sub
```

This code begins by creating a FolderItem object using the `GetOpenFolderItem` method. `GetOpenFolderItem` takes one parameter, a string, and returns an object that represents the file that the user selected. The string is a list of file types that you would like the user to be able to open, in this case PICT and JPEG files. Note that a semicolon separates each item in the list.

The next line of code checks to see whether the user chose a file or clicked Cancel, dismissing the open dialog box without choosing a file type. If the user chooses a file, f is not `nil`.

Finally, the code opens the image with the `OpenAsPicture` method of `FolderItem` and places it in the myPicture property. Because the picture may be a different size than the existing Canvas, it's a good time to resize it. That's the purpose of the following code:

```
//resize the canvas to fit the picture
Canvas1.Width = myPicture.Width
Canvas1.Height = myPicture.Height
//resize the window to fit the canvas
self.Width = Canvas1.Left + Canvas1.Width + 13
self.Height = Canvas1.Top + Canvas1.Height + 45
```

After you assign a picture to `myPicture` and resize the Canvas and window, you can call the `Refresh` method of the Canvas. This forces the `Paint` event of the Canvas to execute, which is where you should put code for drawing the picture.

Drawing a picture in a canvas

To display a Picture object in a Canvas, you need to draw it with the `DrawPicture` method of the Graphics object. `DrawPicture` is a peculiar method. It can take as few as three or as many as nine parameters. Table 8-2 lists the parameters. For now, you need to concern yourself with only the first three.

Table 8-2	DrawPicture Parameters
Parameter	*Description*
Image	Picture you want to draw in the canvas
X	Left position of the picture in the canvas
Y	Top position of the picture in the canvas
DestWidth	Width of the picture in the canvas
DestHeight	Height of the picture in the canvas
SourceX	Used for scaling and cropping
SourceY	Used for scaling and cropping
SourceWidth	Used for scaling and cropping
SourceHeight	Used for scaling and cropping

The first three parameters (`Image`, `X`, and `Y`) are the bare necessities for drawing a Picture object in a Canvas. The `X` and `Y` coordinates are relative to the Canvas, with the top left of the Canvas at (0,0).

To draw the Picture in a Canvas, open the Code Editor to the `Paint` event of the Canvas and enter this code:

```
Sub Paint(g as Graphics)
   g.DrawPicture myPicture,0,0
End Sub
```

This code transfers the Picture named `myPicture` to the Graphics object of the Canvas, causing it to appear on the screen.

Scaling a picture

Using the `DrawPicture` method with only three parameters works great if your Picture object is the same size as the canvas. If the Picture is larger than the Canvas, however, part of your image will not appear. To avoid this problem, you can scale the Picture when displaying it. *Scaling* is a term graphics gurus use to mean change the size.

To scale a Picture so that it fits within a Canvas, you need to add the six remaining properties to the `DrawPicture` method. These six parameters tell `DrawPicture` how wide and tall the final image should be as well as which part of the Picture to copy to the Canvas. If you want to cram a Picture into a Canvas, set the `DestWidth` and `DestWidth` parameters equal to the Canvas width and height. As long as you want to copy the entire picture to the Canvas, set `SourceX` and `SourceY` to 0 and `SourceWidth` and `SourceHeight` to the width and height of the `Picture`. Because this code is presumably in a `Paint` event of the Canvas, you can use the term `me` to refer to the Canvas:

```
g.DrawPicture myPicture,0,0,me.Width,me.Height,0,0,
          myPicture.Width,myPicture.Height
```

Cropping a picture

Cropping works much the same way as scaling. Instead of setting `SourceX` and `SourceY` to 0 and `SourceWidth` and `SourceHeight` equal to the Picture's width and height, however, you use only the portion of the picture that you want. For example, to crop a 100-pixel square of the Picture starting at the point (23,26):

```
g.DrawPicture myPicture,0,0,100,100,23,26,100,100
```

Flicker-free graphics

Sometimes when you work with pictures and Canvas controls, you may notice an unsightly flicker. This happens because the Canvas control updates its appearance at appropriate times (such as when you move a window). When you see the flicker, you are witnessing the redrawing of the Canvas. In most situations, this is unsatisfactory. To get around this problem, use a customized version of the Canvas control with the capability to avoid flicker. Joe Strout, an engineer at REAL Software, provided this excellent procedure for creating a customized flicker-free Canvas:

1. **Create a custom Canvas.**

   Choose File➪New Class.

2. **Set the Super property of the Class to** Canvas.

3. **Add a Picture property called mPicture.**

   Choose Edit➪New Property. In the dialog box that appears, enter

   ```
   mPicture as Picture
   ```

4. **Create a new method called** Draw(g as Graphics).

   Choose Edit➪New Method and then enter this code:

   ```
   g.DrawPicture mPicture,0,0
   ```

5. **Add the following code to the Paint event of the Class:**

   ```
   Draw g
   ```

6. **Create a method named** Redraw. **In it, add this code:**

   ```
   Draw me.graphics
   ```

When you're finished, the control is a cinch to use. Instead of dragging a Canvas control from the Tools window into your interface, drag the custom control from the Project window. Although it will appear as though you dragged a Canvas control from the Tools window, this Canvas is special. It contains all the special functionality you just gave it. To make the Canvas display something, use code like this:

```
Canvas1.mPicture = YourPicture
Canvas1.Redraw
```

If all of this custom control talk makes your head spin, you will be pleased to know that you can get a copy of this custom control on the *REALbasic For Dummies* CD. The CD also contains an example project that demonstrates how to use the custom control to produce flicker-free scrolling graphics.

Saving a picture as a file

Why go through all the hard work of creating and displaying graphics if you can't save them for later? To save a Picture as a file, use the SaveAsPicture method of FolderItem. Before you do that, however, you must get a valid FolderItem that represents the location of the new file. This is the job of GetSaveFolderItem.

GetSaveFolderItem has two parameters: a file type and a default file name. Pass it one of the file types you created previously in this chapter; PICT is a good choice for now. After you have a FolderItem, you can call its SaveAsPicture method:

```
Dim f As FolderItem

f = GetSaveFolderItem("image/x-pict","My PICT File")
if f<>nil then
  f.SaveAsPicture myPicture
end if
```

If you use this code for Windows, the SaveAsPicture method saves as a BMP file, the standard Windows picture format, instead of PICT, the standard Macintosh picture format.

If QuickTime is installed, you can save a Picture also to JPEG format. The code is nearly identical to that of PICT files, but uses the SaveAsJPEG method of the FolderItem instead as well as the image/jpeg file type.

```
Dim f As FolderItem

f = GetSaveFolderItem("image/jpeg","My JPEG File")
if f<>nil then
  f.SaveAsJPEG myPicture
end if
```

Although you can open nearly any type of format for viewing (as long as you have QuickTime), REALbasic allows you to save Pictures only in PICT or JPEG format.

Chapter 9

QuickTime

Apple Computer created the QuickTime technology so that you could play rich multimedia content on the desktop of your favorite Macintosh or Windows computer. This content includes movies, audio, text, as well as 2D and 3D graphics. It's a true multimedia powerhouse that takes care of a lot of programming dirty work for you.

In addition to being one of the most powerful multimedia engines around, QuickTime, with the help of REALbasic, is also one of the easiest multimedia packages to program. With drag-and-drop ease, you can take advantage of QuickTime's many features.

Instead of producing run-of-the-mill applications, you can offer fancy multimedia content — with QuickTime taking care of most of the hassles. This chapter takes you step-by-step through the process of playing, creating, and enhancing QuickTime movies.

Using MoviePlayer

The MoviePlayer control is the heart of multimedia playback in REALbasic. You can add the MoviePlayer control like you do any other controls: by dragging it from the Tools window into your interface. (It's the blue control with a letter *Q* on it).

To create your own private movie theater and production house, begin by opening a new project:

1. **Launch REALbasic or choose File⇨New to create a new project.**

2. **Open the Window Editor for Window1.**

    To open the Window Editor, double-click Window1 in the Project window.

3. Drag a MoviePlayer control from the Tools window to Window1.

Change the properties of Window1 and the new MoviePlayer as follows:

Window1.Width	326
Window1.Height	395
MoviePlayer1.Top	80
MoviePlayer1.Left	13
MoviePlayer1.Width	300
MoviePlayer1.Height	300

If you're in a hurry to see QuickTime in action, drag a movie file into your Project window. Next, select the movie from the Movie popup menu in the Properties window. Choose Debug➪Run. The application displays your movie in all its glory. Press the play button on the movie controller to watch the movie. Without any code at all, you've implemented QuickTime movie playback.

Opening movies

Playing the same QuickTime movie all the time might be desirable if you need a permanent animation in your interface. There will come a time, however, when you want to play another movie or maybe even lots of other movies. To load and play a movie file that is not part of your project, you need to add some code (but not very much).

To update the movie project interface, begin by adding a new PushButton from the Tools window. Place it somewhere above the MoviePlayer you added previously. Figure 9-1 gives you an idea of what the interface might look like.

Figure 9-1:
A simple
movie
playback
interface
with room to
grow.

Installing QuickTime

If QuickTime is not installed on your computer, you can obtain a free copy on the Internet. You can install the QuickTime software in two ways:

- Through an automatic Internet installation
- By downloading the installer

The first method is the most popular. By going to this web address:

```
www.apple.com/quicktime/
     download/
```

you can begin downloading and installing QuickTime directly from a browser window. When the installation is complete, the QuickTime installer asks you to restart your computer to finish the installation.

Sometimes the automatic installation is not desirable. For example, if you don't have an Internet connection, you may want to use another computer to download the QuickTime installer. After you download the installer, you can save it to a disk and use it to install on the computer without an Internet connection. To download the installer, go here:

```
www.apple.com/quicktime/
     download/support/
```

Double-click the new PushButton to open the Code Editor and then enter the following:

```
Dim myFile as FolderItem

myFile=GetOpenFolderItem("video/quicktime")

if myFile<>nil then
    MoviePlayer1.movie=myFile.OpenAsMovie
end if
```

This code allows a user to select a movie for playback using the standard file dialog box. Don't try to test this code just yet, though.

First, you need to define video/quicktime as a file type that your program recognizes. To do so:

1. **Choose Edit⇨File Types.**

   The File Types dialog box appears. To expedite matters, REALbasic offers many file presets.

2. **Expand the menu next to the Name field.**

3. **Scroll down and select video/quicktime.**

   REALbasic instantly puts the proper data in each field of the File Types dialog box.

Chapter 12 discusses this process in depth, but Figure 9-2 should give you enough information to complete the project.

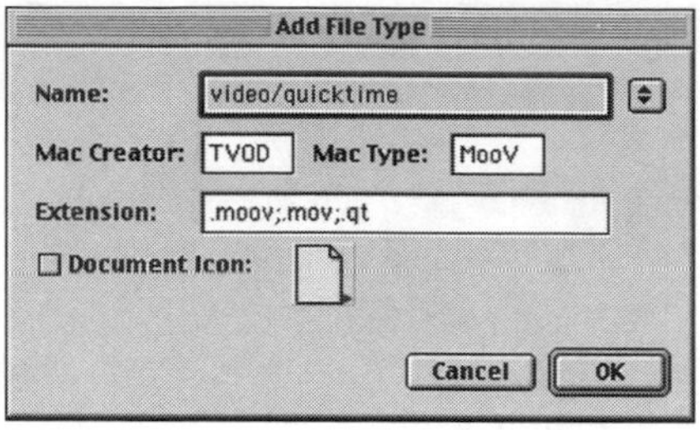

Figure 9-2:
Be sure to
add the
video/quick-
time file
type to your
project.

```
                    Add File Type
Name:        video/quicktime                    ⬍

Mac Creator:  TVOD    Mac Type:  MooV

Extension:   .moov;.mov;.qt

☐ Document Icon:      ▢

                            Cancel    OK
```

Now that you've entered the code and defined the file type, it's safe to test the project. Choose Debug➪Run to give it a whirl. Click the PushButton and open a movie file. If the movie is larger than the Width and Height properties of MoviePlayer1 that you set when you opened the project, part of the movie will be hidden from view. To keep this from happening, you must resize the window to accommodate larger movies.

MoviePlayer1 has a property called AutoResize. When this property is set to TRUE (as it is by default), the MoviePlayer object automatically resizes to accommodate a movie. When this resizing occurs, the ControllerSizeChanged event of MoviePlayer fires. To change the size of the window, simply add code to the ControllerSizeChanged event of Window1:

```
Sub ControllerSizeChanged()

// No need to resize the width of Window1 if the movie
// is 300 pixels wide or smaller
if MoviePlayer1.controllerwidth>300 then
    // leave a 13-pixel border
    // on both sides of the movie
    // 13+13=26
    Window1.width=MoviePlayer1.controllerwidth+26
end if

// To account for the top position(80)
// and bottom edge(13) of MoviePlayer
// 80 + 13=93
// move 80 pixels from the top
// and leave a 13 pixel border at the bottom
Window1.height=MoviePlayer1.controllerheight+93

End Sub
```

Because this code lies within the ControllerSizeChanged event of MoviePlayer, you could use the term Me to talk about the MoviePlayer itself. If this code were not within an event of the MoviePlayer, you would have to refer to the MoviePlayer by name (MoviePlayer1, for example).

In a similar fashion, you could use the term `Self` to refer to the window that holds this code. If this code appeared somewhere else besides within this window (in, say, a module or another class), you would have to refer to the window by name (`Window1`, for example). This isn't absolutely necessary, but it will make your code easier to maintain. For example, if you changed the name of the MoviePlayer control from MoviePlayer1 to MyMoviePlayer, you would have to also change any instance of code that referred to MoviePlayer1.

The simplified code looks like this:

```
Sub ControllerSizeChanged()

// No need to resize the width of Window1 if the movie
// is 300 pixels wide or smaller
if me.controllerwidth>300 then
    // leave a 13-pixel border
    // on both sides of the movie
    // 13+13=26
    self.width=me.controllerwidth+26
end if

// To account for the top position(80)
// and bottom edge(13) of MoviePlayer
// 80 + 13=93
// move 80 pixels from the top
// and leave a 13 pixel border at the bottom
self.height=me.controllerheight+93

End Sub
```

Figure 9-3 shows you the project running with a large movie loaded.

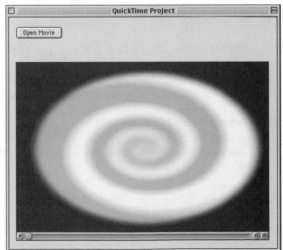

Figure 9-3:
Resize your windows to accommodate large movies.

Starting and stopping movie playback

Up until now, you've controlled the playback of QuickTime movies with the MoviePlayer controller. There isn't any reason why you have to do it this way. You could, for example, play and stop the movie with two buttons. What's more, you could do so without writing a lick of code.

Begin by adding two new PushButtons to Window1. Change the Caption property of each button to read *Play* and *Stop,* respectively.

Next, while holding down the Shift and ⌘ keys on your keyboard, click the Play button (PushButton2). With the mouse still pushed down, drag towards MoviePlayer1. As you drag, a line magically appears. Drag the line until it connects with MoviePlayer1 and then let go of the mouse button. The New Binding dialog box appears, as shown in Figure 9-4.

Figure 9-4:
Add instant
functionality
with the
New
Binding
dialog box.

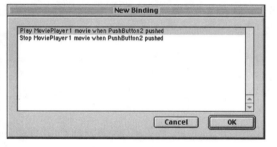

Click OK to dismiss the dialog box. The line you created remains. Press ⌘-Shift again, drag from the button labeled Stop (PushButton3) to MoviePlayer1, and select the second item in the New Binding dialog box:

```
Stop MoviePlayer1 movie when PushButton2.pushed
```

After you click OK in the New Binding dialog box, a small line appears in the Window Editor connecting the two controls. This line, called a *binding,* is very powerful. It provides common functionality without any code. Other controls have this capability to automatically bind with other controls.

The New Binding dialog box displays bindings that are common to the two controls you are trying to bind — in this case a PushButton and a MoviePlayer. Figure 9-5 shows the new MoviePlayer controls with their associated bindings.

To remove bindings from controls, select the binding line in the Window Editor and press the Delete key.

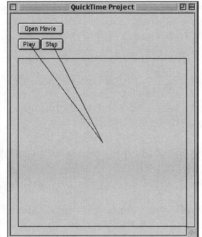

Figure 9-5:
After two
controls are
bound, a
small line
connects
them in the
Window
Editor.

Sometimes bindings won't fulfill your movie-playing requirements. For example, you might want to begin playback from a control or a method that does not support bindings to MoviePlayer. In these cases, add the following code to the Action event of a control to begin playing the movie:

```
MoviePlayer1.Play
```

and this code to make it stop:

```
MoviePlayer1.Stop
```

Important MoviePlayer properties

The MoviePlayer object has several important properties you can set to affect the playback of movies as well as the appearance and functionality of MoviePlayer.

Altering playback

By default, MoviePlayer plays movies only one time. When MoviePlayer reaches the end of the movie, it stops. To make the movie continue playing when it reaches the end, you must set the Looping property of MoviePlayer to TRUE. When the playback head reaches the end of the movie, it automatically jumps to the beginning of the movie and continues playing.

You can set the Looping property of MoviePlayer in two ways:

- In the REALbasic Properties window
- Using code

To set up your MoviePlayer to loop, click it in the Window Editor for your window (Window1, for example). Next, click the Looping check box in the Properties window. Or if you want to set the Looping property with code from the `Action` event of some control:

```
MoviePlayer1.Looping = TRUE
```

When you set the Looping property with code, like this, you need not change the property manually in the Properties window.

If your code resides in the `Open` event of MoviePlayer, use the following:

```
Me.Looping = TRUE
```

Because this code exists in a MoviePlayer event, you don't have to refer to the MoviePlayer by name (`MoviePlayer1`). Rather, refer to it by using the term `Me`.

Setting the Looping property to `FALSE` causes the movie to stop looping. If the movie is already playing, it continues until the end and then stops.

A close cousin to the Looping property of MoviePlayer is the Palindrome property. The Palindrome property causes the movie to loop, but instead loops forwards and backwards. When the movie reaches the end, the playback continues in a reverse direction. When the playback head reaches the beginning of the movie, the movie plays in the standard forward direction.

You set the Palindrome property in the same way you set the Looping property. If both the Palindrome and Looping properties are set to `TRUE`, the Palindrome property overrides the Looping property.

Use the Palindrome property sparingly. It plays in reverse not only the video but also the audio. This can result in some evil-sounding audio, which is sure to cause the neighborhood kids to run screaming. You've been warned! All kidding aside, you can use the Palindrome property for some fun special effects, but most of the time you should just leave it set to `FALSE`.

Position is another important property for controlling QuickTime playback. It's a double number (one with a decimal point) that represents the location of the playback head measured in seconds from the beginning of the movie. You move the playback head to a specific position in the movie, like this:

```
MoviePlayer1.Position = 10.5
```

You can also find out how far into the movie you are by looking at the position of the playback head. To find the position of the playback head, simply move the `MoviePlayer1.Position` code to the opposite side of the equal sign:

```
Dim myPosition as Double
myPosition = MoviePlayer1.Position
MsgBox Str(myPosition)
```

Changing the look and feel of MoviePlayer

In addition to altering MoviePlayer's default behavior, you can also change its appearance and interface elements. For starters, MoviePlayer can optionally display a small black line around the border of a QuickTime movie. This Border property is set to TRUE by default. If you're playing movies for the sake of playing movies, leave it set to TRUE. If you're playing a movie that is not supposed to look like a movie (such as when you use a QuickTime movie disguised as part of your interface), set it to FALSE.

MoviePlayer can also display playback controls. These allow your users to control the playback of movies. The controls encompass the following, which appear in Figure 9-6:

- ✔ **Play and Stop buttons** to start and stop playback
- ✔ **Timeline slider** to both view and set the current position in the movie
- ✔ **Fast forward and rewind buttons** to set the playback in either direction
- ✔ **Speaker** to set the playback volume of a movie

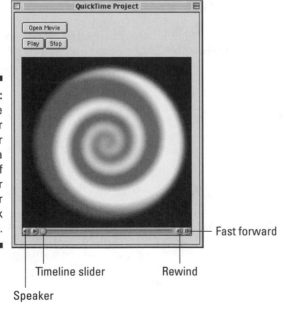

Figure 9-6:
The MoviePlayer controller sports a number of widgets for your playback needs.

Fast forward

Timeline slider   Rewind

Speaker

To display the first three interface elements of MoviePlayer, set its Controller property. The Controller property has three possible settings:

- ✔ 0 is no controller
- ✔ 1 is badge
- ✔ 2 is controller

A *badge* is a small widget that displays the full controller when you click it. Otherwise, the full controller stays out of view.

By default, MoviePlayer displays a controller. You can set the property by selecting one of the settings in the Properties window or in your code:

```
MoviePlayer1.Controller = 2
```

Volume control of MoviePlayer in REALbasic works somewhat differently. Rather than controlling it with the traditional Controller property, you set it by adjusting the Speaker property of MoviePlayer. Set it either by clicking the Speaker check box in the Properties window or with code:

```
MoviePlayer1.Speaker = TRUE
```

Creating Your Own Movies

You can not only play and control QuickTime movies, but also create them with REALbasic. Creating movies with REALbasic involves a few more steps than usual:

- ✔ Create an editable movie
- ✔ Add a video track to the movie
- ✔ Add frames to the video track

Using EditableMovie

EditableMovie is a bit like a movie that you can't play. Instead, you can only create or open one and manipulate it by adding tracks to it. EditableMovies are also somewhat strange because they stick around until your program clears them from memory. You don't actually have to clear them from memory yourself; REALbasic does the job for you.

Your project makes use of variables and properties throughout your code only as long as they remain in memory. If you define a variable (or property) within a particular event, that variable remains in memory only while the event executes. As soon as the event has finished executing, REALbasic erases the variable from memory. In other words, only the code within that event has access to it. No other events do, because they are *out of scope*. What this means to you as a programmer is that you must make special provisions in your code.

To begin adding movie creation functionality to the project in this chapter, follow these steps:

1. **Drag a PushButton and an EditField to Window1.**

   Change the Caption property of the PushButton to read *Create Movie*.

2. **Open the Window1 Code Editor and add a FolderItem property to it.**

   Choose Edit⇨New Property and enter `myFolderItem as FolderItem` in the dialog box that appears. Click OK to dismiss the dialog box. The myFolderItem property is now accessible by all controls and methods in Window1.

3. **Create two methods in Window1.**

   Choose Edit⇨New Method and create a method named `CreateTheMovie`. Repeat this process but name the second method `PlayTheMovie`.

With your foundation laid, you can begin adding code. Double-click the new PushButton (PushButton3) to open its `Action` event in the Code Editor. Add the following:

```
CreateTheMovie
PlayTheMovie
```

This code first calls the `CreateTheMovie` method to, you guessed it, create a movie. Because the instance of EditableMovie used in creating the movie resides solely in the `CreateTheMovie` method, REALbasic automatically closes EditableMovie when the method completes execution.

A *class* is a general description used to create an object. You don't actually create objects when you are writing a program. Rather, when the program runs, it creates the objects. Programmers call each object an *instance* of the class from which it was made. Jargon-loving programmers call this action *instantiation*. Now you know that instantiation is simply the act of creating an object.

If EditableMovie was not closed in this fashion, it would be impossible for the next method, `PlayTheMovie`, to do its work — which, as you can probably guess, is to play the movie. Therefore, you must make special provisions to deal with the problem of scope. The code in the `CreateTheMovie` and `PlayTheMovie` methods both access the same movie file (a FolderItem), so myFolderItem is a property of Window1 to allow both methods access to it.

Now, to add code to these two methods, open the Code Editor, navigate to the CreateTheMovie method, and enter the following:

```
Sub CreateTheMovie()
Dim i,numframes as Integer
Dim myEditableMovie as EditableMovie
Dim myVideoTrack as QTVideoTrack
Dim myPicture as Picture

myPicture=NewPicture(320,240,32)

myFolderItem = GetSaveFolderItem("video/quicktime","My
        REALbasic Movie.mov")
if myFolderItem<>nil then
    myEditableMovie=myFolderItem.createmovie
    myVideoTrack=myEditableMovie.NewVideoTrack
        (myPicture.width,myPicture.height,15)
    numframes = 15 * 4 // 15fps * 4 sec.

for i=1 to numframes
    myPicture.graphics.foreColor=RGB(0,0,0)
    myPicture.graphics.fillrect(0,0,320,240)
    myPicture.graphics.foreColor=RGB(0,255,0)
    myPicture.graphics.TextSize=i
    myPicture.Graphics.TextFont="Geneva"
    myPicture.Graphics.DrawString EditField1.text,10,100
    myVideoTrack.appendpicture(myPicture)
next
end if
End Sub
```

This code incorporates many different functions, so take it one step at a time. For starters, the code creates a number of variables:

- i is an integer to run a For-Next loop
- numframes is an integer used to store the number of frames you will add
- myEditableMovie is an EditableMovie that will become your completed movie file
- myVideoTrack is the video track, which holds all the frames of this movie
- myPicture is a variable to hold a Picture object that is used, in turn, to create the content for each frame of the track

Next, the code creates the Picture object with dimensions of 320x240 and a 32-bit color depth (that is, millions of colors):

```
myPicture=NewPicture(320,240,32)
```

You will create graphics using this Picture object to produce the individual frames of the `VideoTrack` movie. The final preliminary step is to ask the user to specify a location for the movie using the `GetSaveFolderItem` command:

```
myFolderItem = GetSaveFolderItem("video/quicktime","My RB
          Flick.mov")
```

This command takes two parameters: the file type and the default name. In return, it gives you a FolderItem. Because you created the video/quicktime file type previously in this chapter, you can continue to use it without redefining it.

The default name for the movie can be anything you like; it's only a suggestion for your users. They are free to change the name to whatever they want in the Save dialog box.

If the user declines to choose a location for the movie, `GetSaveFolderItem` returns `nil`. If this happens, you have no FolderItem to access, so you must be sure to avoid trying to use it. This is the purpose for the next line of code:

```
if myFolderItem<>nil then
...this code executes if the user selected a file location
...if the user did not select a location, the code proceeds
          to the "end if" statement
```

Now, it's time to create the movie. Commence production by creating EditableMovie. Next, add `myVideoTrack` to `myEditableMovie`, passing the width and height of `myPicture` as well as the rate of this movie in frames per second (15 fps). It is to this `VideoTrack` that you will add frames:

```
myEditableMovie=myFolderItem.createmovie
myVideoTrack=myEditableMovie.NewVideoTrack(myPicture.width,my
          Picture.height,15)
```

To continue, calculate the number of frames that you want to add to the movie. The number of frames is equal to the rate in frames per second (15 fps) multiplied by the number of seconds you want to add to `VideoTrack`:

```
numframes = 15 * 4 // 15fps * 4 sec.
```

Finally, add frames to `myVideoTrack` by running through a simple loop. During each pass through the loop, create a picture with some text in it and add that picture to `VideoTrack` as a frame:

```
for i=1 to numframes
    myPicture.graphics.foreColor=RGB(0,0,0)
    myPicture.graphics.fillrect(0,0,320,240)
    myPicture.graphics.foreColor=RGB(0,255,0)
    myPicture.graphics.TextSize=i
```

```
        myPicture.Graphics.TextFont="Geneva"
        myPicture.Graphics.DrawString EditField1.text,10,100
        myVideoTrack.appendpicture(myPicture)
next
```

The last line terminates the earlier If-Then statement. If the user didn't select a destination for the movie, the code jumps here:

```
End If
```

After the `CreateTheMovie` method has finished executing, REALbasic instantly disposes of `myEditableMovie` from memory but saves the movie that the code has created to disk. Having completed the `CreateTheMovie` method, REALbasic jumps back up to the PushButton3 `Action` event to execute the next line of code:

```
PlayTheMovie
```

The `PlayTheMovie` method has the following code:

```
if myFolderItem<>nil then
    MoviePlayer1.Movie = myFolderItem.OpenAsMovie
    MoviePlayer1.Play
end if
```

If the user selected (and subsequently created) a movie, the code loads it into the Movie property of MoviePlayer1 and plays the movie. You have successfully programmed your own movie!

Adding special effects to a movie

QuickTime has many special effects that you can access with REALbasic. The effects are various types of video transitions. You can find the complete listing of available transitions in the *REALbasic Language Reference* under the `GetQTSMPTEEffect` and `GetQTCrossFadeEffect` methods. To view the *Language Reference,* choose Window➪Reference. For this example, use the SMPTE effect called the 5-Pointed Star (SMPTE effect number 128).

To create a movie with this special effect, first create a new method by choosing Edit➪New Method. Name the method `CreateTheTransitionMovie`. Open this new method in the Code Editor and enter the following code:

```
Sub CreateTheTransitionMovie
Dim i,numframes as Integer
Dim myStartingPicture,myEndingPicture as Picture
Dim myEditableMovie as EditableMovie
Dim myVideoTrack as QTVideoTrack
```

```
Dim myEffect as QTEffect
Dim mySequence as QTEffectSequence

myStartingPicture=NewPicture(320,240,32)
myStartingPicture.Graphics.ForeColor=RGB(0,0,255)
myStartingPicture.Graphics.FillRect 0,0,320,240

myEndingPicture=NewPicture(320,240,32)
myEndingPicture.Graphics.ForeColor=RGB(0,255,0)
myEndingPicture.Graphics.FillRect 0,0,320,240
myEndingPicture.Graphics.ForeColor=RGB(0,0,0)
myEndingPicture.Graphics.TextSize=24
myEndingPicture.Graphics.DrawString "REALbasic",100,100

myFolderItem = GetSaveFolderItem("video/quicktime","My Fancy
        RB Flick.mov")
if myFolderItem<>nil then
    myEditableMovie=myFolderItem.createmovie
    numframes = 15 * 4 // 15fps * 4 sec.

    myEffect=GetQTSMPTEeffect(128)
    mySequence=new
        QTEffectSequence(myEffect,myStartingPicture,myEndi
            ngPicture,numframes)
    myVideoTrack=myEditableMovie.NewVideoTrack
        (myStartingPicture.width, myEndingPicture.height,
        32)

    for i=1 to numframes
        mySequence.Frame=i
        myVideoTrack.AppendPicture mySequence.Image
    next
end if
End Sub
```

You should recognize much of the code from the example in the preceding section. There are, however, are a few notable exceptions. First, in this example, you need two Picture objects. These Pictures store the beginning and ending frames of the movie. The code fills the starting Picture (myStartingPicture) with a blue rectangle. Next, it fills the ending Picture (myEndingPicture) with a green rectangle and prints the word *REALbasic* in black. With a starting and ending image prepared, it's time to create a QTEffectSequence.

QTEffectSequence is a collection of frames that make up a completed special effects transition. To create QTEffectSequence, you must first create a QTEffect object. The number you pass corresponds to a particular effect (in this case the 5-Pointed Star effect):

```
myEffect=GetQTSMPTEeffect(128)
```

Next, create QTEffectSequence, passing the effect, the starting frame, the ending frame, and the frame count to QTEffectSequence:

```
mySequence=new
         QTEffectSequence(myEffect,myStartingPicture,myEndi
         ngPicture,numframes)
```

This call creates a sequence of picture frames that begin with myStartingPicture and end with myEndingPicture. REALbasic creates all the pictures that occur between the beginning and ending frames and places them in mySequence. Now, it's a simple matter to loop through the sequence of pictures and add each one to the VideoTrack of the movie:

```
for i=1 to numframes
    mySequence.Frame=i
    myVideoTrack.AppendPicture mySequence.Image
next
```

To put this code into action, add yet another PushButton to Window1 and add the following code to its Action event:

```
CreateTheTransitionMovie
PlayTheMovie
```

Test the project by choosing Debug⇨Run. Figure 9-7 shows the completed project.

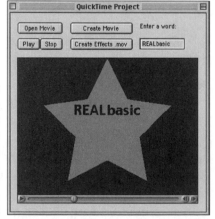

Figure 9-7:
REALbasic can create all kinds of movie special effects.

If you don't feel like entering all the code for the examples in this chapter, you can copy and paste the code from *REALbasic For Dummies* CD in the back of this book. If that still feels like too much work, you can also copy the entire project by dragging from the CD to anywhere in the Finder.

Chapter 10

Sound Off!

· ·

In This Chapter

▶ Playing sounds the easy way

▶ Squeezing audio out of a computer with advanced methods

· ·

*O*ne of the most overlooked features of today's computers is sound. Nothing makes an application feel more professional than adding a bit of sound to it.

Sound is useful for giving a user instant feedback about an action, such as clicking a button. A real-world button clicks, so why not make your virtual buttons do the same? Sound can also enhance the overall presentation of your application. From raucous special effects to subtle background music, sound can make your application stand out.

This chapter takes you through the simple steps of adding sound to your REALbasic projects. As the saying goes, there many ways to skin a cat, and REALbasic sound is no different. Using a variety of techniques, you will have your computer clicking, squeaking, and squawking in no time. Furthermore, REALbasic allows you to create your own software radio to tune in broadcasts from all over the world. By the end of the chapter, you'll have a simple project that demonstrates each of these techniques.

Simple Audio Techniques

REALbasic affords you simple audio production with a modicum of code or effort. To begin building a project for sound production, follow these steps:

1. **Create a new REALbasic project.**

   Begin by starting REALbasic (which creates a new project by default), or by choosing File⇨New.

2. **Open the Window Editor for Window1.**

   Double-click Window1 in the Project window to open its Window Editor.

3. **Drag two PushButtons from the Tools window to Window1.**

   These buttons will contain the code that plays sound.

System Alert sound

The easiest way to play a sound from REALbasic involves only one command:

```
Beep
```

This simple command placed anywhere in your code will produce a sound. What sound? It depends on your operating system settings. On the Macintosh, open either the Sound control panel or the Monitors and Sound control panel (depending on your version of the Mac OS) and choose a system Alert sound. REALbasic plays this sound when you issue the Beep command.

REALbasic Pro users will be glad to know that the Beep command works in Windows as well. To set the sound, open the Sounds setting in the control panel. The sound named Default Sound is the one that your application will play with the Beep command.

To add sound-producing code to your project, double-click one of the PushButtons you created earlier to open its Action event. Into this event, type the Beep command. Choose Debug⇨Run to test the project. Press the button and the system sound plays in all its glory.

System 7 sounds

The Macintosh platform supports a sound file format called a *System 7 sound.* This type of file is native to the Macintosh platform, and REALbasic can read it easily.

To complete the code in this part of the chapter, you need at least one System 7 sound file. You can find these types of sounds on the Internet or you can record your own. Several sounds are also on the *REALbasic For Dummies* CD.

Playing a System 7 Sound is easy to do. You simply send the Play command to the sound file. To add a System 7 sound to your REALbasic project, do the following:

1. **Drag a System 7 sound from the Finder to the Project window.**

   It's usually a good practice to place your sound files in the same folder as your project, so that you always know where they are. Drag the sound file from your project folder into the Project window. The file automatically appears in the Project window. For this example, we use a sound file named ClickSound.

2. **Open the Code Editor for PushButton2.**

   Double-click the second PushButton in your Window Editor to open its `Action` event.

3. **In the `Action` event of PushButton2, enter the following code:**

   ```
   ClickSound.Play
   ```

4. **Save the project by choosing File⇨Save.**

One simple command is all it takes! Now, choose Debug⇨Run to test the project. If all goes well, you should hear `ClickSound` play when you click the button. By now, your project should look something like Figure 10-1.

Figure 10-1:
It's easy to play simple sounds with the Beep and `Play` commands.

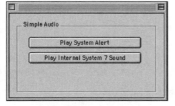

Sometimes you may not want to include a sound file directly in your application. Instead, perhaps you'd like your user to be able to play any sound file. This too is an easy task, but it requires a bit more code.

To play any System 7 sound file, you must do a few things:

- ✔ Create a FolderItem, which is a reference to a file.
- ✔ Create a Sound object to store the sound after you open it.
- ✔ Send the Sound object a `Play` message to play the System 7 sound file.

To implement this list of requirements, the code is a little more involved. For starters, you need a FolderItem. If you know the name and location of the sound file (in the same folder as the project, for example), use the `GetFolderItem` command:

```
Dim f as FolderItem

// "ClickSound" is a sound file in the same folder
// as this project
f = GetFolderItem("ClickSound")
```

If you want users to select a sound file for themselves, use
GetOpenFolderItem. The GetOpenFolderItem command requires you to
tell it the type of file to open. For this example, use sys7 as the file type:

```
Dim f as FolderItem

f = GetOpenFolderItem("sys7")
```

The sys7 file type is a made-up name. It could just as well have been fred
instead. You must define this name as a file type, so REALbasic can recognize
it. To define a file type:

1. **Choose Edit⊅File Types.**

   The File Types dialog box appears. (For an in-depth discussion of file
   types, look at Chapter 12.)

2. **Click the Add button.**

   The Add File Type window opens.

3. **Set the Name, Type, and Creator.**

   Use sys7 for the Name; sfil for the Type; and ???? for the Creator.

4. **Click OK twice to dismiss the dialog boxes.**

Now REALbasic know that a sys7 file is a file with a type of sfil. This is a
System 7 sound file. The ???? setting means that the file could have been created by any application, not one application in particular.

After you have FolderItem representing the System 7 sound file, you open the
sound resource by sending FolderItem an OpenAsSound command. When you
open the sound resource, it returns the sound. To use the sound, you must
create a sound object to store the sound.

After you have opened the sound and placed it in a sound object, you can
send the sound object the Play command:

```
Dim s as Sound
.
.
.
s=f.OpenAsSound
s.Play
```

The completed code for opening a System 7 sound file looks like this:

```
Dim f as FolderItem
Dim s as Sound

f = GetOpenFolderItem("sys7")
// if you know the file name, use GetFolderItem
// f = GetFolderItem("thud")
if f<>nil then
    s = f.OpenAsSound
    s.play
end if
```

Fancy Audio Techniques

Playing System 7 sounds and operating system alerts is fun and all, but sometimes you want to do something flashier. REALbasic combines with QuickTime to produce a virtual jukebox capable of playing MIDI songs, popular audio files, and even audio from the Internet.

MIDI

MIDI is an acronym for Musical Instrument Digital Interface. MIDI files contain the name notes required to play a song. Only the musical notes — not the audio — is actually stored in the file. The sounds already reside on a user's computer. This makes MIDI files quite small but requires the user to have MIDI capabilities. Luckily, QuickTime, which ships with the Mac OS and is a free download for Windows, contains a full MIDI engine that provides full MIDI capabilities, including a synthesizer of dozens of sounds.

To access the functionality of QuickTime, you must use a MoviePlayer control. MoviePlayer plays back MIDI files using the QuickTime synthesizer engine. Although a MIDI file is not a native QuickTime file, QuickTime automatically takes care of opening and converting the file to something it understands. Playing a MIDI file with REALbasic involves these steps:

- ✔ Adding MoviePlayer to your project
- ✔ Loading a MIDI file as a movie
- ✔ Setting the Movie property of MoviePlayer to the MIDI file
- ✔ Playing the MIDI file

Because this method also includes the use of FolderItems, look at the System 7 sound description previously in this chapter for a recap of how to work with FolderItems.

To begin your quest for symphonic excellence, open a Window Editor and add a MoviePlayer control. Figure 10-2 shows a window with a MoviePlayer control.

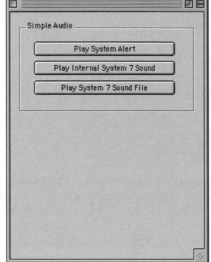

Simple Audio

Play System Alert

Play Internal System 7 Sound

Play System 7 Sound File

Figure 10-2:
With
MoviePlayer,
you can
easily play
MIDI files.

In addition, add a PushButton to your window. Double-click the button to open its Action event and enter the following code:

```
Dim f as FolderItem

f = GetOpenFolderItem("audio/midi")
if f<>nil then
    MoviePlayer1.movie=f.openasmovie
    MoviePlayer1.play
end if
```

Notice that the GetOpenFolderItem command has audio/midi as a parameter. You must add this file type to the File Types dialog box. Again, the previous System 7 example covers how to accomplish this. If you would like a more in-depth look at file types, see Chapter 12.

Other audio files

The MoviePlayer control will also play many other types of files. Any file type that QuickTime supports is playable with the REALbasic MoviePlayer control. Furthermore, as QuickTime adds other audio file type functionality, your REALbasic projects can take advantage of it immediately.

Some of the current file types that QuickTime supports include the following:

- ✔ AIFF (common on the Macintosh)
- ✔ WAV (common on Windows)
- ✔ MP3 (common everywhere!)
- ✔ AU
- ✔ System 7 sound (common on the Macintosh)

To play any of these types of audio files, use the same code as you did for playing MIDI files. Place the following code in yet another PushButton:

```
Dim f as FolderItem

f = GetOpenFolderItem("audio/aiff")
if f<>nil then
    MoviePlayer1.movie=f.openasmovie
    MoviePlayer1.play
end if
```

In this example, the GetOpenFolderItem has audio/aiff as its file type parameter. Again, you must define audio/aiff in the File Types dialog box. By now, your project should look like Figure 10-3.

Figure 10-3:
MoviePlayer can play different types of audio file formats.

Internet

The Internet has unleashed a ton of audio possibilities for you to exploit with REALbasic. Not only is the Internet a great source of all types of audio files, it is also a great new resource of live streaming Internet radio stations.

With only a few short lines of code, QuickTime gives you the ability to tune in any radio station from around the globe. All you need is

- ✔ A MoviePlayer control in your window
- ✔ A URL of some Internet radio content

Adding a MoviePlayer control is something you should be accustomed to by now. Most examples in this chapter have used one. Continue using the existing MoviePlayer.

To find a URL for obtaining Internet audio content, you need to go to the Internet. Many radio stations are offering streaming QuickTime content that you can access. Some sites, such as KRS RadioWorld, at

```
www.krs-radioworld.com/language/home.htm
```

list online radio stations from around the world. For this example, use National Public Radio's online radio address:

```
www.apple.com/quicktime/favorites/npr1/npr1.mov
```

To add Internet radio functionality to your project, begin by dragging an EditField to your Window Editor. This EditField will hold the Web address of the destination to which you would like to connect. Computer nerds refer to a Web address as a *URL,* which is shorthand for Uniform Resource Locator. For convenience, type the URL for National Public Radio into the Text property of EditField.

You could also enter the address when you test the project. But by typing the URL in the Text property of EditField, you won't have to type it every time you test the project.

Next, add a PushButton to the Window Editor. This PushButton performs all the commands necessary to connect MoviePlayer to the URL station. After you add the PushButton, double-click it to open its Action event and add the following code:

```
Dim myURL as String

myURL = EditField1.text
MoviePlayer1.movie=OpenURLMovie(myURL)
MoviePlayer1.play
```

This code first creates a string to hold the URL. Next, it extracts the URL from EditField by looking at its Text property. Finally, the `OpenURLMovie` command loads the movie into the Movie property of MoviePlayer, which immediately plays the movie. Keep in mind that a QuickTime movie doesn't necessarily contain all the media you might associate with a movie. A QuickTime movie can hold pictures, audio, or a combination of both. Your completed audio demonstration project should now look like Figure 10-4.

Figure 10-4:
Your completed audio project can play System 7, MIDI, and AIFF sound files, not to mention tune in radio stations from the Internet.

With only four lines of code, you have harnessed radio stations from anywhere on the planet. And you thought programming would be difficult!

If you are impatient or just don't feel like typing, you can use the copy of the project on the *REALbasic For Dummies* CD.

Chapter 11

Animation Fun

● ●

In This Chapter

▶ Creating sprite animations

▶ Incorporating sprites into games

● ●

After long hours of writing code, you'll eventually want to have some fun. Compared to sleepless nights working on sophisticated utilities, programming games is much more fun. With REALbasic in your hands and a working knowledge of animation, you can make entertaining action games in no time at all.

This chapter takes you through the process of creating a simple arcade game. In the process, you gain a firm understanding of how animation works in REALbasic. Furthermore, REALbasic's new features allow you to make your game animations object-oriented as well.

SpriteSurface Essentials

At the heart of REALbasic animation is the SpriteSurface control. It's a resizable control that takes care of a lot of the dirty work involved in graphics animation.

SpriteSurfaces are two-faced

The SpriteSurface control manages much of the hard work when creating animation. To create animation in REALbasic, you use special objects called sprites. *Sprites* are the various graphical elements you want to animate. The SpriteSurface control keeps track of all the sprites, including refreshing the screen, moving sprites, and detecting collisions.

As you can see, SpriteSurfaces are complex controls indeed. The great part is that all this functionality eases the burden of the programmer because so much of the hard work is complete before you start making a game.

Creating sprites

The first step in working with a SpriteSurface is to create some sprites. As mentioned, a sprite is an object that you want to animate. To create a sprite, you use the `NewSprite` method of the SpriteSurface class. The method takes an image and its initial x- and y-coordinates as parameters.

```
SpriteSurface1.NewSprite mySpriteGraphic, 50, 50
```

This works well enough but can soon become unwieldy. When you create a sprite in this fashion, you must store it as a property of the window in which the SpriteSurface control resides. In this way, code from any event in the window can access the SpriteSurface control. The downside is that you must create a lot of messy code to create a sophisticated sprite example.

A far superior method in terms of ease and elegance is to create sprites in an object-oriented fashion. Don't let the terminology scare you. Object-oriented design makes your programming task much easier to perform. Furthermore, it gives you the ability to do some amazing feats that would be nearly impossible any other way.

Perhaps the most important feature of object-oriented programming, or OOP, can be summed up in one word: encapsulation. When you program with OOP, you create *classes,* which are templates for creating and using an object. A class describes what the object is and how it works. Because all these descriptions are stored in one place (in the class), the information is said to be *encapsulated.* That way, all data and processes associated with an object travel with it and no other part of your program has to keep track of it.

What does this mean to you as a sprite programmer? It means that your sprite code can be streamlined, reusable, and possess many great features. For example, because a sprite object is responsible for its own behavior, appearance, and description, it is a simple matter to create objects that seem to have a mind of their own. (And by OOP standards, they do!) This is extremely difficult and time-consuming to recreate using traditional non-OOP programming methods. It is also easy to create as many of these free-willed objects as you want. You simply use the class as a cookie cutter for creating numerous copies of the same type of objects.

This chapter details the methods required to build a simple arcade game. In it, you are the driver of a small automobile. As you speed along, you discover that some sorry sap has left several traffic cones in the middle of the road. It is your mission to jump each of the cones until you reach the finish line. (Yes, you heard right — a jumping car.) Figure 11-1 shows what the completed game looks like.

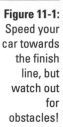

Figure 11-1:
Speed your car towards the finish line, but watch out for obstacles!

The game consists of three custom sprite classes:

- ✔ Car
- ✔ Cone obstacle
- ✔ Flag at the finish line

To begin working with the SpriteSurface, you should create classes for each of the listed sprites. Why? Because classes enable you to store properties to keep track of the sprite's features (such as the car's speed). Launch REALbasic and bring the Project window to the foreground. Choose File⇨New Class to create a new class. In the Properties window, change the Name property of the new class to

```
CarSprite
```

Change the Super property by clicking its popup menu in the Properties window. The Super property gives you the opportunity to inherit functionality from another class. Set it to

```
Sprite
```

That's it! You've created a class! Actually, there's more to it than that, but what you have now is a valid class. Having created and named your CarSprite class, it's time to define its properties and functionality.

Because CarSprite is a special kind of car that possesses jumping capabilities, it needs a Boolean property to keep track of its jumping status. Choose Edit⇨New Property and create a new Boolean property as follows:

```
Jumping as Boolean
```

Furthermore, as the car is jumping, it has a vertical speed that you can store in a Double property of the class. Create another property by choosing Edit⇨New Property:

```
Speed as Double
```

In addition to these properties, this Sprite class automatically inherits the properties of the Super class (which you set to Sprite earlier). *Inheritance* is another important feature of OOP. Because REALbasic has already defined a number of features as part of the Sprite class, you get to take advantage of them for free. Some of the most important properties you inherit are

- ✔ X position of the sprite within a SpriteSurface
- ✔ Y position of the sprite within a SpriteSurface
- ✔ Sprite's image
- ✔ Sprite's Group number, which differentiates it from other sprites

Later, when you create an object from this class, you may want to initialize each of these properties with a default value. To do so, you make use of a constructor. A *constructor* in OOP lingo is simply a method that belongs to a class that executes the instant the code creates an object. It might be helpful to think of a constructor as a type of Open event for an object.

By convention, the constructor usually shares the same name as the class. To create a constructor method, choose Edit⇨New Method and enter the information pictured in Figure 11-2.

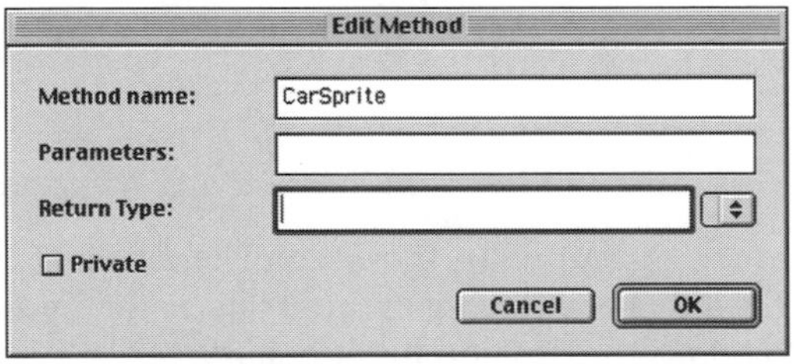

Figure 11-2: The constructor method of a class typically shares the same name as the class itself.

In the constructor of CarSprite, enter the following code:

```
Sub CarSprite()
   Image=Car
   X=150
   Y=215
```

```
   Group=1
   Jumping=FALSE
End Sub
```

This code starts out by defining the CarSprite Image property. `Car` is a graphic file you must drag into the Project window. Next, the X and Y properties indicate the position where CarSprite should begin life. This position is within and relative to SpriteSurface, which will have dimensions of 320 pixels wide by 240 pixels high. Therefore, this position is somewhere near the bottom center of SpriteSurface.

The Group property helps you keep track of which sprites are which. This is important later ,when sprites start colliding into each other. Finally, the constructor initializes the Jumping property of the sprite to `FALSE` because the car will begin life on the ground.

To continue defining the CarSprite class, you need to give some functionality to the car. Your car will jump, move forward and backward, and jump. Create four new methods by choosing Edit⇨New Method. Name the methods

- ✔ Advance
- ✔ Retreat
- ✔ Refresh
- ✔ StartJump

The first two methods take care of moving the car, and the last two redraw it and make it jump, respectively. To each of the methods, add its corresponding code:

```
Sub Advance()
   x=x+2
End Sub

Sub Retreat()
   x=x-1
End Sub

Sub StartJump()
if not Jumping then
   Jumping = TRUE
   Speed=4
end if
End Sub

Sub Refresh()
   y=y-Speed
   Speed=Speed-0.2
```

```
   If y>215 then
     y=215
     Jumping=False
     Speed=0
   End If
End Sub
```

The `Advance` and `Retreat` methods are self-explanatory. They move the sprite to the right or left within SpriteSurface. The `StartJump` method checks to see whether or not the car is jumping. If it isn't, this method initiates the car's jump and sets its vertical speed. Finally, the `Refresh` method takes care of monitoring the car's jump. As the car lifts off the ground, its speed gradually decreases. At some point, its speed becomes negative, which causes the car to fall back to the ground. The ground is at the Y position of 215. If the car's Y position exceeds this number, the car is back down on the ground, and the jumping should cease.

This completes the creation of CarSprite. The next step is to create two more classes:

- ObstacleSprite, a traffic cone
- FlagSprite, a flag at the finish line

Create the two classes just as you created CarSprite, by choosing File⇨New Class. Both classes have only one method each, a constructor method. Thus, add a method to the sprite named `ObstacleSprite` and a method to the sprite named `FlagSprite`. Constructor methods execute only the instant you create an object, so these methods initialize the image, location, and Group for the sprite. Add the following code to the respective method:

```
Sub ObstacleSprite()
   image=cone
   group=2
   x=10
   y=900
End Sub

Sub FlagSprite()
   image=flag
   x=10
   y=900
End Sub
```

The `ObstacleSprite` and `FlagSprite` constructor methods initialize the image, positioning, and Group property of the ObstacleSprite and FlagSprite classes. You must drag two images titled `cone` and `flag` into the Project window for this code to work.

If you don't have these images, the *REALbasic For Dummies* CD accompanying this book has example images you can use.

One peculiarity about the `ObstacleSprite` and `FlagSprite` constructor methods is the fact that they both initialize the classes by setting the Y property to 900. Because the SpriteSurface to which these sprite objects will belong has dimensions of 320x240, these sprites are not within view. I did this on purpose. When the code initializes the sprites, it hides them from view, where they stay until necessary.

This completes the sprite creation process. The code as it stands now doesn't doing anything particularly flashy or even visual. It does, however, lay the groundwork for an exciting and fast-paced arcade game.

Exploring Game Creation

Creating a game is not much different than other tasks. The first task is to make a plan. This is a good time to step away from the computer screen for a moment to write down the process with pencil and paper. Doing so will help you think things through before you get distracted with trying to get your program to do it. By keeping your planning process separate from the creation process, you will save yourself a lot of time and redesign work.

A simple list of the process involved in running this chapter's sample project might include the following:

1. **Create a car, an obstacle, and a flag sprite and attach them to a SpriteSurface.**

2. **Start the game timer.**

   As the game timer periodically fires, the playing field of SpriteSurface refreshes and scrolls the background to simulate movement.

3. **Check for keyboard interaction and act accordingly.**

   As SpriteSurface refreshes, check for pressed keys. If the user pressed a left or right arrow key, move the car appropriately. If the user presses the spacebar on the keyboard, make the car start its jump.

4. **Display an obstacle.**

   At certain points along the road, lay an obstacle on the ground in front of the car. If the car collides with the obstacle, game play ends and a sound plays. If the car jumps over the obstacle, game play continues as normal.

5. Check the finish line.

Is the car at the finish line yet? If so, the game play ends and a victory sound plays. If the car has not reached the finish line, the game play continues by executing Steps 3 through 5 until the games ends.

Now that you have a battle plan, it's a cinch to implement it. Begin by designing an interface for the game. Open the Window Editor for Window1 by double-clicking it in the Project window. To this window, drag a SpriteSurface control from the Tools window (labeled in Figure 11-3).

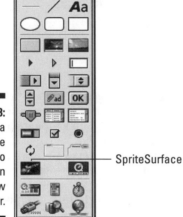

Figure 11-3:
Drag a SpriteSurface control into an open Window Editor.

— SpriteSurface

After you have added the SpriteSurface control to the window, change its properties to match those listed in Table 11-1. By default, when you drag a SpriteSurface control to a window, REALbasic automatically names it SpriteSurface1. In addition, drag a picture that you can use for a backdrop to the game action. Give the graphic the name Scenery. Again, if you need a graphic for the backdrop, one is included on the *REALbasic For Dummies* CD.

Table 11-1	SpriteSurface1 Properties
Property	*Setting*
Left	0
Top	0
Width	320

Property	Setting
Height	240
Backdrop	Scenery
Depth	32

Next, drag a StaticText control as well as a Timer control to Window1. Set the Mode property of Timer1 to 2 and its Period to 1.

To the graphics you added for the sprites and the SpriteSurface backdrop, add two Macintosh sound files. One sound plays when the player wins; the other sounds plays when the player loses.

In addition to images, the *REALbasic For Dummies* CD has sample sounds you can use for this purpose.

This concludes the interface building step. The completed interface should look something like Figure 11-4.

Figure 11-4:
The completed game interface.

To begin adding code for the game, choose Edit⇨New Property and create three sprite properties and one integer property as detailed in Table 11-2.

Table 11-2	Window1 Properties
Property Name and Type	*Stores*
myCarSprite as CarSprite	Car's sprite
myFlagSprite as FlagSprite	Flag sprite
myObstacleSprite as ObstacleSprite	Obstacle sprite
scrollcounter as integer	How far the SpriteSurface has scrolled

Next, create two new methods in Window1. Name them CreateSprites and EndGame. The CreateSprites method does exactly what you might expect: It creates sprites. The EndGame method stops Timer1, which effectively ends game play. It also plays a sound to indicate that the car collided with something and displays a losing message. To these methods, add the following code:

```
Sub CreateSprites()
  myCarSprite = new CarSprite
  SpriteSurface1.attach myCarSprite

  myObstacleSprite = new ObstacleSprite
  SpriteSurface1.attach myObstacleSprite

  myFlagSprite = new FlagSprite
  SpriteSurface1.attach myFlagSprite

  scrollcounter=0
End Sub

Sub EndGame
  Timer1.mode=0
  crashsound.play
  StaticText1.text="You lose!"
End Sub
```

The CreateSprites method creates the CarSprite, myObstacleSprite, and myFlagSprite objects and assigns them to SpriteSurface1 with the Attach method. Don't forget that this simple act causes the constructor method of each Sprite class to execute as well. The scrollcounter variable initializes to 0. To make use of the CreateSprites method, call it from the Open event of Window1:

```
Sub Open()
  CreateSprites
End Sub
```

The game uses the EndGame method to stop the game animation, play a crashing sound, and display a "You lose!" message in StaticText1.

Timer-based animation

To create animation, you draw graphics at different locations on the screen at regular time intervals. As the position of the graphics changes, you see the illusion of movement.

The driving force behind the animation and game action in this project is a Timer control named Timer1. As Timer1 periodically fires, the code within it executes. Only one line of code is necessary to get things going:

```
SpriteSurface1.Update
```

The Update method causes the SpriteSurface to draw the next frame of animation. It also executes the NextFrame event of the SpriteSurface. You can add code to the NextFrame event to change the positions of your animated sprites just before the SpriteSurface draws them on the screen. Timer1 continues to execute until its Mode is set to 0 (zero), in effect stopping the game and animation action (see the EndGame method).

Checking for keyboard action

Now that Timer1 is happily chugging along, telling the SpriteSurface to draw the next frame of animation at regular intervals, what more could you want? Simple, interaction. Animations are nice, but when you or another user controls the animation, it becomes a game. We'll use a keyboard to interact with the game, because all users have one.

To respond to a keypress, you need to continually check to see whether the user has pressed a key. This process of checking for keypresses occurs repeatedly like the redrawing of the frames in the animation, so you can group the code for these two functions together in the NextFrame event of SpriteSurface:

```
Sub NextFrame()
  me.scroll 1,0
  scrollcounter=scrollcounter+1

  Select Case scrollcounter
  Case 500
    myObstacleSprite.x=scrollcounter+320
    myObstacleSprite.y=205
  Case 1000
    myObstacleSprite.x=scrollcounter+320
    myObstacleSprite.y=205
  Case 1500
    myObstacleSprite.x=scrollcounter+320
    myObstacleSprite.y=205
```

```
Case 2000
  myObstacleSprite.x=scrollcounter+320
  myObstacleSprite.y=205
Case 2500
  myObstacleSprite.x=scrollcounter+320
  myObstacleSprite.y=205
Case 2700
  //Display the finish line flag
  myFlagSprite.x=scrollcounter+320
  myFlagSprite.y=205
Case 3000
  //Stop the game - we have a winner!
  Timer1.mode=0
  Crowd.play
  StaticText1.text="You Win!"
End Select

if spriteSurface1.keytest(123) then //left arrow key
  mycarSprite.Retreat
end if
if spriteSurface1.keytest(124) then //right arrow key
  myCarSprite.Advance
end if
if spriteSurface1.keyTest(49) then //jump=spacebar
  myCarSprite.StartJump
end if

if myCarSprite.Jumping then
  myCarSprite.Refresh
end if
if myCarSprite.x<(scrollcounter+10) then
  myCarSprite.x=(scrollcounter+10)
end if
if myCarSprite.x>(scrollcounter+280) then
  myCarSprite.x=(scrollcounter+280)
end if

End Sub
```

The first two lines of code scroll the BackDrop of SpriteSurface1. The picture stored in the BackDrop property wraps around when it scrolls out of the bounds of SpriteSurface1. If you make the BackDrop image correctly, you'll barely notice the fact that the same background keeps scrolling by (think of those wonderfully repeating backgrounds in Fred Flintstone cartoons). As the BackDrop scrolls, the scrollcounter property increments to keep track of how far SpriteSurface1 has scrolled so far.

```
me.scroll 1,0
scrollcounter=scrollcounter+1
```

Next, a large `Select` statement makes the decision of when to place an obstacle in the path of the car. It uses the scrollcounter property to denote milestones along the way. When the scrollcounter reaches a milestone (such as 500 or 1000), ObstacleSprite appears in the bottom-right corner of SpriteSurface1. Keep in mind that right before ObstacleSprite appears in SpriteSurface1, it's out of sight at Y=900. Because SpriteSurface1 continues to scroll, the obstacles continue to advance on the unsuspecting car.

If the car manages to bypass all obstacles and reach the final flag, the game is over and the player wins. The code then halts the game play, plays a victory sound, and displays a winning message in StaticText1:

```
Select Case scrollcounter
  Case 500
    myObstacleSprite.x=scrollcounter+320
    myObstacleSprite.y=205
  Case 1000
    myObstacleSprite.x=scrollcounter+320
    myObstacleSprite.y=205
    .
    .
    .
  Case 2700
    //Display the finish line flag
    myFlagSprite.x=scrollcounter+320
    myFlagSprite.y=205
  Case 3000
    //Stop the game - we have a winner!
    Timer1.mode=0
    Crowd.play
    StaticText1.text="You Win!"
End Select
```

With the animation of the game proceeding at a nice pace, it's time to check for user interaction. For this game, the user maneuvers the car using the left and right arrow keys for acceleration and the spacebar for jumping. To detect keypresses, you must pass keycode values to the `KeyTest` method of SpriteSurface1.

The numbers that you pass can differ for some keyboards. A great way to discover the keycode values you will need is to use a utility such as Theodore Smith's RB Helper. The utility displays the keycode for any key you press. It also performs other useful REALbasic-specific functions. You can download it at the following address:

```
www.thsmith.dircon.co.uk/programmer/downloads/rbhelper.sit
```

The code in the listing checks for a user pressing the left and right arrow keys as well as the spacebar on a U.S. Macintosh keyboard. You might need to alter the code if you are using a keyboard from another country.

```
if spriteSurface1.keytest(123) then //left arrow key
  mycarSprite.Retreat
end if
if spriteSurface1.keytest(124) then //right arrow key
  myCarSprite.Advance
end if
if spriteSurface1.keyTest(49) then //jump=space bar
  myCarSprite.StartJump
end if
```

The final step is to call the `Refresh` method if the car is jumping. This updates the appearance of the car while it is air-bound. Furthermore, if the car manages to reach the upper or lower limits of SpriteSurface1 in the X direction, the code forces the car back on the screen:

```
if myCarSprite.Jumping then
  myCarSprite.Refresh
end if
if myCarSprite.x<(scrollcounter+10) then
  myCarSprite.x=(scrollcounter+10)
end if
if myCarSprite.x>(scrollcounter+280) then
  myCarSprite.x=(scrollcounter+280)
end if
```

Detecting collisions

In your game, you need to be able to determine whether the car successfully jumped the cone or just drove straight through it. If the car jumps each cone and reaches the finish line, the player wins. But if the car collides with a cone, the game is over and the player loses.

Fortunately, SpriteSurface figures out for you whether a car collides with the obstacle. Each time two sprites collide, the `Collision` event of SpriteSurface executes. All you need to do is write a few lines of code to determine whether the two things that collided are the car and an obstacle; if they are, end the game. You can determine this by comparing the groups of the two colliding sprites.

The completed code for the `Collision` event looks like this:

```
Sub Collision(s1 as Sprite, s2 as Sprite)
  if s1.group=2 and s2.group=1 then
    EndGame
  end if
End Sub
```

Now that you have completed the coding for the game, it's time to test the code. Choose Debug⇨Run to give the game a whirl. If the code does not work, check whether

✔ Your typing was accurate

✔ You included all external files (graphics and sound files) in the Project window

✔ You created all necessary sprite classes

If you still can't get the code to work, never fear. A copy of the Sprite project used in this chapter is included on the *REALbasic For Dummies* CD along with the various graphics and audio support files.

Chapter 12

Working with Files

· ·

· ·

*N*early every desktop personal computer made today comes with some sort of permanent storage device, such as a hard drive, a CD-ROM, or one of an assortment of removable media. The main purpose of all these devices is to store and retrieve data.

To use data, your computer stores it on your drive in a variety of formats, called files. REALbasic is adept at handling all types of files. It has simple-to-use functions for creating and using many common file formats including text, graphics, and QuickTime movies.

Your applications access different types of files depending on the desired functionality. For example, graphic applications allow you to view and alter graphic files, whereas word processors permit you to manipulate text files.

This chapter begins by looking at the characteristics that all files share. The remainder of the chapter steps through the various specific file types and how to create and reuse them.

Features Common to All Files

Your hard drive is a sophisticated hierarchical structure of files. Don't let this kind of terminology scare you, though, because all it really means is that your computer keeps track of data in an organized fashion. Furthermore, the manner in which is organizes the data is much like an office filing cabinet. A filing cabinet can hold numerous folders. These folders, in turn, might also store other folders or documents. The computer's filing system works in a similar fashion.

A computer's file system is comprised of the following items:

- ✔ **Volumes,** which are storage devices, such as a hard drive or a CD-ROM
- ✔ **Folders,** which are containers within a volume
- ✔ **Applications,** which are the software you access each time you use your computer, for example, REALbasic, Netscape, Photoshop, or an application you made with REALbasic
- ✔ **Documents,** which are files that you create with applications, for example, text files, preference files, MP3 files, REALbasic project files

You can rest assured that these are the only types of creatures you will encounter when working with files. REALbasic can create each item in this list, with the exception of volumes. If you know of an application that can create hardware, please let me know!

For the remainder of this chapter, the term *volume* means hard drives, CD-ROMs, floppies, and any other device you can use to store or retrieve permanent data.

The FolderItem

FolderItems are the foundation for working with files in REALbasic. A *FolderItem* is an object you create to represent a file on a volume. It can represent all types of files, that is, folders, applications, and documents.

GetFolderItem

Sometimes, you need to access a file in the same folder as the program you have created. Perhaps you have a file with some helpful information in it for the user. Accessing this type of file is easy; simply pass the name of the file to the `GetFolderItem` function. The function returns a FolderItem that represents the file whose name you passed to it:

```
Dim f as FolderItem
f = GetFolderItem("MyFile")
```

In this example, `MyFile` is the name of a file that resides in the same folder as your project while you test it in REALbasic and later in the same folder as your application.

Pushing it to the limit

Have your ever wondered how many files you can open at a time or how large a file can be? The answer depends on the format of your hard drive. You have two choices for formatting your Mac OS hard drive:

- **HFS,** also known as Mac OS Standard
- **HFS+,** also known as Mac OS Extended

If your hard drive is formatted with HFS, you can safely open as many as 348 files simultaneously. Using HFS+, the number climbs dramatically to 8,169 simultaneous open files! Keep in mind that the any application (including the Finder) can, and often does, open files. Thus, the total number of files that your own application can open may be a few less.

None of this explains why you would ever *need* to open so many files. The numbers have been set high so that all running applications can open several files at the same time.

When it comes to file size, HFS has a limit of 2 gigabytes. HFS+ combined with Mac OS 9 can produce files as large as 9 *exobytes* — that's 9 billion gigabytes! Of course, no storage systems exist that can store such monstrously large files. Apple's just getting ready for when there are! Unless you are creating extremely long QuickTime movies or high-resolution pictures as large as a football field, these file size limits are preposterously large. Still, it's good to know that the capability is there.

FolderItem (f) represents the MyFile file, whether MyFile exists or not. Therefore, the GetFolderItem command has two purposes:

- To refer to an existing file
- To refer to a new file that you want to create

If you're uncertain whether or not a file exists, the Exists property of FolderItem will tell you. It returns a Boolean value of TRUE if it the file already exists or FALSE if it doesn't. For example, to continue with the preceding code:

```
Dim f as FolderItem

f=GetFolderItem("MyFile")

if f.Exists then
    MsgBox "File exists"
else
    MsgBox "File does not exist, but FolderItem does!"
end if
```

What if there is no file with the name you passed? Well, it turns out that GetFolderItem still returns a valid FolderItem representing a file. You are probably wondering what good that will do. It's very useful when you want to create a new file with that name. You find out more about this later in the chapter.

If the file already does exist, the returned FolderItem represents an actual file and you can easily find out some other information about it. To figure out whether the file is an application, a document, or a folder, you could enhance your code like so:

```
Dim f as FolderItem

f=GetFolderItem("MyFile")

if f.Exists then
    MsgBox "File exists"
    if f.Directory then
        MsgBox "This FolderItem represents a folder"
    else
            MsgBox "This FolderItem represents an application
                or a document."
    if f.MacType = "APPL" then
        MsgBox "It's an application"
    else
        MsgBox "It's a document"
    end if
end if
else
    MsgBox "File does not exist, but FolderItem does!"
end if
```

This code introduces a couple of new FolderItem properties worth mentioning:

- **Directory.** Returns TRUE if FolderItem is a directory (a folder).

- **MacType.** All files in a Macintosh file system are associated with a 4-letter type; APPL is the Macintosh file type of an application.

If the FolderItem you obtain is a folder, or directory, you can inquire about its contents. The Count property returns the number of items in the folder. Use this number to loop through each item in the folder. The Item property gives you access to each item within the folder, and it requires an Index number. By passing the Index to the Item property, REALbasic returns a FolderItem within the folder. The following code example counts the number of items in MyFolder and outputs the name of each one:

```
Dim f as FolderItem
Dim j, thecount as Integer

f = GetFolderItem("MyFolder")
if f<>nil then
thecount = f.Count
MsgBox "There are "+str(thecount)+" in the folder."
for j=1 to thecount
    MsgBox "Item #"+str(i)+"="+f.item(i).name
next
end if
```

So far, you have worked with only a specific file or folder name. The application knows where to look for this file because it resides in the same folder as the application. To describe the precise location of a file, computers use a path. A *path* begins with the name of a drive followed by the folder names that contain the file in question. Separate each level with a semicolon. For example, the Fonts folder is located in the System folder of hard drive. Therefore, you would write its path like this:

```
Macintosh HD:System Folder:Fonts:
```

Keep in mind that because the Fonts folder is a folder, you must follow its name with a semicolon. This long description of a location of a file is an *absolute path*.

When an application can find the file in relation to itself, you can use a *relative path* instead. In this case, you needn't list the entire path of the file. Instead, you can simply refer to the file according to its location in relation to the application. For example, if your application needs to access a text file named MyFile that resides in the same folder as your application, you can simply refer to it by name:

```
MyFile
```

If the file resides in another folder on the same volume, you can specify the location like this:

```
f=GetFolderItem(":MyFolder:MyFile")
```

In this situation, MyFile is in a folder named MyFolder, which is in the same folder as the application that calls this code.

When you need to look at the exact location of file, as opposed to the relative location, use the AbsolutePath property of FolderItem:

```
Dim f as FolderItem
f = GetFolderItem("MyFile")

MsgBox f.AbsolutePath
```

This code might yield a MsgBox like the one in Figure 12-1.

Figure 12-1:
The AbsolutePath property of a sample FolderItem.

My Volume : MyFolder : MyFile

OK

If all this talk about relative and absolute paths is making your head spin, you're in for a treat. A REALbasic FolderItem has two important methods that simplify matters quite a bit. They are

- ✔ `Parent` returns a FolderItem in the hierarchy one level higher. For example, if you have a folder called Applications on a volume called Macintosh HD, the Parent property of the Applications FolderItem is Macintosh HD. If the result is `nil`, `Parent` is a volume because a volume is at the top of the hierarchy.
- ✔ `Child (Name as String),` when passed to a FolderItem, returns a FolderItem of the file you have named. The Child resides in the folder to which you attach this method.

In other words, these two commands effectively allow you to traverse up and down through your hard drive, folders, and folders within those folders. A volume (such as your hard drive) is the ultimate parent of any file, application, or folder that resides on it. Everything below it (application, folders, and files) is a child of the parent. This continues down the hierarchy. Each file within a folder is a child of that folder.

For example, suppose your hard drive is named Macintosh HD. Within Macintosh HD is a folder titled Applications, and within that folder is a text file named Read Me. To obtain a FolderItem for Applications, for example, you could use code like this:

```
Dim f as FolderItem

f = GetFolderItem("Read Me").Parent
MsgBox f.name
```

Accessing the System folder and other special folders

REALbasic has a several commands that return FolderItems of commonly used folders, as listed in Table 12-1. These FolderItems represent common folders in the Mac OS. They perform only one function, but they save you a lot of time.

Table 12-1	Common Operating System FolderItems	
Method	*In Mac OS*	*Represents in Microsoft Windows*
AppleMenuFolder	Apple Menu Items folder	N/A
ControlPanelsFolder	Control Panels folder	N/A

Method	In Mac OS	Represents in Microsoft Windows
ExtensionsFolder	Extensions folder	Windows/System
FontsFolder	Fonts folder	Windows/Fonts
PreferencesFolder	Preferences folder	Windows
StartupItemsFolder	Startup Items folder	N/A
TemporaryFolder	Temporary Items folder	Windows/Temp
TrashFolder	Trash folder	N/A

These commands are handy to have in your programming toolbox. For instance, they make finding the number of control panels installed in a System Folder a cinch:

```
Dim f as FolderItem
Dim Count as Integer

f=ControlPanelsFolder

if f<>nil then
    Count = f.Count
    MsgBox "There are "+Str(Count)+" Control Panels
           installed."
end if
```

Selecting a file with the Open File dialog box

So far, this chapter has examined only how to obtain a FolderItem based on a file name or one of the nifty System FolderItems. At some point, you'll want your users to be able to select their own file using the standard Open File dialog box rather than always knowing the name of the file you want to work with. REALbasic has a command suited exactly for this task: GetOpenFolderItem.

GetOpenFolderItem has one parameter — a list of file types from which to choose. Therefore, before you get knee-deep in the inner workings of GetOpenFolderItem, you need to know about file types.

What files types can REALbasic recognize and use? Easy. It recognizes any file types that you tell it about. You must define a file type before you can use it with the GetOpenFolderItem command.

To create a QuickTime file type, follow these steps:

1. **Choose Edit➪File Types.**

   The File Types dialog box appears with a list of file types that your application currently recognizes.

2. **Click the Add button.**

   The Add File Type dialog box appears.

3. **In the Name field, choose video/quicktime.**

   REALbasic automatically fills in all the fields in the Add File Type dialog box, as shown in Figure 12-2.

4. **Click OK.**

   The video/quicktime file type appears in the File Types dialog box. You have successfully added a file type for accessing QuickTime files.

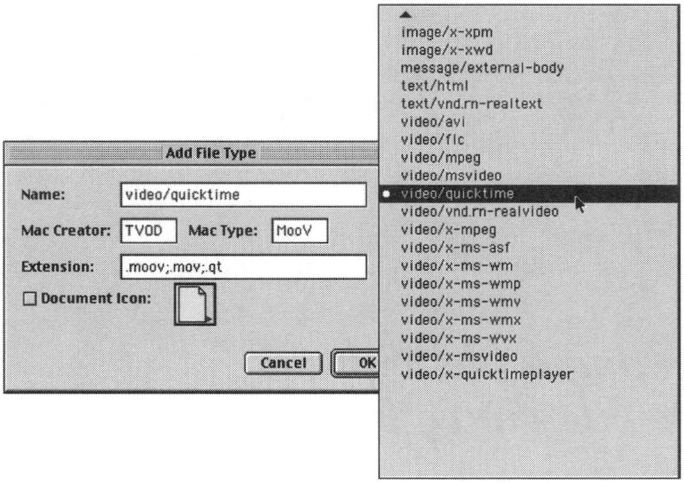

Figure 12-2:
REALbasic has many pre-made file types.

After you define a file type, you can safely use the `GetOpenFolderItem` command. The file type you created can now be referred to by the text that appears in the Name field of the File Types dialog box. For example, to put the QuickTime file type you created to use, enter this code in a PushButton:

```
Dim f as FolderItem

f = GetOpenFolderItem("video/quicktime")

if f<> nil then
    MsgBox f.name
end if
```

This code presents the user with a standard Open File dialog box and allows the user to open any QuickTime file, as pictured in Figure 12-3.

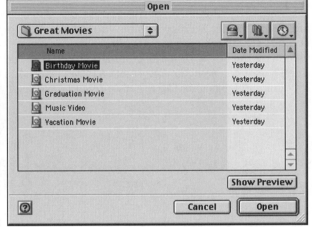

Figure 12-3:
The video/
quicktime
file type
allows you
to open any
QuickTime
file.

Note that you can open only a QuickTime file. If you want to open other file types, you must define each type in the File Types dialog box. After you have defined other types, you can string them together in the `GetOpenFolderItem` parameter list to allow a user to open multiple types of files. For example, this code allows you to open a QuickTime file or a PICT file:

```
Dim f as FolderItem

f = GetOpenFolderItem("video/quicktime;image/x-pict")

if f<> nil then
    MsgBox f.name
end if
```

What happens if the user clicks the Cancel button in the Open File dialog box? The returned FolderItem is empty, or *nil,* so there is no point in trying to do anything with it. Therefore, you need to check whether the FolderItem is nil before proceeding:

```
if f<> nil then
.
.
.
end if
```

If you are the curious type and did try to use the FolderItem when it was `nil`, REALbasic would display a NilObject Exception error. The moral here is that you should always check to see whether you have a valid FolderItem before attempting to use one.

Selecting a folder with the Select Folder dialog box

You can allow users to select not only a particular file, but also a specific folder. This can be handy, for example, when you want your application to process a folder full of pictures, search for a file in a specific folder, or count the number of items in a folder. Use the SelectFolder command to make a dialog box appear with which a user can navigate and select a folder. The code for the SelectFolder command looks a lot like other code you have seen:

```
Dim f as FolderItem

f=SelectFolder
if f<>nil then
    MsgBox "The folder you selected is named " + f.name
end if
```

Displaying and using the Save File dialog box

Finally, if you are itching to save a file, you can display the Save File dialog box with the GetSaveFolderItem command. This command allows a user to select a file name and location for a file. You use the returned FolderItem to create the file.

As parameters to this command, you must pass not only a file type but also a default file name. This default file name appears in the Save dialog box, as shown in Figure 12-4.

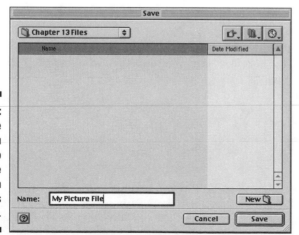

Figure 12-4:
The file name you pass to GetSave FolderItem appears here.

Creating and Using Files

Okay, now that you know all about getting a FolderItem, what do you do with it? FolderItems are the basis for your work with any kind of file, including both reading and creating them. The FolderItem function you call depends on what type of file you want to create. REALbasic can natively create several types of files:

- Text files
- Picture files
- QuickTime files

Accessing text files

Perhaps the first type of file you'll want to read or write is a text file. Text files have a million uses, and there isn't a computer around that can't use them. On the Macintosh, for example, SimpleText can open, edit, and create text files. They're like a universal file type (though that's not completely true.) Accordingly, REALbasic can create and read text files in a flash.

Opening a text file

To open a text file, you must use a TextInputStream object. TextInputStream works much like a vacuum. When you turn it on, it sucks up text from a file into a variable in your application. Instead of continuous suction, however, you control the sucking in short bursts. To open the pathway and let the text flow, you issue the ReadLine command to TextInputStream. Continue issuing this command until you reach the end of the file. The EOF property of TextInputStream signals the end of the file (hence, the abbreviation).

To open a text file, follow these four easy steps:

1. **Define a file type for text files.**

   REALbasic may have already created one for you, but check anyway by selecting File⇨File Types.

2. **Create a TextInput object in your code as follows:**

   ```
   Dim TextIn as TextInputStream
   ```

3. **Send a FolderItem the OpenAsTextFile message as follows:**

   ```
   f.OpenAsTextFile
   ```

4. **Read each line of the text file until you reach the end as follows:**

   ```
   TextIn = f.ReadLine
   ```

A finished product that places the text into an EditField might look like this:

```
Dim f as FolderItem
Dim TextIn as TextInputStream
Dim myText as String

f=GetOpenFolderItem("text")

if f<>nil then
    TextIn = f.OpenAsTextFile
    While Not(TextIn.EOF)
        myText = TextIn.ReadLine
        EditField1.text = EditField1.text + myText+chr(13)
    Wend
end if
```

Creating a text file

Creating a text file is not much different than opening one, just in reverse. Instead of the TextInputStream class, you use the TextOutputStream class. Instead of being like a vacuum, a TextOutputStream is more like a garden hose for text. The text flows through TextOutputStream from your application to a file. The `WriteLine` method of TextOutputStream controls the flow of text to the file, as the nozzle on a hose controls the flow of outgoing water.

Furthermore, instead of opening a file with the `GetOpenFolderItem` command, you can utilize the `GetSaveFolderItem` command to save a text file to a user-defined location, though this isn't mandatory. You application can decide the destination of the text file as well.

This example creates a text file of the names of the last three United States presidents as of 2000:

```
Dim f As FolderItem
Dim TextOut As TextOutputStream
f=GetSaveFolderItem("text","My Presidential List")

if f<>nil then
    TextOut=f.CreateTextFile
    TextOut.WriteLine "Bill Clinton"
    TextOut.WriteLine "George Bush"
    TextOut.WriteLine "Ronald Reagan"
    TextOut.Close
end if
```

Accessing graphics files

REALbasic is great at reading and writing graphics to a file. In particular, it is well suited to PICT files. If your user has QuickTime installed, you can read and write other types of graphics too.

Opening a graphics file

Again, you must define a file type for all the types of graphics formats you want to open. Next, create a FolderItem using the familiar `GetOpenFolderItem` or `GetFolderItem` command, passing all file types you want the user to have access to. Then, simply open the graphics file by calling the FolderItems `OpenAsPicture` function. The result is a Picture object. In this example, the picture is being placed for display in the backdrop property of a Canvas control:

```
Dim f as FolderItem
Dim myPicture as Picture

f = GetOpenFolderItem("image/x-pict;image/jpeg")

if f<>nil then
    myPicture = f.OpenAsPicture
    Canvas1.backdrop=myPicture
end if
```

Saving a graphics file

Saving graphics is just as simple to accomplish by following these simple steps:

1. **In the File Types dialog box, define the graphics format you want to save.**

2. **Use GetSaveFolderItem to get a valid FolderItem.**

3. **Call the** `SaveAsPicture` **method of the FolderItem and pass it the Picture object you want saved.**

For example, to save the graphics currently displayed in the Backdrop property of a Canvas control called Canvas1, use code like this:

```
Dim f as FolderItem

f=GetSaveFolderItem("image/x-pict","My Picture File")

if f<>nil then
    f.SaveAsPicture(Canvas1.Backdrop)
end if
```

Saving and opening graphics files in Microsoft Windows works just as well. When you use PICT files, REALbasic automatically converts them to a format Microsoft Windows can use. Thus, when you compile for Microsoft Windows, the PICT file should appear in your application just as it would in Mac OS. Microsoft Windows applications that you make with REALbasic can also handle many other graphics formats, as long as you have QuickTime installed on the Microsoft Windows computer where you want to use the program.

Chapter 13

Printing with REALbasic

• •

• •

For many years, computer advocates have insisted that the idea of a paperless society was just around the corner. Imagine all the money, not to mention trees, spared when the computer somehow manages to do everything that paper can. As you probably already know, this is still a dream. Paper use is alive and well. Not only is paper etched deep in the conscience of our culture, it's also just so darned useful. You can take paper with you anywhere. It doesn't require any power and it's relatively inexpensive.

Given the popularity of paper, is it any wonder that printing from a computer is also very popular? In fact, many computers come with a printer as a standard option. Personal computers are so adept at desktop publishing these days that almost anyone can produce professional looking results with a minimum of effort.

As a programmer, this leaves you with the necessary task of including printing functions in your own applications. Computer users are a fussy bunch, and they expect certain functions. Printing is one of those functions. Leave it out and you stand to lose an audience.

REALbasic somewhat eases the task of including printing functions in your applications. Although printing is not one of REALbasic's strengths, it does support the common printing interface of the Mac OS and gives you a way to output text and graphics data to a printer. This chapter briefly describes how to add printing functionality to your own applications using a small demonstration project.

Setting Up the Print Job

When it comes to printing, nearly every application in existence has the same two menus:

- ✔ Page Setup menu item under the File menu
- ✔ Print menu item under the File menu

These two menus correspond to the process users should follow to print a document. The first step involves adjusting the printer's settings for options such as paper size, scaling, margins, and page orientation. These settings vary from printer to printer, but they are always accessible from the File⇨Page Setup menu. It's common practice to make these settings once and never change them.

Figure 13-1 shows a typical Page Setup dialog box for a LaserWriter printer. Keep in mind that your Page Setup dialog box will look different than the one pictured in Figure 13-1 (unless you have this model of LaserWriter printer, of course). Each manufacturer includes its own version of the Page Setup dialog box for setting the various features available on a particular printer. After the page setup is complete, the user dismisses the dialog box and proceeds to print a document by choosing File⇨Print.

Figure 13-1:
A standard
Page Setup
dialog box.

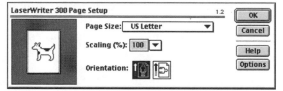

Making printer settings

To display the Page Setup dialog box, users commonly choose File⇨Page Setup. So, to add this feature to your own project, begin by creating a File⇨Page Setup menu. Open the Menu Editor by double-clicking it in the Project window. In the editor, add a new menu item under the File menu by entering the following text:

```
Page Setup...
```

The three periods that follow the words *Page Setup* indicate that a dialog box appears when the user chooses this menu. In this case, the Page Setup dialog appears.

Actually, this is not the strict user interface definition of the three periods, or ellipses. They indicate that additional steps follow the selection of this menu. Those *additional steps* usually mean that a dialog box will appear, requiring the user to enter more information before the menu command can complete its task.

Now go ahead and create a menu item that reads

```
Print...
```

As you can probably guess, this menu will be the home to the dialog box used for printing after the Page Setup step is complete. When you add the Print menu item, be sure to change the CommandKey property to P in the Properties window because this is the preferred keyboard shortcut for printing. Figure 13-2 displays the completed menus in the Menu Editor.

Figure 13-2:
Create the
Page Setup
and Print
menu items
in the Menu
Editor.

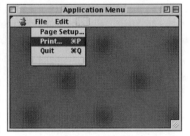

After you create the menus, don't forget to enable them. Open the Window1 Code Editor and navigate to the `EnableMenuItems` event. Enter the following code:

```
Sub EnableMenuItems()
   FilePageSetup.Enable
   FilePrint.Enable
End Sub
```

When you entered *Page Setup...* and *Print...* as the Text of the menu items, REALbasic automatically named the menu items FilePageSetup and FilePrint, respectively. Next, add menu handlers for each menu item by choosing Edit⇨New Menu Handler (or by pressing ⌘-Option-H). See Figure 13-3.

With the menus in place, it's time to add some code. Displaying a Page Setup dialog box is a simple matter of creating a PrinterSetup object and calling its `PageSetupDialog` method. If the user dismisses the Page Setup dialog box by clicking the OK button, the `PageSetupDialog` method returns a value of `TRUE`. If the user instead clicks the Cancel button, it returns a value of `FALSE`.

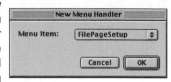

Figure 13-3:
Add a new menu handler for the Page Setup and Print menu items.

When the user dismisses the Page Setup dialog box, the PrinterSetup object stores the settings the user made in its SetupString property. The settings consist of a string of varying length that looks like gibberish. You don't need to be able to read this string because it's used by the printing mechanism in REALbasic. However, you need a place to store these settings, so create a new string property in Window1 by choosing Edit➪New Property (or by pressing ⌘-Option-P). Name the property PageSettings, as shown in Figure 13-4.

Figure 13-4:
The PageSettings property stores the settings from the Page Setup dialog box.

Next, open the Window Editor for Window1 by double-clicking it in the Project window. Drag a StaticText control into this window (REALbasic names it StaticText1 by default). Change the Multiline property of StaticText1 to TRUE and change its dimensions as follows:

- ✔ Width = 275
- ✔ Height = 95

This StaticText control is merely a display for viewing the Page Setup settings later.

Finally, navigate to the FilePageSetup menu handler you created previously and add this code:

```
Function Action As Boolean
   Dim PrinterOptions as PrinterSetup

   PrinterOptions=New PrinterSetup
   If PrinterOptions.PageSetupDialog = TRUE Then
     PageSettings=PrinterOptions.SetupString
   End If
   StaticText1.text=PageSettings
End Function
```

Here's how the code works. It begins by creating a PrinterSetup object:

```
Dim PrinterOptions as PrinterSetup

PrinterOptions=New PrinterSetup
```

Then, the code calls the `PageSetupDialog` method of the PrinterSetup object (named PrinterOptions). If the method returns a value of `TRUE`, the SetupString property of the PrinterSetup object is stored in the PageSettings property you created:

```
If PrinterOptions.PageSetupDialog = TRUE Then
   PageSettings=PrinterOptions.SetupString
End If
```

Finally, the string is output to StaticText1:

```
StaticText1.text = PageSettings
```

To test this code, choose Debug⇨Run. While running the test, choose File⇨Page Setup and change some settings. Dismiss the dialog box by clicking the OK button. If you see some unintelligible string of characters like that shown in Figure 13-5, you did everything correctly. This string of characters holds the settings you just made in an encoded format. If you don't see any text, you probably clicked the Cancel button.

Figure 13-5:
The Page
Setup
settings are
an
unintelligible
mess of
characters.

Now choose the File⇨Page Setup menu again. Note that when you do, the settings you made previously do not appear in the dialog box. It's bad form to force your user to update the dialog box each time, so more code is necessary. Just as you can retrieve the settings by looking at the SetupString property of a PrinterSetup object, you can set the property to display particular settings.

The following code sets the SetupString property to the settings stored in the PageSettings property:

```
PrinterOptions.SetupString=PageSettings
```

After incorporating this feature, the revised code for your FilePageSetup menu handler should look like this:

```
Dim PrinterOptions as PrinterSetup

PrinterOptions=New PrinterSetup
PrinterOptions.SetupString=PageSettings

If PrinterOptions.PageSetupDialog = TRUE Then
   PageSettings=PrinterOptions.SetupString
End If
StaticText1.text=PageSettings
```

Test the project again by choosing Debug⇨Run. Choose File⇨Page Setup, change some settings, and dismiss the dialog box by clicking OK. Open the Page Setup dialog box again and notice that this time the settings remain.

Saving printer settings

After going through all the work of setting up a printer, users expect the settings to be there tomorrow when they turn on their computers and launch your application. Because of this, it takes a bit more work to properly implement printing functions in your project. You must worry about saving the settings where you can find them later. The Preferences Folder, which resides in the Mac OS system folder, is a perfect location.

A *preference file,* by convention, is a binary file. Before you start working with a preference file, though, you must first add a file type so that REALbasic recognizes the file. Choose Edit⇨File Types and create a new file type named myPrefsFile. Fill in the other information as pictured in Figure 13-6.

Next, create a new method in Window1 by choosing Edit⇨New Method (or by pressing ⌘-Option-M). Name the method CreatePreferencesFile and click OK. In this method, add the following code:

```
Sub CreatePreferenceFile()
Dim BinStream as BinaryStream
Dim theString as String
Dim Prefs as FolderItem

Prefs = PreferencesFolder.Child("Printing Chapter
          Preferences")

BinStream = Prefs.CreateBinaryFile("myPrefsFile")
BinStream.Write PageSettings
BinStream.Close
End Sub
```

This code first creates a FolderItem reference to your new preference file, named
Printing Chapter Preferences. Next, the code calls the CreateBinaryFile
method of FolderItem, passing to it the myPrefsFile file type you just created.
This returns a BinaryStream to which you can output data.

Finally, the Write method of BinaryStream adds the PageSettings string to
the file and then closes the file. Although this method conveniently saves the
Page Setup settings in a preference file, your project is not making use of the
code yet. To use this method, add it to the end of the FilePageSetup menu
handler. The updated menu handler should now read as follows:

```
Dim PrinterOptions as PrinterSetup

PrinterOptions=New PrinterSetup
PrinterOptions.SetupString=PageSettings

If PrinterOptions.PageSetupDialog = TRUE Then
  PageSettings=PrinterOptions.SetupString
End If
StaticText1.text=PageSettings
CreatePreferencesFile
```

The settings are now securely stored in a preference file.

Loading the saved settings

Saving settings in a preference file is of no use if you can't retrieve them for use later. Fortunately, this is a trivial matter. Create another method titled OpenPreferencesFile and add the following code:

```
Sub OpenPreferencesFile()
  Dim BinStream as BinaryStream
  Dim Prefs as FolderItem

  Prefs = PreferencesFolder.Child("Printing Chapter
          Preferences")
  if Prefs.Exists then
    BinStream = Prefs.OpenAsBinaryFile(FALSE)
    PageSettings = BinStream.Read(BinStream.Length+1)
    BinStream.Close
    StaticText1.text = "Page Settings=" + PageSettings
  else
    CreatePreferencesFile
  end if
End Sub
```

This code first creates a FolderItem reference to the preference file. If the FolderItem exists, it opens the file. Otherwise, it creates one.

It opens the file by calling the OpenAsBinaryFile method of the FolderItem. The OpenAsBinaryFile method has a FALSE parameter, which indicates that the file opens with read-only access. If you need to write to the file, set the method to TRUE.

```
Dim BinStream as BinaryStream
  Dim Prefs as FolderItem

  Prefs = PreferencesFolder.Child("Printing Chapter
          Preferences")
  if Prefs.Exists then
    BinStream = Prefs.OpenAsBinaryFile(FALSE)
```

Next, the code calls the Read method of BinaryStream. It takes an integer as a parameter, indicating the number of characters to return. Because you want the entire contents of the file, pass a value equal to the entire length of the BinaryStream plus 1.

REALbasic doesn't care if the number you supply to the Read method is too large. If you do, it simply reads to the end of the file.

The code then stores the data in the PageSettings property, as usual:

```
PageSettings = BinStream.Read(BinStream.Length+1)
```

Finally, the code closes the file and displays the contents of the PageSettings property in StaticText1, just to show you that it worked:

```
BinStream.Close
StaticText1.text = "Page Settings=" + PageSettings
```

To use this new `OpenPreferencesFile` method, call it from the `Open` event of Window1:

```
Sub Open()
  OpenPreferencesFile
End Sub
```

Now, whenever the application launches, it automatically opens the preference file and retrieves the saved Page Setup settings.

Executing the Print Job

Until now, you have only set up the printer. To get something out of the printer, you must call one of the two global printing methods available in REALbasic:

✔ OpenPrinter

✔ OpenPrinterDialog

Both methods return a Graphics object, which represents the printed page. To print something on a page, you simply draw to this Graphics object, exactly as you would with the Graphics object of a Canvas.

Printing the quick and dirty way

The easiest way to print something is to use the `OpenPrinter` method. By calling this method and then drawing text or graphics to the Graphics object it returns, your printer will output a printed page. Keep in mind, however, that this method will not display the standard Print dialog box, to which you may be accustomed.

Printing without Page Setup

The `OpenPrinter` method takes an optional parameter. Omitting it will have no effect other than to use the default PrinterSetup settings. The following example prints a red square and a blue circle somewhere near the top of the page:

```
Dim g As Graphics
g  = OpenPrinter()

g.ForeColor = RGB (255,0,0)
g.FillRect 10,10,50,50

g.ForeColor = RGB (0,0,255)
g.FillOval 100,10,50,50
```

As you can see, you can use the same code to draw on a printed page as you do to draw graphics on a Canvas. As soon as this code executes, the printer spits out the finished page.

Printing with Page Setup

Having wrestled with the intricacies of the Page Setup dialog box previously in the chapter, it's time to put those settings to work. Because the settings are stored in the PageSettings String property that belongs to Window1, the settings are always accessible. To use the settings, first create a PrinterSetup object and populate its SetupString property with the stored settings:

```
Dim PrinterOptions as PrinterSetup

PrinterOptions=New PrinterSetup
PrinterOptions.SetupString = PageSettings
```

You can then pass the PrinterSetup object to the `OpenPrinter` method so that it takes advantage of the settings:

```
g  = OpenPrinter(PrinterOptions)
```

The finished code prints text using different fonts and sizes. It should look like this:

```
Dim PrinterOptions as PrinterSetup
Dim g As Graphics

PrinterOptions=New PrinterSetup
PrinterOptions.SetupString = PageSettings

g  = OpenPrinter(PrinterOptions)

g.ForeColor = RGB(0,0,0)
g.TextFont = "Helvetica"
g.TextSize = 24
g.DrawString "REALbasic For Dummies",10,50

g.TextFont = "Times"
g.TextSize = 36
g.DrawString "REALbasic For Dummies",10,(g.Height\2)
```

Printing the standard way

It's usually a good idea to follow standard interface guidelines. Therefore, to add printing functionality, your application should always display the standard Print dialog box before printing. This gives users a chance to make duplicate copies as well as tweak the page setup of the printed page. You can accomplish this with the OpenPrinterDialog method.

Printing without Page Setup

Like the OpenPrinter method, you can call the OpenPrinterDialog method without PrinterSetup settings. If you do, OpenPrinterDialog uses default PrinterSetup settings. For example, to print your name somewhere near the middle of the page, use code like this:

```
Dim g As Graphics
g  = OpenPrinterDialog()

if g<>nil then
   g.DrawString "Jane Doe", (g.width\2), (g.height\2)
end if
```

One different part of this code that you might notice is the line

```
if g<>nil then
```

and its corresponding

```
end if
```

This extra bit of code is an absolute necessity when dealing with the OpenPrinterDialog method. When the standard Print dialog box appears, the user always has the option of clicking the Cancel button to halt the printing process. If this should happen, OpenPrinterDialog doesn't return a Graphics object. Later in the code, when you try to draw to a non-existent Graphics object, your program will generate a NilObject Exception error. By first checking to see whether the object exists, this code squishes a potential bug.

Printing with Page Setup

The most complete (and generally preferred) method of printing is to pass page setup information to the OpenPrinterDialog method. As before, this requires that you create a PrinterSetup object, populate its SetupString property with the saved settings, and finally print using the OpenPrinterDialog method. Open the FilePrint menu handler you created previously in the chapter and add this code:

```
Function Action as Boolean
Dim PrinterOptions as PrinterSetup
Dim g As Graphics

PrinterOptions=New PrinterSetup
PrinterOptions.SetupString = PageSettings

g   = OpenPrinterDialog(PrinterOptions)
g.DrawPicture Face,100,100
End Function
```

Before you test the code, be certain to drag a PICT file named Face into your Project window. If you don't have a PICT file, you can use the one on the *REALbasic For Dummies* CD accompanying this book.

Chapter 14

Creating Internet Applications

● ●

In This Chapter

▶ Linking to the Web with your favorite browser

▶ Linking with other browsers

▶ Sending email messages

▶ Creating a chat application

● ●

*W*hen personal computers first became popular, they were independent boxes of electronics components sitting on the desk in the basement of some hobbyist. Slowly, they matured, with manufacturers adding more features and updating the hardware. This progress continued for many years, with personal computer use exploding not just in the office but in the home as well. Then, a strange thing happened. Someone decided that it would be a great idea if you could connect all of these computers into a giant network. The Internet was born, and the rest, as they say, is history.

Personal computers, rather than being slaves to their own capabilities, can now take advantage of the functionality of thousands of computers from anywhere on the planet using the Web. Need a telephone number of your favorite pizza joint in Carbondale, Illinois? Looking to take a tour in Bremen, Germany? Want to send your friends in Pueblo, Mexico a floral bouquet? All of these functions are possible from the confines of your own home using the Internet.

To connect to the world's computers, you must use specialized software. The most common examples are Web browsers and email clients. You, too, can add Internet capabilities to your own applications. This chapter walks you through some common REALbasic networking functions and shows you how to add them to your own projects.

Linking to Your Favorite Web Browser

Adding the capability to link to a Web site from your own REALbasic projects is an easy task to accomplish using the ShowURL method. Pass a URL (www.apple.com for example) to the ShowURL method and it instantly

directs your favorite Web browser to the URL. For example, to go to the
...*For Dummies* Web site, use code like this:

```
ShowURL "http://www.dummies.com"
```

This code is a tad on the plain side. True, it does transport you to a Web site
within a browser, but it leaves a lot to be desired when it comes to interface
design. Namely, there is no interface. Therefore, to make this code act more
like a traditional Web link, you need to build a small interface.

Launch REALbasic as usual and open the Window Editor for Window1, the
default window that comes with every new project created in REALbasic. To
this window, add a Canvas control. Why a Canvas control and not something
more suited to text like a StaticText control, you ask?

Although it is true that a StaticText control seems like the obvious choice
because the link will be text, it is missing some features that prevent its use
as a Web link. A StaticText control, for example, is not a good control for
responding to mouse clicks. Besides that, a Canvas control is adept at displaying text (among other things), so your users will never even know that it
is a Canvas rather than a StaticText control.

Change the properties of the Canvas control to match those in Table 14-1.

Table 14-1	Initial Properties of a Linkable Canvas
Property	*Setting*
Name	myURLCanvas
Left	13
Top	13
Width	150
Height	25

With a Canvas foundation in place, it's time to display something in it.
Double-click the Canvas, now named myURLCanvas, and add some code to its
Paint event:

```
g.ForeColor = RGB(255,0,0)
g.DrawString "Dummies Web Site",10,10
```

This code snippet sets the text color to red and displays the "Dummies Web
Site" string at the point (10,10) in the Canvas. If you are the apprehensive
type, feel free to test the project by choosing Debug⇨Run. The canvas displays the text, but not much else. To get the text to behave like a standard
Web link, it must respond to a click within it.

Responding to a click is a simple matter of adding code to the MouseDown event of the Canvas:

```
Function MouseDown(X As Integer, Y As Integer) as Boolean
   ShowURL "http://www.dummies.com"
End Function
```

Finally, choose Debug⇨Run to see the effects. Clicking the text should cause your Web browser to open and the Web site to load.

This is all fine and dandy, but you want a link that changes color when the mouse button is down and opens the page when you release the mouse button. Fortunately, a few color changes are all it takes. Change the MouseDown event code to

```
Function MouseDown(X As Integer, Y As Integer) as Boolean
   me.graphics.ForeColor = RGB(0,0,255)
   me.graphics.DrawString "Dummies Web Site",10,10
   return TRUE
End Function
```

This snippet changes the text color to blue and redraws the string whenever a user clicks the Canvas. The final statement, return TRUE is necessary so that the MouseUp event executes when the MouseDown event has finished executing. The MouseUp event changes the color back to red and loads the Web page.

To complete the illusion of a Web link, it's customary to change the cursor shape whenever the cursor is over a link. The first step is to create a few cursors. To do so, you need to use a resource editor. Several are available, but the one from Apple, named ResEdit, is freely available. You can download it here:

```
www.versiontracker.com/redir.fcgi/kind=1&id=417/ResEdit_2.1.3
              .sea.bin
```

After you have a resource editor, launch it and create a new CURS resource. This resource will hold your cursor. ResEdit opens a cursor editor that allows you to draw a black-and-white cursor, as shown in Figure 14-1. Create a cursor that appears when you drag the mouse over a link. By default, ResEdit gives a new CURS resource an ID of 128.

Figure 14-1: ResEdit makes it a snap to create cursors.

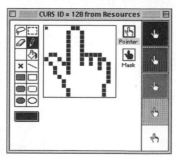

With your link cursor created, save the resource file, paying careful attention to accurately name the file Resources. You must name the resource file exactly in this manner. Otherwise, REALbasic will not be able to use it properly. Drag this new resource file into your REALbasic project.

To use the cursor you just created, you need only two lines of code. Change the cursor to the new pointer cursor by setting the MouseCursor property of the application object. The GetCursor method of the resource fork of the application object loads the cursor from the Resources file.

Macintosh files are composed of two forks. Like Windows files, there is a data fork. Unlike Windows, however, Macintosh files may also contain a resource fork. The resource fork holds all types of data common only to Macintosh files.

Place the following code in the MouseEnter event of the Canvas link:

```
App.MouseCursor = App.ResourceFork.GetCursor(128)
```

If the user moves the mouse away from the link, be sure to reset the cursor. REALbasic provides a few of the common cursors you may encounter. Placing the following code in the MouseExit event of the Canvas link, for example, sets the standard arrow mouse cursor:

```
App.MouseCursor = ArrowCursor
```

Linking to Any Web Browser

The ShowURL method is convenient for loading a Web page in a browser, but it has one drawback. Only your favorite browser loads the page. To set the favorite browser to a different one, you must change the setting in the Internet control panel of the Mac OS, as shown in Figure 14-2.

To load a Web page in any browser you choose, you must approach this task another way. Most Web browsers are scriptable, so AppleScript makes a good choice for loading a Web page with any type of browser.

Another option is to use two scripts on the *REALbasic For Dummies* CD. Just drag the OpenNetscape and OpenExplorer scripts into your project, and they'll be functional commands in your project.

To direct Netscape Navigator to a Web site, add the following line of code:

```
OpenNetscape "http://www.dummies.com"
```

For Internet Explorer, use:

```
OpenExplorer "http://www.dummies.com"
```

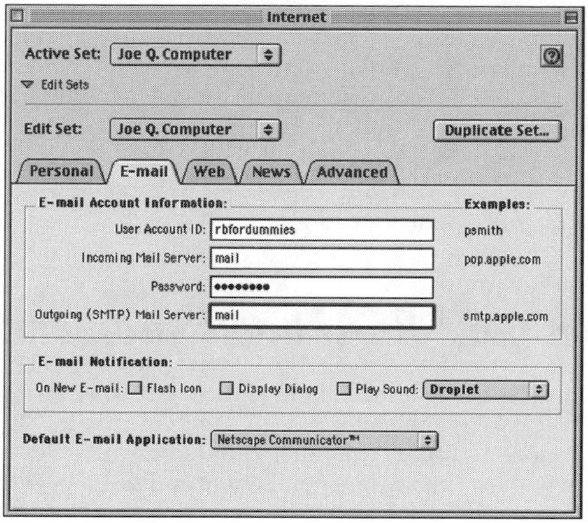

Figure 14-2: Set your default browser using the Internet control panel.

Email Features

In addition to directing your users to useful Web sites, you may also want to offer the possibility of sending email messages. This is handy for giving your users a way to contact you.

Email from your favorite client

The easiest way to implement email links in your project is to use the ShowURL method. Because the ShowURL method accepts a Web address as its sole parameter, it is legal to include additional standard HTML parameters. Don't worry if you don't know HTML, though. The tags are simple enough and knowledge of HTML is not required. To send a message, construct a string of mailto: followed by an email address. This code opens a new email message in your preferred email client:

```
ShowURL "mailto:rbfordummies@longlivethemac.com"
```

If you'd like the message sent to more than one person, you can also use the CC (carbon copy) parameter of the mailto: tag as follows:

```
ShowURL "mailto:rbfordummies@hotmail.com?cc=
          rbfordummies@longlivethemac.com"
```

What's more, you can load the subject header of the email message with anything you like:

```
ShowURL "mailto:rbfordummies@hotmail.com?subject=REALbasic is
         fun!"
```

Providing users a chance to send you feedback is a fantastic way to spruce up the About Box of your application.

Email from your REALbasic project

Linking to a new message in an email client is nice, but sometimes you may want to take care of sending the email as well. Sending email with your own code is quite a bit more complex. You must know some specifics about how the email protocol works. This is time-consuming and not a beginner's topic.

Luckily, some competent REALbasic programmer's have gone through all the hard work of wrestling the email protocol for you. Now you can add email capabilities to your own projects with only a modicum of effort. One excellent example is the Nubz SMTP Socket from Matthijs van Duin at Nubz Development. You can find the code for it on the CD included with this book.

Using the Nubz SMTP Socket isn't tough as long as you follow two important steps:

1. **Add the Nubz SMTP Socket modules and classes to your project.**

   Drag each of these components into your project's Project window:

Encoding Tools	Module
SendMailUtils	Module
SMTPSocket	Class
SMTPTransaction	Class
SendMailSocket	Class
SendMailEnvelope	Class
MimeEnvelope	Class

2. **Add a SendMailSocket to your interface.**

   SendMailSocket is one of the components you added in the first step. To add it to your interface, drag it from the Project window into an open Window Editor. Make certain that you set the Super property of the new SendMailSocket to SMTPSocket if REALbasic doesn't automatically.

When you add new components to a project, REALbasic can sometimes lose track of a few settings from when you originally created the project. For this reason, you should check the SMTPSocket and SendMailSocket classes in the Project window for accuracy. When you choose SMTPSocket in the Project window, set the Super property to Socket. Likewise, set the Super property of the SendMailSocket to SMTPSocket. If either of these is in error, correct the problem and repeat Step 2.

With the guts of your email project in place, you need to add a few parts to your interface. In particular, you need a PushButton to send the email and five EditFields for the

- Email address of the recipient
- Email subject
- Content of the email message
- Emil address of the sender
- SMTP server address of the sender

Figure 14-3 shows a simple example.

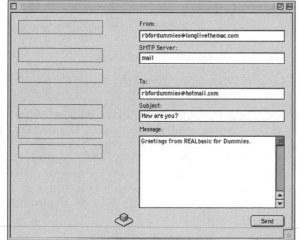

Figure 14-3: Add EditFields to complete the email interface.

The final step in completing your email masterpiece is to add the source code. The following code sends a bare-bones email message. It has all the essentials for a minimal email message, but nothing more. Still, it works fabulously every time. Double-click the PushButton you added earlier. In its Action event, add this code:

```
Dim mail as SendMailEnvelope
Dim message as string

mail = new SendMailEnvelope

mail.sender = FromField.text
mail.server = SMTPServerField.text
mail.headers.append "X-Mailer: SendMailSocket Test"
mail.recipients = ToField.text
mail.subject = SubjectField.text
message = MessageField.text
mail.body = new MimeEnvelope("multipart/mixed", "")
mail.body.append new MimeEnvelope("text/plain", message)

SendMailSocket1.Post mail
```

If you don't understand what all this code means, don't worry. The beautiful thing about it — and one of the lessons you should take away from this example — is that you don't need to understand it all. Many people use automobiles every day and don't know how they work under the hood.

The code isn't that tough to decipher if you take it in steps. To begin, we create a space for a SendMailEnvelope object and a string in memory:

```
Dim mail as SendMailEnvelope
Dim message as String
```

Next, the code creates a SendMailEnvelope object:

```
mail = new SendMailEnvelope
```

This object is part of the components you added to the project previously. It's a structure that takes care of sending your email. The rest of the code deals primarily with populating the various properties of the SendMailEnvelope object. This is almost completely analogous to sending a traditional letter. First, you prepare the envelope by writing the sender, recipient, and post office information on the envelope. Then you add a letter to the envelope and send it on its way. This code does the same thing but with a virtual envelope:

```
// The return address
   mail.sender = FromField.text
   mail.server = SMTPServerField.text

// The recipient's address
   mail.recipients = ToField.text
   mail.subject = SubjectField.text

// stuff a message in the envelope
   message = MessageField.text
```

```
    mail.body = new MimeEnvelope("multipart/mixed", "")
    mail.body.append new MimeEnvelope("text/plain", message)

// send the letter
    SendMailSocket1.Post mail
```

You might want to add an indicator when your program has sent the message successfully. To do this, add code to the PostDone event of the SendMailSocket1 object, like so:

```
Sub PostDone(post as SendMailEnvelope)
    MsgBox "Message successfully sent."
End Sub
```

The MsgBox command displays a window containing the accompanying text.

In this example, I do not consider attachments. Attachments are more involved, and the example project from Nubz Development illustrates the process nicely. Furthermore, this example is a bit simplistic. Typically, the email interface for the sender information is separated from the recipient information, often in different windows. However, for simple email messages, this method works flawlessly and quickly.

Other Networking

In addition to common Internet and email functions, REALbasic is wide open to a host of other networking possibilities. As you may have recognized throughout this chapter, the Socket control is the heart of all networking operations in REALbasic. You can use this Socket control to send and receive data over the Internet and most local area networks.

Standard protocols

When you conduct communications over TCP networks, it is customary to create a small language that both sides of the conversation can understand. Computer geeks call these small languages *protocols*. Hundreds of protocols are available for participating in all types of communication.

Protocols present the information you are sending or receiving in a way that other computers everywhere can understand. Standards committees make decisions about what should go in each protocol and publish their decisions in freely available documents called RFCs. If you would like more information about the various protocols, type RFC into your favorite search engine or check the following:

```
www.cis.ohio-state.edu/hypertext/information/rfc.html
```

If you have spent any time using the Internet, you have probably used several Internet protocols without knowing it. Internet protocols are involved in the data transfers that take place behind the scenes each time you access a Web page, upload a file to a server, or chat with a friend. Some of the more common protocols are

- ✔ FTP to transfer files
- ✔ POP to receive email
- ✔ SMTP to send email
- ✔ HTTP for Web pages

SMTP is the protocol that the Nubz code uses. Describing the remaining protocols listed here, among dozens of others, is beyond the scope of this book. REAL Software's own FTP server is a good place to start looking for Socket projects that incorporate existing TCP protocols:

```
ftp.realsoftware.com
```

Custom communications

The REALbasic Socket control enables you to use not only standard protocols but also custom protocols for your own communication needs. To explore the possibilities of the Socket control, in this section you build a small chat application server and client, though no real protocol is necessary.

Because communication is a two-way process, it follows that two applications are involved in network communications. One application is the *server* because it traditionally serves, or sends, data to other applications called *clients*. Clients can also send data, but it is the server that agrees to the communication in the first place. Because this server example is rudimentary, you can adapt it to create the client application. When your chat server and client applications are finished, you will be able to send text messages back and forth between the server and the client.

To begin creating the chat server, launch REALbasic. In the Project window, double-click Window1 and design its interface to look like Figure 14-4. The control that looks like a small globe is a Socket. You can find it in the Tools window. You should be familiar with the remaining interface elements.

To begin communicating, your code must initialize the Socket and begin listening on port 200. A *TCP port* is analogous to a television channel. Only those applications on the network that are listening and sending on the port can communicate with each other. The Socket listens for other computers (also known as *clients*) to connect to it. Open the Code Editor by double-clicking ListButton. In its Action event, enter the following code:

```
Sub Action()
if me.caption="Listen" then
  Socket1.Address=AddressField.text
  Socket1.Port=200
  Socket1.listen
  me.caption="Disconnect"
  SendButton.enabled=TRUE
else
  Socket1.Close
  me.caption="Listen"
  SendButton.enabled=FALSE
end if
End Sub
```

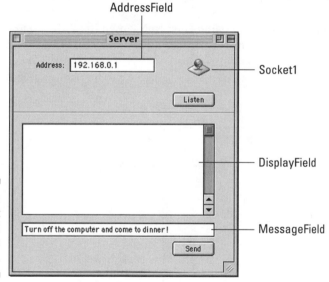

AddressField

Socket1

DisplayField

MessageField

Figure 14-4:
A chat
server need
not be
complicated.

When the Socket control receives data from another computer, the control's `DataAvailable` event fires. You capture the incoming data using the Socket's `ReadAll` method and then display it in an EditField:

```
Sub DataAvailable()
 Dim s as string
 s=me.ReadAll
 DisplayField.text=DisplayField.text+"Client:"+s+chr(13)
End Sub
```

After the server has a connection with a client, it can send messages to the client by calling the `Write` method of the Socket. Place this code in the `Action` event of SendButton:

```
Sub Action()
Socket1.write MessageField.text
DisplayField.text=DisplayField.text+MessageField.text +
         chr(13)
MessageField.text=""
End Sub
```

That's all the code there is for the server! Save this project and build the server application by choosing File⇨Build Application.

The next step is to build a chat client application. Fortunately, the client version is nearly identical to the server. The main difference is in the initial connection. While the server sits and listens for a connection, the client requests a connection. Other than that, the client works much like the server, sending and receiving messages.

Create a new project by choosing File⇨New. Open the Window Editor for Window1 by double-clicking it in the Window Editor. In Window1, build an interface that looks like Figure 14-5.

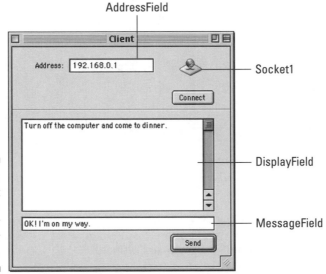

AddressField

Socket1

DisplayField

MessageField

Figure 14-5:
The client application looks similar to the server application.

Because you haven't made a connection yet, you don't want your users to send any data. To prevent them from doing so, disable the SendButton in your interface by selecting the SendButton and changing its Enabled property to FALSE in the Properties window. In ConnectButton, enter this code:

```
Sub Action()
if me.caption="Connect" then
   Socket1.Address=AddressField.text
   Socket1.Port=200
   Socket1.Connect
   me.caption="Disconnect"
   SendButton.enabled=TRUE
else
   Socket1.Close
   me.caption="Connect"
   SendButton.enabled=FALSE
end if
End Sub
```

As you can see, the code is nearly identical to that of the server's ListenButton. The main difference is that the client sends the Connect message to the Socket to initiate communications. When the client Socket successfully connects to the server, the `Connected` event of the Socket fires. This is an excellent place to display some information in your interface indicating a successful connection:

```
Sub Connected()
DisplayField.text=DisplayField.text+"Connected to
          server..."+chr(13)
End Sub
```

After the connection takes place, the Socket sits and waits for incoming data. When it receives data, the `DataAvailable` event fires. As before, capture the data and display it in the interface:

```
Sub DataAvailable()
dim s as string
s=me.readall
DisplayField.text=DisplayField.text+"Server:"+s+chr(13)
End Sub
```

Finally, the client can send messages to the server just as the server can send messages to it. To send a message, add this code to the `Action` event of SendButton:

```
Sub Action()
Socket1.write MessageField.text
DisplayField.text=DisplayField.text+"Client:"+MessageField.te
          xt+chr(13)
MessageField.text=""
End Sub
```

You have just completed the chat client!

Choose File⇨Build Application to build the client version of the application. To test the chat capabilities, launch both the server and the client at the same time. In the AddressField of the server, enter your IP address. If you don't know your address, you can find it in the TCP control panel. Next, click the Listen button to begin listening.

With the server sitting there listening, activate the client application and click the Connect button. If all goes well, the Connected to server... message should appear in the field set aside for display. The server has heard your request to chat and allowed the client to connect. Now you can freely send messages between the two applications.

Go ahead and try sending a message from the client to the server and vice versa. To use this in the real world, the client and server applications would be on different computers.

The chat program makes a great addition to a home network for messaging family members without yelling across the house. This should make mothers the world over very happy. Furthermore, you can use this program to send messages between two computers in an office, over a local network, or even on opposite sides of the Earth through the Internet.

Part IV

Getting REAL
Fancy with
Advanced Topics

The 5th Wave   By Rich Tennant

"I failed her in Algebra but was impressed
with the way she animated her equations
to dance across the screen, scream like
hyenas and then dissolve into a clip art image
of the La Brea Tar Pits."

In this part . . .

Besides the standard functionality you expect from most applications, REALbasic has many fantastic advanced features. The makers of REALbasic knew that they would never be able to add every imaginable function, so they enabled you to supplement the features of REALbasic with those from AppleScript as well as dozens of readily available REALbasic plugins. In this part, you find out how to take advantage of this expandability.

Another important professional feature of REALbasic is its advanced database capability. REALbasic gives you convenient methods for storing and retrieving all sorts of data in its own database file format as well as many other common database formats. In this part, you discover how to create, store, and retrieve database information in your REALbasic applications.

Perhaps the juiciest of all of REALbasic's features is its capability to create applications for several different kinds of computers and operating systems without changing one line of code. The part concludes by showing you the necessary steps for creating applications for Microsoft Windows and Apple's newest operating system — Mac OS X.

Chapter 15

AppleScript in REALbasic

● ●

In This Chapter

▶ Exploring the basics of AppleScript

▶ Adding AppleScript functionality to your own projects

▶ Sending and receiving data with AppleScript

● ●

They say that good artists borrow and great artists steal. Well, my friend, you are about to become a regular Picasso! Although the theft will not require any illegal activities, it will make you feel like you are getting away with murder. The heist I am speaking of is AppleScript.

AppleScript adds an enormous list of features to the Mac and comes with default installations of the Mac OS. REALbasic, in one of the greatest coups ever, can reach its paws into the AppleScript box of tools and take advantage of its functionality. This means you can instantly add all the power of AppleScript to your own REALbasic applications with little effort.

AppleScript has the amazing capability to carry on conversations with practically every application on your Mac. Like a human conversation, AppleScript can converse in one of three ways. First, it is adept at barking commands. This allows you, for example, to tell an application to do a series of functions that would be either tedious or repetitious to do by hand.

After you have finished telling applications what to do, you might want to listen a bit. If you pay close attention, applications, with the help of AppleScript, will tell you information. With only a small amount of effort, you can have the Finder telling you all sorts of interesting information about your Macintosh.

The final method of conversation using AppleScript is a true dialogue. Shout a command at an application and it replies with an answer.

In this chapter, I do not provide you with an exhaustive tutorial about AppleScript. Many publications and Web resources do that job well. Rather, this chapter shows you how to exploit the amazing powers of AppleScript to supercharge your own REALbasic applications.

AppleScript on Steroids

AppleScript is a set of tools provided by Apple with the Mac OS to allow the exchange of information between applications through an English-like scripting language. Although this language is relatively simple to use, tasks become difficult to manage when you reach any level of complexity.

REALbasic allows you to utilize all the power of AppleScript while it takes care of the hard parts. As you will see, this makes wrestling with AppleScript a fight you can win. Furthermore, with REALbasic providing the front end to your AppleScript back end, you have access to unlimited interface possibilities that would be tedious if not impossible to access with AppleScript.

To begin examining some of the nifty possibilities of AppleScript, you need to use the Script Editor. Apple's Script Editor is an application to write and create scripts for AppleScript. Other applications are available for creating scripts, but the Script Editor is included for free with the default AppleScript installation.

Load the Script Editor application by double-clicking its icon. It typically resides in the Apple Extras folder at the root of your hard drive. Script Editor begins by default with a new script document. A *script* is a list of instructions that AppleScript and the Script Editor can understand and execute.

Installing AppleScript

So you'd like to take advantage of AppleScript but didn't install it when you installed the latest gee-whiz version of the Mac OS. Or, if your home is like mine, maybe a small ten-fingered creature has somehow managed to send your AppleScript software into the great void.

Never fear, help is here! Follow these easy steps and you will be unleashing the awesome power of AppleScript on your unsuspecting REALbasic projects in minutes:

1. **Insert your Mac OS CD into the CD-ROM drive and then run the Mac OS installer.**

2. **Proceed through the license agreements and press the Customize button to customize the Mac OS installation.**

3. **When presented with a list of items that are installed by default, deselect all components except Mac OS 9.**

4. **Change the Installation Mode for Mac OS 9 to Customized Installation.**

   A dialog box appears with a listing of items to be installed for the Mac OS 9 component.

5. **Deselect all features of the Mac OS 9 custom installation. Expand the Utility feature section and select AppleScript. Click OK and start the installation.**

6. **When you are finished with the installation, restart your Mac.**

AppleScript is now ready to go.

You may be wondering why you would want to use AppleScript in the first place. Suppose you wanted to create a REALbasic application that searched for and deleted unneeded files on your hard drive. Although REALbasic has built-in functionality for moving files to the Trash, it doesn't include a command to empty the Trash after the files are placed there. AppleScript, however, does.

Into the new document, enter the following script:

```
on run {}
    tell application "Finder"
        Empty Trash
    end tell
end on
```

The beginning of the script might look a bit strange to you. This is simply a requirement for using the script with REALbasic. Later, something will appear in the braces, but for now leave it empty. The last line of the script ends the `on run` statement. Enclosed within the `on run` statement is the meat of the script. First, the `tell` statement explains that this command will be directed at the Finder. It should be obvious that the next line of code empties the trash. Finally, the `tell` statement is closed with a corresponding `end tell` command. The final step in creating this script is to save it. Choose File⇨Save and save the script with the settings shown in Figure 15-1.

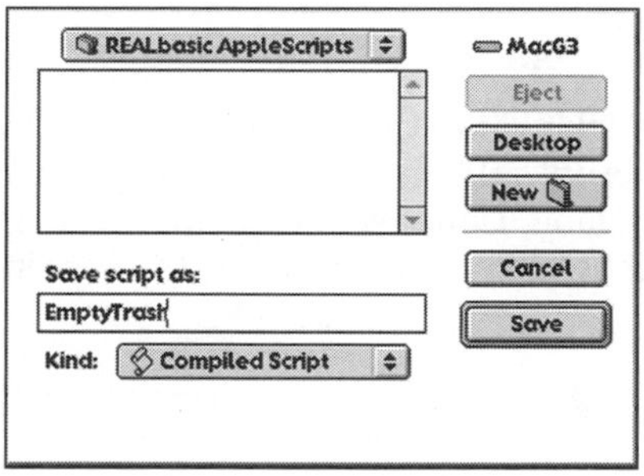

Figure 15-1:
The
EmptyTrash
script Save
settings.

Believe it or not, you have just extended REALbasic's capabilities. REALbasic by itself does not have a command to empty the trash, but with the script you just made, it does. To demonstrate, in the next section you create a small utility toolbar project.

Using AppleScripts in Your Project

REALbasic makes utilizing AppleScripts a cinch. To include a script in your project, simply drag it into the Project window. Follow these steps to begin the utility toolbar project:

1. **Start the REALbasic application.**

   To run the application, double-click it in the Finder. A new window opens by default.

2. **Add the script to the project.**

   To include a script in your project, simply drag it from the Finder into your new Project window. By now, your project should look something like Figure 15-2.

3. **Build an interface and enter some code.**

   Open Window1 by double-clicking it in the Project window. Drag a PushButton from the toolbar onto the opened Window1. The PushButton is named PushButton1 by default. Double-click PushButton1 to open the Code Editor and enter the following code into its Action event:

   ```
   EmptyTrash
   ```

   That's all there is to it!

4. **Test the project.**

   To see the fruits of your labor, choose Debug⇨Run and click PushButton1. The Finder magically empties the trash. Save the project.

I realize that although emptying the trash a useful task, it's not very exciting. Fortunately, AppleScript is loaded with goodies that you can exploit. For example, the Finder alone has more than fifty commands for you to fiddle with, not to mention the endless ways you could use those commands.

To see which commands the Finder — or any other application for that matter — knows, open the Script Editor application and choose File⇨Open Dictionary. A list of the scriptable features of that application appears. Figure 15-3 shows the Finder Dictionary.

Figure 15-3:
The Finder
Dictionary.

To spice up the utility toolbar you are creating, think of other functions that might be useful for instant access. For example, it might be nice to shut down the computer without accessing the Special menu. Following a method similar to the one you used to add EmptyTrash functionality, four simple steps will give you the desired functionality:

1. **Create an AppleScript.**

   Start the Script Editor application and enter the following code into a new script window and save it as a compiled script, remembering the filename for later. For this example, the script is named ShutDown.

   ```
   on run {}
    tell application "Finder"
     shut down
    end tell
   end run
   ```

2. **Add the script to the project.**

   Again, drag the ShutDown script into the utility toolbar project window. By now, your project should be looking something like Figure 15-4.

Figure 15-4:
The Project
window
with the
EmptyTrash
and
ShutDown
Apple-
Scripts in it.

3. **Add an interface element and enter some code.**

Open Window1 by double-clicking it in the Project window. Drag another PushButton from the toolbar to the opened Window1. This time the PushButton is named PushButton2 by default. Double-click PushButton2 to open the Code Editor and then enter the following code in the Action event:

```
ShutDown
```

Now, wasn't that easy?

4. **Test the project.**

You can test your project now, but be warned that this test might have dire consequences if you are not prepared. This function shuts down your computer! So, be sure to go through all your applications and save anything you might need to save, including this project. Finally, choose Debug⇨Run and click PushButton2.

Hey, your Mac shut down! Good. If everything went smoothly, you should be staring at a blank screen right about now. Restart your Mac, take a snack break, and come back when you're ready to continue.

Sending and Receiving Info

Are you back? Great! As you can see, adding AppleScripts to REALbasic projects is both easy and useful. Thus far, however, you have been telling the Finder to do something. Suppose you wanted the Finder to tell you the amount of RAM installed in the computer. Or maybe you would like to pass some text to the Finder and then have the Finder speak that text. Now things are getting interesting.

AppleScript is capable of conversing with applications by

- Sending a command to an application
- Receiving information from an application
- Sending information to and receiving information from an application immediately

To get the Finder to tell you some information, your AppleScript must include the `return` command. This command makes AppleScript send to REALbasic whatever information you want.

For example, it is relatively easy to find out the amount of RAM installed in a computer using AppleScript. AppleScript can then return that number to REALbasic, so your REALbasic application can make use of it.

To illustrate, create another script in Script Editor and enter the following code:

```
on run {}
    tell application "Finder"
    set m to (computer memory available)/1048 div 1000
        return m
    end tell
end run
```

Most of this script should appear familiar. The `on run` and `tell` commands are standard fare for AppleScripts in REALbasic. The next line, however, is new. The `set` command sets the value of the variable `m` to that whole mess that appears after `to`. The term `computer memory available` should be easy to understand. It represents the amount of physical RAM installed in the machine but in bytes. When it comes to RAM, a byte is such a small unit of measure these days. To convert it into something a bit more palatable, you first divide it by 1048 and then by 1000 to get it in units of megabytes. With `m` now set to the amount of RAM in megabytes, it's time to send it back to REALbasic for further use. This is the goal of the `return` statement. Save the script, naming it `GetRam`.

AppleScript is also proficient at speaking text. You must have Apple's Text to Speech software installed for this to work. Create a fourth script and enter the following code:

```
on run {thisphrase, thisvoice}
    tell application "Finder"
    say thisphrase using thisvoice
    end tell
end run
```

This time something different is happening. This script passes values the thisphrase and thisvoice values to AppleScript. They are used to indicate what text to speak and with which voice to speak it. Any values that you want to pass to an AppleScript from REALbasic must follow the on run statement and appear separated with commas and enclosed in two braces { and }. You can then use these values in the rest of the script.

The remaining script should be routine. The say command does exactly what you think it does, using the thisvoice voice variable. Save the script, naming it SayThis.

Now that you have created one script that sends information to REALbasic from AppleScript and one that sends information to AppleScript from REALbasic, it's time to add this functionality to the utility toolbar. Open your REALbasic project and drag the two new scripts into the Project window.

Next, open Window1 and drag a new PushButton onto the window, changing its caption to read How much RAM?. Double-click this PushButton to open the Code Editor. In the Action event of the button, enter the following:

```
dim AmountOfRAM as string
dim theVoice as string

AmountOfRAM=GetRam()+ " Megabytes of ram is installed."
theVoice=Popupmenu1.text

SayThis AmountOfRam,theVoice
```

The first two lines of code create two new strings. AmountOfRam stores the RAM total returned by the GetRam AppleScript and any other text to be spoken. The variable named theVoice stores the name of the voice. It gets its value from a popup menu, which you have not added yet.

To add a PopupMenu to Window1, drag one from the toolbar onto Window1. Click EditButton in the InitialText Property text box of the Properties window. Enter a few of the voice names. Figure 15-5 shows the process.

Having entered some voice names into PopupMenu1, click OK and dismiss the InitialValue property dialog box. Next, change the ListIndex property through the Properties window to a value of 0.

This bit of code selects the first name in the list when the application runs because no PopupMenu item is selected by default.

Now, your project should be ready to test. Choose Debug⇨Run and click the How much RAM? button. If all goes well, your Mac should speak the amount of RAM to you.

Figure 15-5:
Adding
voice names
to a Popup-
Menu.

The final feat to your bag of AppleScript tricks is a script that both receives information from REALbasic and sends information back to REALbasic. Finally, a true dialogue! Actually, not much is new here. You have already essentially accomplished this feat but in a disjointed manner. If you put both techniques together into one script, you can accomplish this functionality. Perhaps an example would better demonstrate the power of this method.

Until now, you have been solely concerned with bossing around the Finder. The beauty of AppleScript is that most applications can be ordered around to varying degrees. In fact, you can command some applications to do dozens of functions and to yield all sorts of data.

Again, to get a real appreciation for the scriptability of any application, open its dictionary in the Script Editor.

One fabulous example of real power is in the scripting dictionary of Netscape. One particularly useful command is GetURL, which returns the URL of any open Netscape window. You tell AppleScript which window to look at, and it replies with the URL. Finally, a true dialogue!

To demonstrate, create a new AppleScript:

```
on run {x}
    tell application "Netscape"
        GetUrl of Window x
        return result
    end tell
end run
```

Save the script and name it GetURLFromWindow. As you can see, this script receives a window number, called x. The GetURL command uses this number. The return result statement gives the URL to REALbasic. REALbasic speaks, and Netscape listens and replies with an answer.

To add this script to your utility toolbar project, open the project and its Window1. Drag a new PushButton to Window1 and double-click the PushButton to open the Code Editor. In the Action event of PushButton, enter a few lines of code. This code is nearly identical to previous examples:

```
dim s as string
s=GetURLFromWindow(1)
MsgBox s
```

GetURLFromWindow sends 1 to mean the foremost window. The script replies with the URL of the foremost window.

Now that you have the basics behind you, it's easy to imagine hundreds of uses for AppleScript in your REALbasic projects. For example, you might want to spell check some data from a REALbasic application. Instead of reinventing the wheel, why not use an existing spell checker? AppleWorks has extensive scripting capabilities, including access to its spell checker. Send it some text to spell check, and it returns a list of misspelled words and their locations within the string.

To demonstrate, create a new script in Script Editor. To the script, add the following code:

```
on run {x}
    tell application "Appleworks"
        set z to check spelling of x
        return z
    end tell
end run
```

This script accepts text and checks its spelling. The result is a list of all misspelled words and their positions. This string is then returned to REALbasic. Save the script, naming it checkspelling.

Next, open the REALbasic utility project you've been creating in this chapter. Open Window1 and drag two EditFields and one PushButton onto it. For both EditFields, change the Multi-Line property to TRUE.

The first EditField (EditField1) will hold the text you want to spell check. You use the second EditField (EditField2) to display the results of the spell check. AppleScript returns the results as a comma-separated list. Before you display the results in EditField2, you must scan through each item in that list.

To add spell-checking functionality, double-click the PushButton to open its Code Editor. To its `Action` event, add the following code:

```
dim s as string
dim f as string
dim i as integer

s=checkspelling(editfield1.text)

for i=1 to countFields(s,",")
    f=NthField(s,",",i)
    editfield2.selstart=len(editfield2.text)
    editfield2.seltext=f+chr(13)
next
```

The first three lines define three new variables: two strings and one integer. The next line sends the text from EditField1 to the `checkspelling` script. The script replies with a list of misspellings, and the result is stored in the `s` variable. The list also contains positions of each misspelled word between each misspelled entry. Thus, the list is formatted like this: word, position, word, position, and so on. The For-Next loop splits that data apart so that you can display it easily, with one entry per line.

The first line in the loop shows that the loop runs from 1 to the number of fields that are separated by commas, in other words, the number of items in the list. The `NthField` command returns a particular field (field number `i`) from the `s` string. The following two lines put the field data into EditField. Instead of simply assigning the text to EditField, this method prevents flickering of the text during update. Finally, a `chr(13)` (a newline character) is appended to EditField. The last line of code ends the loop.

The final step required to use the script is to add it to the project. Drag the script from the Finder into the Project window. To test the project, choose Debug⊏>Run. Enter text into EditField1 and press PushButton5. EditField2 should now display a list of misspelled words. Figure 15-6 shows the completed project for this chapter.

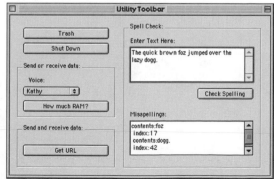

Figure 15-6:
The completed toolbar project.

Granted, the spell check example is not suited for commercial use or shareware, but it is beneficial for rapid development or a tool specific to your needs. Furthermore, it shows an example of using AppleScript to add a new function to your REALbasic application. Now it is up to you to explore the countless possibilities of AppleScript.

Be sure to scour the scripting dictionaries of your favorite applications and never forget that the Finder is an application itself. Exploiting the AppleScript features of different applications can save you hours of development time and give you amazing powers with very little effort.

You can find loads of useful AppleScripts and tutorials for using AppleScript on the Internet. Most notably, Apple's own AppleScript site provides a lot of information about using AppleScript, sample scripts, and links to AppleScript resources all over the Web:

```
www.applescript.com
```

The great folks at ResExcellence also dedicate a portion of their Web site to reader-submitted AppleScripts in their AppleScript Archive:

```
www.ResExcellence.com/applescripts/
```

Not to be outdone, MacCentral also hosts a number of AppleScript tutorials:

```
www.maccentral.com/columns/briggs.shtml
```

Finally, you don't even have to access the Web to get help for using AppleScript. The Mac OS has documentation and tutorials for using AppleScript built-in. To access this information, choose Help⇨Mac OS Help from the Finder and search for the topic AppleScript.

Chapter 16

Databases

*T*here may come a time in your programming career when you need to handle large amounts of information. Typical programming efforts would be unwieldy or simply ineffective. Suppose that you need to store a list of your 10 favorite movies, their release dates, and a brief synopsis of each movie. This seems easy enough to accomplish with a Listbox and a simple text file. Now consider what would happen if the number of movies you need to store increases to 1,000, or even 100,000! Clearly, you need another solution. Meet your friend the database.

A *database* is a container for storing information — and lots of it. You've probably encountered databases many times without even knowing it. For example, when you purchase something on the Internet or look up a book at the library, you're accessing a database. Similarly, the address book in your email program is an example of a database. Databases are great for organizing large amounts of data. Furthermore, they can swiftly and accurately search through the data and find specific tidbits of information.

REALbasic is adept at working with data from many types of databases. This chapter explores working with databases in REALbasic, paying particular attention to REALbasic's own variety of database.

Types of Data

Databases are large containers for information or data. To store information in them, however, you must follow a few rules.

Like variables, databases expect data expressed according to type. REALbasic can work with many different types of information in a database, including

- ✔ Numbers
- ✔ Date and time
- ✔ Strings

Before embarking on database creation, you must first decide what types of data you want to work with. Databases, like computers in general, are fussy when it comes to data. They must know all about the kind of data you will be feeding to and requesting from them.

It's a good idea to write a list that details the various information you want to work with. Then, assign a data type to each item in your list. This is an important step because changing a data's type later can be difficult. It's better to take time in the beginning to plan things accurately than it is to discover later that you forgot to include some important information.

Numbers

REAL databases can handle several types of numerical data, including numbers with or without decimal points. You encounter these types of numbers when dealing with variables.

Numbers without a fractional part, or decimal point, are integers. For REAL databases, they include

- ✔ **Integer.** Any number between -32766 and +32766
- ✔ **Smallinteger.** An integer that takes up less space than a standard integer

Integers are excellent for storing information such as your age (30), your IQ (150), or the number of sit-ups you can do (250). A smallinteger is the same as a standard integer, except it can represent only a fraction of the range of an integer. Because of this, a smallinteger consumes less memory (RAM) than an integer type.

Programming geeks love to make their code as efficient as possible, and smallintegers make this possible. Fortunately, the examples in this book don't require you to be a super geek, so you can disregard smallintegers. A standard Integer stores any number that a smallinteger can (and more).

Because your first databases will not tax your computer's memory or hard drive, you're safe to stick with integers.

When you need to store in a REAL database a number that has a decimal point, use one of these data types:

- ✔ **Double.** A double precision number.

- ✔ **Float.** A decimal number in which you can define the position of the decimal point. Because you can change the location of the decimal point within the number, the decimal point is said to *float*.

These data types are perfect for storing things such as money amounts ($8.15), your body temperature (98.6 degrees), or the exact distance from your home to the nearest beach (700.329 miles). For now, you need to be concerned only with doubles because they serve all your needs for the included examples.

The presence of a number in your data does not necessarily mean that the data type should fall in the numerical category of data. For example, most people have a telephone number, but it doesn't consist of numbers in strictest sense. You wouldn't perform a mathematical operation, for example, on a telephone number. Rather, a telephone number is more like a string of characters. Addresses are another example of a string in number clothing. Although your address may contain a number, it's shouldn't be a number data type. For these cases, you need to use another data type explained later in this section: Varchar.

Dates and times

When you want to store dates or times, REAL databases offer the Date and Time data types. These data types are ideal for storing things such as birthdays, the time you woke up each day, or your next scheduled dental appointment.

Strings

Sometimes you may need to store something other than a bunch of numbers and dates. When this happens, it's time to break out the Varchar type. Varchar variables can store strings of text such as your name, address, telephone number, and favorite kind of ice cream.

Varchar is so named, because it contains a *variable* length of characters. Many other databases (but not REAL databases) have a Char type, which holds a fixed number of characters. Varchar, on the other hand, can change size to accommodate any number of characters that you throw at it. For REAL databases, you always use Varchar. It can handle all sizes of strings, including a single character.

Creating Your First REAL Database

Now you know that you can store different types of data in a database, but it might not occur to you why you'd want to do so. Databases help you by storing information in an ordered manner. This gives you the ability to find information quickly. For example, you've probably purchased software that has a serial number or code for registering the software. Over time, as you register more software, it's easy to lose track of all this registration information. A database can help you store this information in an organized fashion.

Now that you have an idea about the types of data you can store in a REAL database and why you might want to store data, it's time to make your first database. You can create a REAL database in one of two ways:

- Using the tools included with REALbasic
- Writing code

For now, concern yourself only with the former. REALbasic has a set of tools that allow you to design databases directly in your project. To do so, begin by adding a data source to your project:

1. **Choose File⇨Add Data Source⇨New REAL Database.**

   This creates a new REAL database in your project.

2. **Name the database.**

   REALbasic prompts you to name and save your new database somewhere on your hard drive. It's customary to append .rdb to the filename to denote a REAL database. For this example, use a name such as `myRegistrationDatabase.rdb`.

3. **Click OK.**

   REALbasic creates a new database and displays it in the Project window.

Your brand new database is a shell of a database. It can store all kinds of information, but not until you specifically tell it what type. This is where the true design aspect of databases comes into play. Now is the time you should get out a pencil and paper and jot down the different kinds of data you want to store. After you have made that list, go through each item in the list and give it a data type as discussed previously.

This chapter walks you through the steps of creating a small database to store the serial numbers of your favorite applications. Such a database might include information such as

✒ Software's title (Title)

✒ Price you paid for the software (Price)

✒ Date you bought the software (PurchaseDate)

✒ Software's serial or registration number (SerialNumber)

First, name each element in the list. Use a name that describes the data, contains only alphanumeric characters, and is not the same as a REALbasic command (to avoid confusion).

Having named each item in the list, you must now give each element a data type. Table 16-1 lists these elements and the data types each requires.

Table 16-1	Serial Number Database Design
Data Name	*Data Type*
Title	Varchar
Price	Double
PurchaseDate	Date
SerialNumber	Varchar
ID	Integer

Note the final item in Table 16-1: an element not listed in the original design. It's commonplace to store a unique number for each item in a database. This number uniquely identifies each piece of software. Although you might be able to uniquely identify each piece of software by the title alone, you may run into problems. Suppose, for example, that you have two versions of an application that share the same name. How will you possibly keep them separated? The ID will take care of this. It is vital that at least one element in the list uniquely identifies the software. Not only does it keep thing straight for you, but REALbasic also requires it, as you will soon discover.

With your list of data types in hand, you can go back to the computer and begin entering them into the database. To add each of these data types, you must first create a table. In database lingo, a table is special container that holds a set of related data. For example, you may want to create a table called `myRegistrationTable` in which you can place each of the data types listed in Table 16-1. You can the use this table to store as many serial numbers as you wish.

To add a table to your existing REAL database:

1. **Double-click the database in the Project window to open it.**

   A dialog box appears listing all of the tables in the database. So far, you should see none, because you haven't created any yet.

2. **Click the New button to display the New Table dialog box, as shown in Figure 16-1.**

3. **In the Name field, type a name for your new table.**

   Having given the table a name, it is time to add each of the data types to the table. Database aficionados call these data types *fields*.

4. **Click the Add button.**

   A New Field dialog box appears, as shown in Figure 16-2.

5. **For each name in Table 16-1, enter it into the dialog box, assign it a type from the Type popup menu, and click OK. For the final item in the list (ID), click the Primary Key check box in the New Field dialog box.**

   The Primary Key field of a table uniquely identifies a set of data; each table requires one. When you have completed entering each field in the table, the New Table dialog box should look like Figure 16-3.

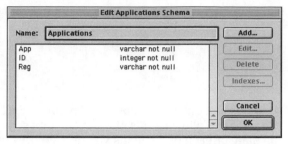

Figure 16-3:
The
completed
table,
entitled
myRegistra-
tionTable.

6. **With the table design complete, click OK to add the table to your database.**

The database now has a structure to which you can add data.

Adding Data

With the database design behind you, it's time to add some data to the database. REALbasic doesn't allow you to enter data directly into your database. Rather, you have to add data to a table using REALbasic code.

The first step in working with databases is to let your project know which database to work with. It's common to create a property of a window that refers to the database, and then use that property throughout your code. To do this, open the code editor for Window1 by double-clicking its Window Editor. Choose Edit➪New Property and then create a property as shown in Figure 16-4.

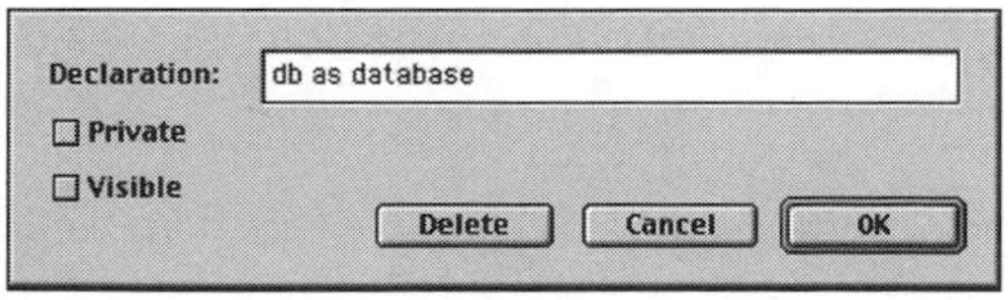

Figure 16-4:
Create a
Database
property
called db
that you can
refer to
in the
Window1
code.

After you have created the db property, define it in the Open Event of Window1:

```
Sub Open()
   db = myRegistrationDatabase
End Sub
```

REALbasic databases, like most databases, consist of records. Each *record* is a unique item in the database. Following this chapter's database design, a record would contain data for each of the fields you defined previously. For example, one record might contain the data as shown in Table 16-2.

Table 16-2	An Example Database Record
Field Name	*Data in the Field*
Title	REALbasic
Price	$350.21
PurchaseDate	15Aug1999
SerialNumber	#123-456-789
ID	1

To add this data to the database, you must first create a DatabaseRecord object, like this:

```
dim rec as DatabaseRecord
rec = New DatabaseRecord
```

Next, populate the record with each piece of data in the list. Place each item, or field, into its own column in the table. Title has its own column, Price has its own column, and so forth. The Database Record object has methods to help you. To add string data to your table, use the Column method of the Database Record class like this:

```
Dim rec as DatabaseRecord
rec = New DatabaseRecord

rec.Column("Title") = "REALbasic"
rec.Column("SerialNumber") = "#123-456-789"
```

For numerical data, use the DoubleColumn and Integer methods to set the fields of a record:

```
rec.DoubleColumn("Price") = 350.21
rec.Integer("ID") = 1
```

In other words, use the `Column` method for strings, the `Integer` method for integers (numbers without a decimal portion), and `Double` for doubles (numbers with a decimal portion).

Date information requires a little extra work before you can add it to a database table. When you store a date in a REAL database, it must be in the form of a REALbasic Date object, not a string of text as you might expect. Fortunately, REALbasic provides a nifty method called `ParseDate` that converts a date in string format (which you can easily read) into a REALbasic Date object. It returns a Boolean value of `TRUE` if it was able to successfully convert the string to a Date object. Furthermore, `ParseDate` takes a Date object as a parameter, where it will store the newly created Date object:

```
Dim rec as DatabaseRecord
Dim DateConversionWorked as Boolean
Dim theDate as Date

rec = New DatabaseRecord
theDate = new Date
DateConversionWorked = ParseDate("15Aug1999",theDate)
if DateConversionWorked then
  rec.DateColumn("PurchaseDate") = theDate
else
  MsgBox "There was a problem creating the date object."
end if
```

After you have populated the database record with all the necessary information, it's time to add this record to the table. To do so, simply include the following line of code:

```
db.InsertRecord("myRegistrationTable",rec)
```

The InsertRecord method of the database does exactly what it says. It inserts the record, called rec, into the myRegistrationTable table. The completed code for adding a record to a table should look something like this:

```
Dim rec as DatabaseRecord
Dim DateConversionWorked as Boolean
Dim theDate as Date

rec = New DatabaseRecord
rec.Column ("Title") = "REALbasic"
rec.DoubleColumn ("Price") = 349.95
rec.Column ("SerialNumber") = "#123-456-789"
```

```
theDate = new Date
DateConversionWorked = ParseDate("15Aug1999",theDate)
if DateConversionWorked then
  rec.DateColumn("PurchaseDate") = theDate
else
  MsgBox "There was a problem creating the date object."
end if
rec.IntegerColumn("ID") = 1
db.InsertRecord("myRegistrationTable",rec)
```

You may have noticed in the preceding code listing that the different fields of the database record appear out of order from the original table definition. For example, you defined `SerialNumber` in the table before `PurchaseDate`, but the listing has the `PuchaseDate` assignment after `SerialNumber`. When you are *populating* a record (that's fancy database programmer talk, by the way) with data, the order doesn't matter. The REAL database doesn't care, as long as you issue an `InsertRecord` command to the database, passing to it the table's name and the database record you have populated.

So far, you have gone to extraordinary lengths to add only one record to the table. This serves a purpose for a programming example, but is bad form for a few reasons.

First, programmers hate the idea of having information hard-coded in a program. What happens later if your country decides to change money denominations? You'll have to go through all your old code and change every instance of the old currency and replace it with a new one.

Second, this method of putting data directly in your code is a bad practice because it allows only a REALbasic whiz (like yourself) to add data to the database later. What if your grandma wants to add her own data to your database? With all you newfound REALbasic knowledge, it's simple to make the data entry more generic and, consequently, easier to maintain and use.

Bring the Project window to the foreground by choosing Window➪Project. Double-click Window1 in the Project window to open its Window Editor. Like all other projects in this book, create an interface for entering data into your database. Figure 16-5 shows an example interface.

To simplify your life later, name each of the elements in the interface something you'll remember. For example, the EditField for entering the title of a piece of software might be named TitleField, similar to the name of the field in the database. Do the same for each EditField in the interface.

Database programmers, like most programmers, love jargon. When you create an interface for accessing a database, database pros often call this interface a *front end.* The database itself is the *back end.* Resist the urge to insert the appropriate sophomoric joke here.

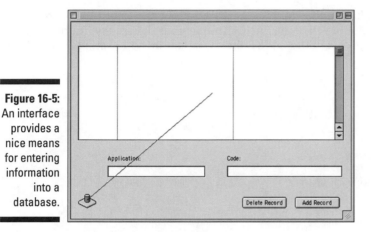

Figure 16-5:
An interface
provides a
nice means
for entering
information
into a
database.

The front end is what you see; the back end is what you don't. The front end is the interface and pretty stuff that will make your database such a joy for others to use, but the back end is the powerhouse of the whole setup. It does all the work of shuffling data around, keeping track of it, and so on. Be certain not to neglect either aspect of database design. A poor implementation of either can cause your database application to fail. Who cares if your application looks pretty if it doesn't do what it's supposed to? Conversely, who cares if your application can handle 10,000 users at a time if the user interface is confusing and, consequently, unusable?

Luckily for you, REALbasic does most of the back-end work for you. It worries about the difficult tasks of data management. The front end, however, is up to you. So, now that you are becoming a database pro yourself, feel free to toss around your new lingo: "Oh, I just thought the front end lacked something, but that back end. . . ." Your computer friends will all know what you're talking about, but no one else will, and that always make you sound important.

You should note a few things about this code example. First, all data from the preceding code example has been replaced with the Text property of the corresponding EditField in the interface. When the data is not text (Price and ID), the Val command precedes the Text property of the EditField. Val converts the text data to a number.

Second, the user must provide a number for the ID field of the table. This is less than ideal because users must supply a unique number for each entry. Sure, you can enter records one by one, increasing the number each time, but what happens when you come back to the database a month or even a year from now? You'll have no way to know just how many records are in the table and, therefore, no idea what ID numbers you can use. This sets the stage for the next section of the chapter — retrieving data from a database. By getting information back out of the table, you'll be able to tell what ID numbers are unused and thus valid. Moreover, you can remove the task altogether, allowing REALbasic to provide a unique ID number.

With your database entry interface built, it's a trivial matter to make the code more generic. Double-click the PushButton in your data-entry interface to open its Action event in the Code Editor. Change the code listing from before to read:

```
Sub Action()
Dim rec as DatabaseRecord
Dim DateConversionWorked as Boolean
Dim theDate as Date

rec = New DatabaseRecord
rec.Column("Title") = TitleField.text
rec.DoubleColumn("Price") = Val(PriceField.text)
rec.Column("SerialNumber") = SerialNumberField.text

theDate = new Date
DateConversionWorked =
            ParseDate(PuchaseDateField.text,theDate)
if DateConversionWorked then
   rec.DateColumn("PurchaseDate") = theDate
else
   MsgBox "There was a problem creating the date object."
end if
rec.IntegerColumn("ID") = Val(IDField.text)
db.InsertRecord("myRegistrationTable",rec)
End Sub
```

Retrieving Data

All of this data entry has been for a purpose — looking at the data later. You normally store information in a database so that you can access and use it in the future. Why else would you spend hours tediously entering all those serial numbers?

An introduction to the language of databases (SQL)

REALbasic offers a few different methods for retrieving data from a database, but all have one thing in common: SQL. SQL stands for Structured Query Language, but don't let the name scare you away. It is simply a small computer language resembling English that allows you to talk to (query) databases. SQL lets you ask the database questions, such as "Hey database, when did I buy my REALbasic software?"

If the idea of learning another language is enough to drive you crazy, relax. You must know only a few SQL commands to perform most REALbasic database tasks. Furthermore, REALbasic has a number of features that take away some of the extra SQL work for you.

At the heart of SQL is the Select statement. Select permits you to get information from a database table. Its general form is

```
Select <some data> from <some table>
```

This is simplifying matters, but it's important to understand this reduced command. You must provide the text shown in *italics*. For example, you might substitute with information from the table that you have created:

```
Select Title from myRegistrationTable
```

This instruction — and here's the tricky part — returns a list of every Title found in myRegistrationTable. When your database grows to be very large, this can be troublesome, so SQL gives you a few more tricks you can use. Consider this:

```
Select <some data> from <some table> where <some condition is
             true>
```

The where keyword in SQL helps you narrow down your search for the data. Suppose you wanted to look at the title of an application with an ID of 1. To accomplish this in SQL:

```
Select Title from myRegistrationTable where ID=1
```

There! That wasn't so bad, was it? Now, suppose you wanted to get the title and the purchase price of the same ID. SQL allows you to include multiple items in the Select statement, separated by a comma:

```
Select Title, Price from myRegistrationTable where ID=1
```

An important and frequently used shortcut in SQL is the asterisk (*). It's a wildcard character that essentially translates to *everything*. For instance, consider this Select statement:

```
Select * from myRegistrationTable where ID=1
```

This statement returns the following data from the database record with ID=1:

- ✔ ID
- ✔ Title
- ✔ Price
- ✔ PurchaseDate
- ✔ SerialNumber

As you can see, this SQL statement returns everything about the record. You can prune the `Select` statement even further to retrieve everything single item from the database:

```
Select * from myRegistrationTable
```

This statement returns every record and every field within every record.

SQL also has tons of other commands that give you the capability to create tables, update them, and more. This book doesn't cover them, but many fantastic resources are available for you to explore. REAL Software recommends *SQL For Dummies,* 3rd Edition, by Allen Taylor (published by Hungry Minds, Inc.) as well as the Web-based SQL tutorial at the following site:

```
http://w3.one.net/~jhoffman/sqltut.htm
```

Until now, you have looked at the basics of the SQL `Select` statement. As stated previously, the `Select` statement is great at retrieving data from databases, but you still don't know how to incorporate SQL into your REALbasic projects.

Control binding saves the day

Just when you think SQL is going to get the best of you, REALbasic comes along and gives you a powerful way to utilize SQL without a lot of the hassle associated with retrieving and displaying the information. REALbasic has a useful control in its Tools window called the DatabaseQuery. The DatabaseQuery control does just what its name implies: It queries a database. The beautiful part is that is does a lot of the work for you. Not only does it talk to the database on your behalf, but it also interfaces nicely with controls for displaying the output. Figure 16-6 shows the location of the DatabaseQuery control in the Tools window.

When you retrieve information from a database, you need to display it somehow. A Listbox makes a perfect choice for displaying data from a database. Because a Listbox readily displays multiple columns of information, the fields from a database table line up nicely, with each record occupying one row in the Listbox.

Figure 16-6:
The
DatabaseQu
ery control
helps you
retrieve and
display data
without all
the hassles.

—DatabaseQuery

What's more, Listboxes can bind with the DatabaseQuery control. Binding causes the data to instantly appear in the Listbox each time the DatabaseQuery control executes a query. In other words, you need to create only one SQL statement — REALbasic does the rest.

To continue updating this chapter's project, open the Window Editor of Window1 again. Drag a DatabaseQuery control from the Tools window to any-where in Window1. The DatabaseQuery control is an invisible control. Although it's visible in REALbasic while you design your project, it becomes invisible when you test the project, as well as when you build your final application.

By default, REALbasic names the DatabaseQuery control as DatabaseQuery1. After you have added the DatabaseQuery control to Window1, change its SQLQuery property in the Properties window to read

```
Select ID, Title, Price, SerialNumber, PurchaseDate from
        myRegistrationTable
```

The control will use this SQL statement to query the database. Pay particular attention to the order of the items in the Select statement. This is the order in which your program will display the data. Should you want to change the order or even the number of displayed items later, you would do so here.

In addition, select your database from the popup menu of the Database prop-erty of the DatabaseQuery1 control. Your database must be present in the Project window for it to appear in the Database property of DatabaseQuery1. Figure 16-7 shows the property settings of the DatabaseQuery1 control.

Next, you need someplace to display the data that DatabaseQuery1 retrieves. This is where the Listbox comes into play. Drag a Listbox from the Tools window into the Window Editor of Window1. Because the Select statement presented in Figure 16-7 retrieves five items from myRegistrationTable, change the ColumnCount value of the Listbox to 5. By default, the Listbox dis-plays all columns with equal widths. If you would like to change the widths of the columns, change the ColumnWidths property of the Listbox as well.

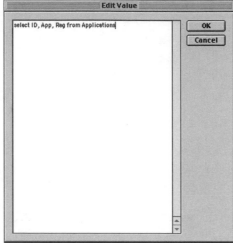

Figure 16-7:
Enter the
SQL
statement
and choose
a database
for
Database
Query1
in the
Property
window.

Percentages make a convenient unit of measure for defining Listbox columns, but be sure not to exceed 100%. If you do, some of your data will not be properly displayed. In fact, REALbasic programmers sometimes use this trick to hide data from the user. Conversely, a ColumnWidths of 0% also hides data, although it is still technically there. For now, set the ColumnWidths property of the Listbox to match Figure 16-8.

Change the property to match this

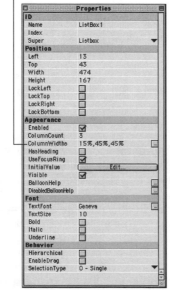

Figure 16-8:
Change the
ColumnWidt
hs property
of the
multicolumn
Listbox to
display data
in different
ways.

This completes the interface-building step of retrieving the data, but how does DatabaseQuery1 stick the information in Listbox? The answer is control binding. By using simple drag-and-drop methods, you can bind DatabaseQuery1 to Listbox. This has the effect of automatically displaying the results of the query in the Listbox.

To bind the two controls, begin by selecting the DatabaseQuery1 control. Then press and hold the Shift and Controls keys and drag from the DatabaseQuery control to the Listbox. A small line appears as you drag. When you reach the Listbox with the line, the Listbox becomes highlighted. When it does, let go of the mouse button and a New Binding dialog box appears. This is where you define how the DatabaseQuery and the Listbox bind. Select the first item in the list, which should read (as shown in Figure 16-9.):

```
Bind Listbox1 with list data from DatabaseQuery1 results
```

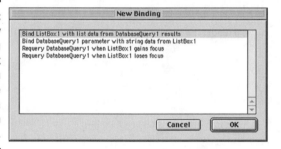

Figure 16-9:
The New Binding dialog box lets you select the function of a custom binding.

With this step completed, it's time to see how the project works. Test your project by choosing Debug⇨Run. When you run it, the Listbox should automatically populate with all the records in myRegistrationTable. Choose File⇨Quit to stop testing the project.

A few small changes to the code will improve its operation. For starters, keep in mind that users must supply unique ID data for each record they create in the table. This is troublesome, particularly when the number of records is extremely large. The only way a user will know if a number is unique is to search through all current records. You can easily remedy this problem by looking at the number of records in the table and, subsequently, the Listbox that displays the data from the table.

The Listbox control has a property called ListCount. As its name implies, it's the count of the number of items in the Listbox. If you get this count and add 1 to it, it can form a unique ID number for a new record. In this manner, you always base the new ID on a number 1 larger than the number of records in the table. For example:

```
rec.IntegerColumn("ID") = ListBox1.listcount+1
```

Each time you create a record, you can be certain that the ID number is unique.

The next change you should make to the code involves the DatabaseQuery1 control. When you add a record to the table in your database, you undoubtedly want to display the new information that you just added. To do so, simply send the DatabaseQuery control a `RunQuery` message, like this:

```
DatabaseQuery1.RunQuery
```

This causes the DatabaseQuery control to requery the database and update the Listbox in the process. Thus, the updated `Action` event of the PushButton in your interface should look like this:

```
Sub Action()
Dim rec as DatabaseRecord
Dim DateConversionWorked as Boolean
Dim theDate as Date

rec = New DatabaseRecord
rec.Column("Title") = TitleField.text
rec.DoubleColumn("Price") = Val(PriceField.text)
rec.Column("SerialNumber") = SerialNumberField.text

theDate = new Date
DateConversionWorked =
          ParseDate(DateFieldDateField.text,theDate)
if DateConversionWorked then
  rec.DateColumn("PurchaseDate") = theDate
else
  MsgBox "There was a problem creating the date object."
end if
rec.IntegerColumn("ID") = ListBox1.listcount+1
db.InsertRecord("myRegistrationTable",rec)
DatabaseQuery1.RunQuery
End Sub
```

Deleting Data

While excitedly entering dozens of software registrations in the database, your users are bound to screw up at some point. So far, you have not given them a way to correct a mistake. This section shows you how to remove a record from the table.

To begin making changes to existing records, you need to get comfortable with the DatabaseCursor class. A DatabaseCursor works like a spreadsheet in that it arranges information in rows and columns and lets you look at one record at a time. When you're looking at a record with DatabaseCursor, you can easily delete or even change it. To use DatabaseCursor, begin by defining one with the following code:

```
dim cur as DatabaseCursor
```

Next, send the DatabaseCursor object a SQL statement to retrieve all columns from the record. To decide which record to retrieve, use the Cell property of Listbox to get the ID column of the currently selected row in Listbox. The ID field is stored in the first column of Listbox, which is column number 0.

```
dim s as string
dim cur as DatabaseCursor

s=Listbox1.Cell(Listbox1.listindex,0)

cur = db.SQLSelect("select * from myRegistrationTable where
        ID=" + s)
```

Now that DatabaseCursor holds the currently selected record, it's a trivial task to delete the record using the `DeleteRecord` method of the DatabaseCursor class:

```
cur.deleteRecord
```

Don't forget to close DatabaseCursor and rerun the query of the DatabaseQuery control to update the Listbox so that it reflects the changes you made:

```
cur.close
DatabaseQuery1.RunQuery
```

To properly add this code to the interface, add another button to the Window1 Window Editor. To avoid a lot of extra messy code, form a control binding between PushButton and Listbox by pressing ⌘-Shift and dragging from the new PushButton to Listbox. In the New Binding dialog that appears, select:

```
Enable PushButton2 when Listbox1 has a selection
```

This causes the Delete PushButton to become active whenever you select something in Listbox. If you don't add this extra step and someone comes along and clicks PushButton without a Listbox selection, an error will occur.

Next, double-click the new PushButton to open the Code Editor. Then add the finished code to its `Action` event:

```
dim s as string
dim cur as DatabaseCursor

s=Listbox1.Cell(Listbox1.listindex,0)
cur = db.SQLSelect("select * from myRegistrationTable where
          ID=" + s)
cur.deleteRecord
cur.close
DatabaseQuery1.RunQuery
```

As is often the case when you program, adding features can sometimes break an existing feature. This code properly deletes records as intended, but a new problem jumps out if you test the project enough. Adding a new record after you have deleted a record makes the project function incorrectly.

The reason? In the original code for adding a record, you used the Listbox ListCount property to come up with a new and unique ID number. When you start removing records, this trick stops working because after you remove a record from anywhere but the end of the list, the ID numbers no longer correspond with the row numbers in the Listbox.

To correct this discrepancy, you can no longer simply rely on the ListCount property of Listbox to obtain a new and unique ID number for a new record in the table. Rather, you should look at the ID number of the last record in the list and add 1 to that. Change the code for PushButton1 to the following:

```
Sub Action()
Dim rec as DatabaseRecord
Dim DateConversionWorked as Boolean
Dim theDate as Date

rec = New DatabaseRecord
rec.Column("Title") = TitleField.text
rec.DoubleColumn("Price") = Val(PriceField.text)
rec.Column("SerialNumber") = SerialNumberField.text

theDate = new Date
DateConversionWorked =
          ParseDate(DateFieldDateField.text,theDate)
if DateConversionWorked then
  rec.DateColumn("PurchaseDate") = theDate
else
  MsgBox "There was a problem creating the date object."
end if
rec.IntegerColumn("ID") =
          Val(ListBox1.cell(Listbox1.ListIndex,0))+1
db.InsertRecord("myRegistrationTable",rec)
DatabaseQuery1.RunQuery
End Sub
```

This code retrieves the ID number from the last item in Listbox and adds 1 to that value. This ensures a unique ID each time you add a record to the table. Having completed the final code, test it by choosing Debug⇨Run. If all goes well, you should be able to add records to and delete records from the database table. The finished project should look like Figure 16-10.

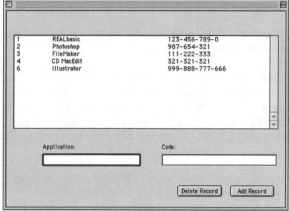

Figure 16-10: The completed serial number database project.

To add the capability to update records, check the REALbasic documentation on the *REALbasic For Dummies* CD. The *Language Reference* found within REALbasic itself also details this procedure.

Using Other Data Sources

In addition to connecting to the native REALbasic database format, REALbasic applications can connect also to a host of other databases, such as Oracle and 4D Server, to name a few. Besides that, the code for connecting to other databases and to a REALbasic database is nearly identical.

The main difference you'll encounter when working with data sources other than REALbasic databases is when you connect to the database. Each type of supported database has its own REALbasic method for connecting to it. This is because each type of database comes from a different manufacturer. Because different products have different features (including the connecting feature), REALbasic has methods tailored to each type of database it supports.

For example, to connect to an Oracle database, use the `OpenOracleDatabase` method:

```
db = OpenOracleDatabase("Erick@IDG", "arugula")
```

`OpenOracleDatabase` takes two parameters, which are related to the security scheme in Oracle databases:

- ✔ Username
- ✔ Password

Because this method is specific to Oracle databases, the parameters may differ for other types of databases.

After you have connected to an Oracle database, you can continue to use it by sending it queries just as you did with a REALdatabase. This is the beauty of working with external databases in REALbasic: You can often use the same code to work with many types of databases. (By the way, the password in the preceding code example, arugula, is a type of herb. But, don't ask me how to pronounce it!)

To find out how to connect to other types of databases, consult the *Language Reference* by choosing Window⇨Reference or by pressing ⌘-1.

Chapter 17

Extending REALbasic with Plugins

. . . .

In This Chapter

▶ Installing and using REALbasic plugins

▶ Looking at some of the most popular plugins

▶ Building your own plugins

. . . .

*T*here may come a time when you find that REALbasic doesn't perform a function you need. REAL Software realized this in advance and built in a way for programmers to extend the capabilities of REALbasic using plugins.

Plugins give you instant access to additional controls, methods, and classes created by other programmers (or you, for that matter). This chapter takes you quickly through the process of using plugins. It also gives you a brief overview of what's available. What's more, you can find many of the plugins mentioned in this chapter on the *REALbasic For Dummies* CD, complete with example projects. And if that's still not enough, many of the plugins are free. (I knew that would get your attention.) Finally, the chapter wraps up with some resources for getting started programming your own plugins.

Going beyond REALbasic

REALbasic plugins are special files that add functionality to the REALbasic language. REALbasic loads them into memory each time it launches.

Installing plugins

For REALbasic to find these plugins, however, you will have to perform three quick steps:

1. **Open the folder entitled Plugins located in the same folder as the REALbasic application.**

2. **Drop any plugin you want to use into the Plugins folder.**

3. **Launch REALbasic to make the plugins take effect.**

Figure 17-1 shows you what your REALbasic development folder should contain as a minimum.

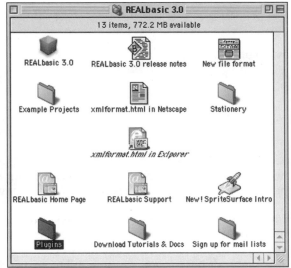

Figure 17-1:
Be sure to
place all
plugins
within the
Plugins
folder in the
same folder
as your
REALbasic
application.

After you have launched REALbasic with the plugins installed, the functionality of each plugin is automatically added to REALbasic. Some common types of functionality you might find include

- ✔ **Global methods.** These are simple commands that you can call from any code.

- ✔ **Custom controls.** Some plugins add custom controls to the Tools window. To use them, simply drag them into your interface as you would any other control.

- ✔ **Custom classes.** Plugin authors sometimes add functionality to existing REALbasic classes. For example, if a plugin updates the MoviePlayer control (one of the included plugins does just that), it simply has more properties, methods, or events. You use the updated class just as you would the regular class.

Plugin compatibility

REALbasic plugins must be compatible with your intended target platform. In other words, if you're developing for computers that run Mac OS 8, you need a PowerPC or 68K version of the plugin. If Windows is your forte, get your hands on a plugin that's compatible with Windows. Table 17-1 lists the various types of REALbasic plugins you might encounter.

Table 17-1	Plugin Compatibility Chart	
Plugin Compatibility	*Operating System*	*Computer*
68K	Mac OS 7, 8, 9	68K, PowerPC
PPC	Mac OS 7, 8, 9, X	PowerPC
FAT	Mac OS 7, 8, 9	68K, PowerPC
Carbon	Mac OS 8.6, 9, X	PowerPC
Windows	Win 95, 98, NT, 2000	x86

You might run into a few more plugin combinations in addition to those listed in Table 17-1. Some include compatibility for a combination of Macintosh and Windows platforms. For example, it's not uncommon to find a REALbasic plugin that's compatible with both PowerPC and x86. Before using a plugin in a program, you must know what kind of compatibility the plugin has for a particular platform.

By now, I bet you're wondering how to figure out a plugin's type of compatibility. The first place to look is the documentation that came with the plugin. If you've misplaced the documentation, simply open the plugin with a resource editor and look for the resources listed in Table 17-2. If a resource for the platform is present, it's compatible with that type of system.

Table 17-2	REALbasic Plugin Resources
Resource	*Compatibility*
PL68	68k Macintosh
PLPC	PowerPC Macintosh
PL86	Windows x86
PLCN	PowerPC Macintosh - Carbon (OS-X)

Are you in need of a resource editor? Check these links:

- ✔ **ResEdit** is the free resource editor from Apple. Apple halted development some years ago, but it still works like a charm. And did I mention that it's free? To download it, go to VersionTracker at

  www.versiontracker.com

  and search for ResEdit to find its current home on Apple's servers.

- ✔ **Resorcerer** isn't free, but it is more current. If you plan to do any serious work with Macintosh resources, you will probably need this one day. If you are just a beginner, stick with ResEdit. Go to the following site:

  www.mathemaesthetics.com/

Figure 17-2 shows a plugin's guts exposed. Based on Table 17-2, can you guess which platform this plugin is compatible with? If you answered 68k, PowerPC, and x86, you're correct!

Figure 17-2:
Some of the
resources
you should
look for
when trying
to figure out
a plugin's
compatibility.

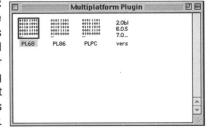

One final caveat is that REALbasic plugins are sometimes compatible with only specific versions of REALbasic. If you happen to see an error like that shown in Figure 17-3, you might be experiencing problems from a plugin incompatibility. If this happens, check to see whether the latest release works with your version of REALbasic. If not, you may be out of luck, unless you can convince the developer to remedy the situation (bribes usually work in this case).

Figure 17-3:
Time to
update your
plugin, your
version of
REALbasic,
or both.

Runtime Error: Could not get plugin's table of
contents.

Now that you know the difficult way to check plugin compatibility, you'll be glad to know that a utility on the Web takes care of all the dirty work for you. You can download it at the following:

```
www.realbasic.com/files/utilities/REALbasicPlug-
        inInspector.sit
```

Top Plugins of the Pros

A wealth of REALbasic plugins are available on the Web. They run the gamut from freeware to shareware and commercial products. To get you started, this section details some of the most important, useful, and downright cool plugins available today.

You can find demos and full working versions of the plugins in this section on the *REALbasic For Dummies* CD. All of them come complete with documentation and example projects to get you up and running quickly.

Einhugur Software

```
www.einhugur.com/Html/memberdl.html
```

Considered by many to be the king of REALbasic plugins, Einhugur provides dozens of plugins covering everything from graphics to files to custom controls. The custom ListBoxes are not to be missed. He is a co-author of the RB Plugin Plunger, an open source application useful for learning about the functionality of a plugin.

Michio Ono, PhD

```
hp.vector.co.jp/authors/VA009277/rb/index_e.htm
```

One of the hottest Japanese REALbasic plugin programmers around, Michio Ono creates REALbasic plugins for icons, graphics, QuickTime, string manipulation, and many other areas. Be sure to take a look at his QuickTime plugin; it makes REALbasic's implementation of QuickTime shine. Best of all, his plugins are free.

Thomas Tempelmann

www.tempel.org/rb/

Another REALbasic author that many revere, Thomas hosts a gaggle of plugins on his site. He also co-created the RB Plugin Plunger and was one of the first to offer Windows compatible plugins for REALbasic. Do not miss this site.

Essence Software

www.essencesw.com

A longtime promoter of REALbasic plugins, Essence Software offers several unique plugins. From 3D graphics to video capture, Essence Software always produces commercial quality plugins. Their Super Socket plugin has been a huge hit in the REALbasic community for the way it spices up REALbasic network communications. And before the revamping of the SpriteSurface, their MadPlug was one of the only ways to play background music within games. It's still a favorite.

Nubz

www.nubz.org

Nubz provides a number of useful plugins. Although tailored mainly for more advanced users, beginners are sure to find something they need here too.

Doug Holton

http://people.vanderbilt.edu/~doug.holton/basic/plugins/

Doug Holton is another one of those REALbasic geniuses that roam the planet looking for ideas that he can turn into code and give away free. His site includes plugins for AppleScript, XML, and others, but the real winner is his WasteField plugin, which implements the ever-popular Waste Text Engine as a REALbasic plugin. Never before has stylized text been so easy, nor so beautiful.

Fabian Lidman

`http://homepage.mac.com/fabianl/development/`

Although not really a REALbasic plugin programmer, Fabian Lidman has a famous TBFinder application that's a must for any REALbasic programmer's toolbox. It quickly finds and creates the appropriate syntax for REALbasic `Declare` statements, which can be used in your REALbasic code to mimic much of the functionality formerly reserved only for plugins.

RealVision

`www.cabanis.com/realvision/en/download/index.cfm`

If you're into music, make sure to check out RealVision, which offers the venerable DxMidi plugin. This plugin allows you to implement full MIDI function in your REALbasic application. RealVision also has a few nice custom controls that resemble sliders on popular music gear.

ZegSoft

`http://zegsoft.tripod.com/realbasic.html`

ZegSoft produces an important printing plugin for REALbasic that finally lets you get high-resolution output from REALbasic 2 applications.

Joe's REALbasic Page

`http://strout.net/info/coding/rb/intro.html`

A REAL Software employee by day, Joe sometimes masquerades as a REALbasic programmer in his free time. (He must really love REALbasic, eh?) Although his site is mostly about standard REALbasic projects, he does have a cool screen capture plugin available. His 3D graphics and game examples can't be beat either.

REAL Software

Finally, you should be aware of one additional plugin resource. REAL Software maintains a list of currently available plugins. Be sure to check their site for the latest list.

Creating Your Own Plugins

One day you may find yourself longing after a function or control that's not available in REALbasic. That's when you must look into REALbasic plugin programming.

Plugin programming is not for everyone. It is time-consuming, not always well-documented, fly-by-the-seat-of-your-pants programming. More importantly for readers of this book, though, is the fact that plugins must be created in another language called C++. If you are starting to sweat or are thinking of tossing this book out the window, please skip the rest of this chapter.

You're still reading, so you must be interested in plugins. In the remainder of this chapter, I don't go into the details (some might even call it gore) about REALbasic plugin programming. Instead, I outline some resources.

REALbasic plugin SDK

As the adage goes, "When all else fails, read the instructions." The REALbasic plugin SDK (Software Developer's Kit) is the first place you should look for information about REALbasic plugin programming. It features an extensive list of features and available functions, as well as many sample plugins. Many of your questions will be answered by this document alone. It's included on the *REALbasic For Dummies* CD.

MacTech magazine

www.mactech.com

MacTech magazine provides a steady stream of REALbasic programming information, including articles about plugin programming. They also have an online presence where you can download source code for each of their articles.

Thomas Tempelmann

```
http://www.tempel.org/rb/
```

Thomas Tempelmann has created a fantastic starter kit for REALbasic plugin programming. The kit includes a sample CodeWarrior project that you can use as a template for all your plugins. You also get CodeWarrior plugins that allow your code to compile plugins for the Windows x86 platform. This may be the second most important place to find information about plugins in REALbasic, after the SDK itself.

REALbasic plugins mailing list

```
http://www.realbasic.com/support.html
```

Imagine a place where all REALbasic plugin programmers go to discuss current plugin issues, ask each other questions, offer tips, and generally help each other out. Now, stop imagining, and go sign up for the REALbasic Plugins mailing list. This email list, maintained by REAL Software itself, allows you to post questions about your REALbasic plugin needs. You can learn a lot more, sometimes by eavesdropping on unsuspecting programmers as they unload all their tricks and secrets. They also frequently answer questions for plugin newbies, so don't be shy.

Chapter 18

Special Mac OS X and Windows Considerations

*R*EALbasic began life as a Classic Mac OS-based programming environment for PowerPC and 68K Macintosh computers. Therefore, Mac OS features sometimes overshadow the other great features in REALbasic. Ever since Version 2.0, REALbasic has offered the capability to create applications that run on Windows 95, 98, NT, and 2000 operating systems. With the release of REALbasic 3.0, REALbasic also offers you the chance to create applications that run on the latest Macintosh operating system, Mac OS X.

Because Mac OS X and Windows are very different than the classic Mac OS, it stands to reason that the applications that run on each system would also be quite different. In fact, they are so different that applications from one operating system will not work with another. REALbasic gives you all the tools you need to create each type of application. It also has a number of features that help you focus your efforts on each of the different target platforms.

This chapter examines how to build Mac OS X and Windows applications. It also gives you a few pointers about what to watch out for when you begin programming these types of applications.

While you read this chapter, keep in mind that these multiplatform features are limited to the Professional version of REALbasic. If you bought the Standard version instead of the Professional version, these features work, but your applications will run only for a demo period of five minutes.

Adding Code for a Specific Platform

REAL Software designed REALbasic with the intent that you could write code only once yet create applications for multiple platforms. In theory and more often than not in practice, this is true. When you add any of the standard interface controls, write code, and make use of variables (all standard fare for computer programs), REALbasic readily supports your multiplatform endeavors. Then reality hits.

It turns out that this claim of "write once, compile many times" is not always true. This is no fault of REAL Software. Rather, it's due to the fact that the target operating systems are so different. Some of these differences are purely cosmetic; others are fundamentally related to features of the operating system or hardware itself. Luckily, REAL Software had enough foresight to include some tools to help you when the operating systems begin to compete for your code.

Your main tool of defense in fighting the multiplatform code war is the #If statement. The #If statement tells the REALbasic compiler that builds your final application to use or disregard certain segments of source code. It works just like a normal If-Then statement but is reserved for the task of targeting particular platforms directly in your code.

For example, suppose you want a few lines of code to work for Mac OS applications and another set of code for the Windows platform. The #If statement allows you to do just that. It acts as a sort of source code shunt during the creation of your application by the REALbasic compiler.

To illustrate, consider this example:

```
#If TargetMacOS then
   MsgBox "Hello! I'm a Classic MacOS application"
#else
   MsgBox "Hello! I'm not a Classic MacOS application"
#EndIf
```

When you decide to build a Classic Mac OS application, REALbasic looks through this code and uses the MsgBox "Hello! I'm a Classic MacOS application" statement. On the other hand, if you are building a Mac OS X or Windows application, it uses the MsgBox "Hello! I'm not a Classic MacOS application" statement instead. As you can see, a close ally of the #If statement is the Target command. REALbasic has a full set of Target commands to cover each type of application you can create. Table 18-1 lists the complete set of commands for targeting each type of application.

Table 18-1	Commands for Targeting Platforms
Command	*Operating System and Platform*
Target68K	Classic 68K Macintosh
TargetPPC	Classic PPC Macintosh
TargetMacOS	Classic 68K Macintosh, Classic PPC Macintosh
TargetCarbon	Carbon PPC Macintosh
TargetWin32	Windows 95/98/NT/2000 x86

When to use each of these Target commands will become clearer as you progress through this chapter. Just keep in mind that this is how you write code for specific platforms. Most times, you won't need these commands because REALbasic performs most tasks equally on all platforms.

Some Mac OS X–Related Gotchas

Apple's newest operating system is entitled (or better yet, enumerated) Mac OS X. By the way, that's a Roman numeral 10, not the letter *X*. It changes lots of things about the Macintosh operating system we all know and love (and maybe sometimes loathe). It offers many outstanding improvements over previous versions of the Mac OS in the form of

- Dynamic memory
- True multithreading
- A revamped and stunning interface called Aqua
- Elimination of system freezes
- And much more

To take advantage of these new features, however, you must make your applications work with them. This is the purpose behind *Carbon* applications. Carbon applications are not much different from their recent Mac OS brethren. (Some older versions of the Mac OS can run Carbon applications if you configure them properly.) Carbon applications can take advantage of all the new features in Mac OS X. Classic Mac OS applications will run in Mac OS X but don't get the added benefits of Mac OS X. Rather, they run just as they always have — with crashes, the old interface, and the usual memory requirements.

The beautiful part about REALbasic is that you may not need to change any of your code to get instant Carbon compatibility. Simply build a new version for the Carbon target and your application automatically takes advantage of all the new features in Mac OS X. When this isn't the case, break out the #If statement to help isolate Carbon-only code.

Carbon code

The following may require you to add code for only the Carbon version of your application:

- Carbon-compatible REALbasic plugins
- Declare statements
- System-specific information

Plugins

REALbasic plugins come in a variety of flavors. Be sure to use only Carbon-compatible versions when creating Carbon applications. Sometimes developers create plugins with Carbon capabilities combined with other platform targets. In these cases, you can use the same code for each platform that the plugin supports. If the plugin does not support multiple platforms, you may have to use a plugin from another source to cover the functionality not found in the Carbon plugin. This is when the #If statement becomes vital.

For example, suppose that you have three different plugins. Each comes from a different vendor and each performs the same function but for one specific platform: Mac OS PPC, Mac OS 68K, or Carbon Mac OS. Because each plugin comes from a different vendor, it's likely that each plugin has a different command for the same function. This example shows how you might enter code for each of the platforms:

```
#If TargetMacPPC then
   DoThePPCFunction
#Endif
#If TargetMac68K then
   DoThe68KFunction
#Endif
#If TargetCarbon then
   DoTheCarbonFunction
#Endif
```

Declare statements

Just as plugins can help you add cool features to your REALbasic projects, Declare statements provide you with access to direct calls to the code of a particular operating system. These calls stem from information in special files called *libraries*. Each operating system has a different set of built-in libraries, so it should make sense that `Declare` statements differ depending on which platform you are targeting, including Mac OS X.

Because Carbon applications are so closely related to their predecessors, the code often looks identical to the Classic version but with a change to the library name. For example, the following call adjusts the volume of the system alert sound for both Classic and Carbon-compatible Macintosh operating systems:

```
Dim osErr as Integer
Dim lvlBlock as MemoryBlock

lvlBlock=NewMemoryBlock(4)
//Set the left channel (max. of 256)
lvlBlock.short(2)=256
//Set the right channel (max. of 256)
lvlBlock.short(0)=256

#If TargetCarbon then
Declare Function SetSysBeepVolume Lib "CarbonLib" (level as
          Integer) as Integer
#else
Declare Function SetSysBeepVolume Lib "InterfaceLib" (level
          as Integer) as Integer
#endif

osErr=SetSysBeepVolume(lvlBlock.long(0))
If osErr<0 then
  MsgBox "System Beep Volume Error: "+Str(osErr)
end if
```

Notice that the `SetSysBeepVolume` function is identical for both platforms, requiring only a change in the name of the code library (`CarbonLib` versus `InterfaceLib`).

System-specific issues

The release of Mac OS X brings with it a number of unique system-specific issues that you must address when building applications for it. Some of these issues include

- ✔ Locations for key operating system files
- ✔ Multiuser capabilities

The locations of files in the Classic Mac OS environment do not always have an equal or meaningful counterpart in the world of Mac OS X. Furthermore, now the Mac OS can have multiple users. All users of a single computer can have their own set of preferences, bookmarks, desktop background, installed applications, among many other differences. Don't forget to take into account some of the new changes in the Mac OS architecture when designing Mac OS X applications.

Introducing Aqua!

Along with all the new functionality, Mac OS X brings with it a new user interface named Aqua. While steeped in the tradition of Apple's award-winning interface, Aqua makes some significant changes. Aqua alters the color and appearance of virtually every element of the Macintosh interface (see Figure 18-1).

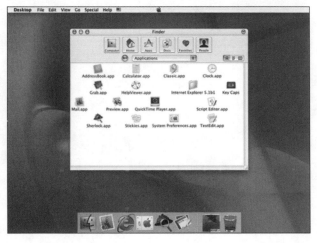

Figure 18-1:
Aqua changes the "look-and-feel" of the Mac OS in significant, yet beautiful ways.

REALbasic makes the transition to the new Aqua interface a snap. Simply compile your application for the Carbon target platform, and your interface instantly acquires all the new and improved spiffiness of Mac OS X, without altering one line of code.

The design of your interface, however, must change a bit. Controls in Aqua are generally a few pixels longer and wider than their Classic Mac OS counterparts. To compensate for this difference between operating systems, design the interface with Aqua in mind and the Classic Mac OS version should look just fine. Despite the small amount of work you must do to prepare for Aqua, your interfaces will instantly gain all of its handsome features.

Some Windows-Related Gotchas

When REALbasic added the capability to create Windows applications using the same code as Macintosh applications, a new era of rapid application development emerged. No longer was it necessary to painstakingly translate a lot of system-specific source code and interface issues from one platform to another. Simply write an application once and create a Macintosh or Windows version with only one mouse click.

This works in theory, but in practice, you may find that the nirvana of cross-platform development is not always so simple to attain. Before you head for the safety of one platform or, heaven forbid, go back to your previous cross-platform programming methods, relax in knowing that in most cases you can handle most issues with little effort.

What works

If you're shy about treading the waters of cross-platform development, you can follow a path that limits your exposure to potential problems. REALbasic provides a rich set of tools for creating Macintosh and Windows applications. The more rigid you are in using only these elements, the less changes you'll need to make for a particular platform. These tools include

- All standard REALbasic windows and controls
- REAL databases
- Cross-platform plugins
- Graphics, audio, and movies (requires QuickTime)
- Macintosh sound files
- Menus
- Custom controls

As you can see, a majority of REALbasic's features are cross-platform already. Stick to this list and you can usually guarantee compatibility between Macintosh and Windows versions of your projects.

What doesn't work

Again, REALbasic began as a tool for Macintosh development. As such, it can take advantage of several Macintosh technologies that have no appropriate Windows parallel. These include

- AppleScript
- Hypercard XCMDs
- Macintosh-only plugins
- Apple events

If you rely on any of these technologies to perform some important functionality, you'll be out of luck when it comes to Windows projects. Because of their reliance on principles of the Macintosh operating system, these technologies simply will not work. This is not to say that there isn't a way to accomplish some of the same tasks another way. You just have to hunt for solutions when they raise their ugly heads. For example, you can reproduce many functions that these technologies provide using `Declare` statements or Windows-compatible plugins.

One other place where Windows and Macintosh applications differ, sometimes wildly, is in their menus. The functionality of menus is no different, but the text that appears within them surely is. To make your REALbasic Windows application look like a Windows application, be sure to change the various menu items to match those of common Windows applications. Table 18-2 details some of the common similarities and differences between Macintosh and Windows menus.

Table 18-2	Common Macintosh and Windows Menus	
Menu	*Macintosh Shortcut*	*Windows Shortcut*
Open	⌘-O	Control+O
Save	⌘-S	Control+S
New	⌘-N	Control+N
Close	⌘-W	Alt+F5
Quit (Mac), Exit (Windows)	⌘-Q	Alt+F4
Copy	⌘-C	Control+C
Paste	⌘-V	Control+V

Building and Testing Mac OS X and Windows Applications

After you have narrowed down and eliminated cross-platform code and interface issues, its time to build the final application. As usual, the aim of REALbasic is to offer a simple one-step creation process, and it delivers on that promise. Building final versions of your application works just as it does for the Classic Mac OS: choose File⇨Build Application (or press Shift-⌘-M), make your final settings, and click OK.

This should work fine, given that you followed the recommendations in this chapter. If you look closely at the Build Settings, however, you'll notice a few options that vary for each intended target. This section explains what you need to know about each of these settings.

Mac OS X

Mac OS X versions of your REALbasic projects should compile and run just like the Classic Mac OS versions, with a few minor differences. For starters, Mac OS X applications don't have the traditional memory-setting requirements of their Classic Mac OS predecessors. Mac OS X offers dynamic memory allocation features, which is just a fancy way of saying that you never again have to assign a chunk of memory for each of your applications. Rather, Mac OS X grabs whatever amount of memory it needs whenever it needs it. Therefore, the memory settings have no effect when you go to build a final application with the Build dialog box in REALbasic, as shown in Figure 18-2.

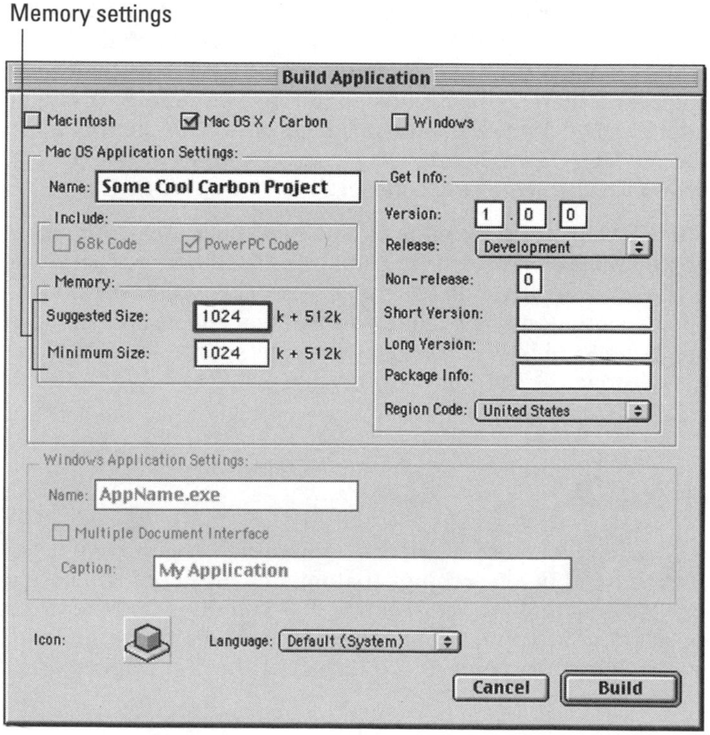

Figure 18-2:
Memory settings are a thing of the past for Mac OS X applications.

Be careful before you carelessly toss those memory requirements by the way-side just yet. Although Mac OS X offers numerous improvements over ver-sions of the Classic Mac OS, Mac OS X/Carbon applications are capable of running in Mac OS X and Classic Mac OS environments. When you intend to have your Mac OS X/Carbon application run on a version of the Mac OS before Mac OS X, be sure to make the memory settings just as you always have. Earlier versions of the Mac OS still rely on them, and forgetting to set the memory requirements appropriately is an easy way to make your applica-tion crash. If you're building applications for only Mac OS X or newer, how-ever, just go ahead and forget about your memory!

With your final Mac OS X application sitting there staring you in the face, you can finally test and ultimately use it. That was your goal for creating the REALbasic project in the first place, wasn't it? To test Mac OS X applications, you have a number of choices:

- **Mac OS X.** Mac OS X can run Carbon and Classic Mac OS applications. Only the Carbon versions display the Aqua makeover and updated oper-ating system features.

- **Mac OS 8.5 through Mac OS 9.** Versions of the Mac OS from 8.5 on up can run Carbon applications, as long as the Carbon Extension is present in the Extensions folder of System folder. Unlike with Mac OS X, however, your carbonized applications do not take advantage of the new Aqua interface and Mac OS X advanced features. They simply appear as Classic Mac OS applications. Of course, Classic versions of your REALbasic projects run as usual.

- **The REALbasic environment.** The REALbasic environment emulates applications as if they were running on a standard Macintosh computer. If you are using REALbasic under Mac OS X, your test environment sports all the Aqua eye candy and advanced features of Mac OS X. If you are using REALbasic on a Classic version of the Mac OS, you see the Classic Mac OS Platinum appearance.

Windows

It's easy to build and test Windows-compatible versions of your application with REALbasic, but a few things that might cause confusion are worth men-tioning. The final build process works like as it does for Mac brethren. Choose File➪Build Application, and REALbasic displays the Build Application dialog box. Select Windows as the target, as shown in Figure 18-3.

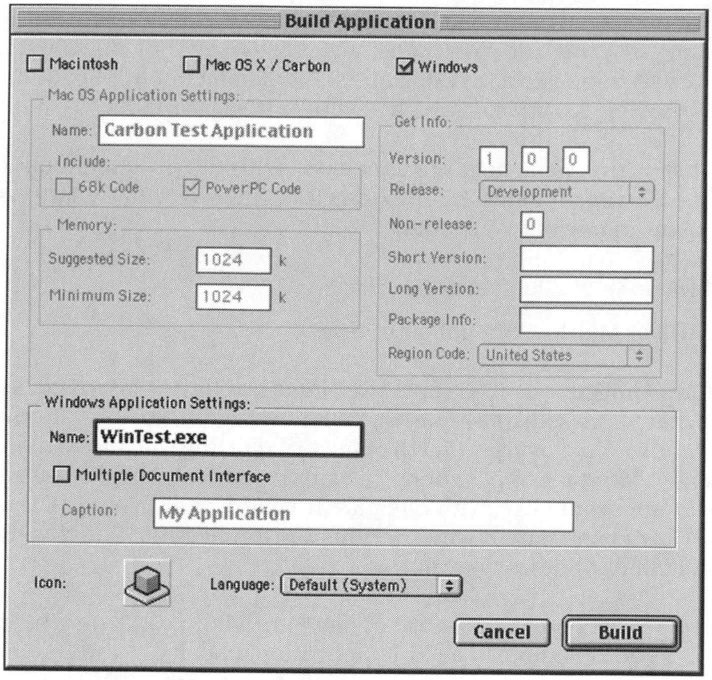

Figure 18-3:
A simple click is all it takes to get your REALbasic project to speak the language of Windows.

To set the icon for your final application, you need to copy an appropriate graphic to the Clipboard. You can accomplish this in a few ways:

- **Use a graphics application.** Fire up your favorite graphics application and create a graphic that has equal width and height. (This guarantees that it will scale properly if it's larger than standard icons.) Next, copy the graphic to the Clipboard by choosing Edit⇨Copy.

- **Use the Mac OS.** The Mac OS, unlike Windows, has always been handy for shuttling around icon graphics. If you see file with an icon that you like in the Finder, click it. Then, choose File⇨Get Info to gain access to the icon. A window appears with information about the file. In this window, select the icon in the top-left corner and choose Edit⇨Copy. This has the effect of copying the icon graphic to the Clipboard.

- **Assign the icon to your final build.** See the small picture in Figure 18-3? That's the icon for your final application. Select it and choose Edit⇨Paste to put your new icon in place of the default one.

This process changes the icon of your final application for Windows and Mac OS targets as well. Having set the icon, the next step is to give your application a name. This is the name end users will see when they use your application. It's customary to append the suffix .exe to Windows applications, indicating that they are *executable,* which is to say they do something rather than just sit there like a text document. To name your application, enter a title in the Name EditField, which is shown in Figure 18-3.

Right below the Name field is a check box with the peculiar sounding words Multiple Document Interface adjoining it. It turns out that Windows applications come in one of two flavors:

  ✔ SDI, or Single Document Interface
  ✔ MDI, or Multiple Document Interface

Windows applications that sport the Single Document Interface, as the name somewhat implies, display only one window at a time. This one window is the application, and closing it has the effect of quitting the application. Multiple Document Interface applications can simultaneously display as many windows as you would like, with one parent window containing all the child windows. Closing the parent window quits the application, but closing the various child windows does not.

If your application will make use of only one window, SDI may be the way to go. For a good example of an SDI application, check out the Calculator or WordPad application that comes with all installations of Microsoft operating systems. If you need multiple windows, or if you are unsure just what all this really means, use MDI. MDI provides a nice visual window backdrop to your application, and it won't ever steer you wrong. You'll probably use it the majority of the time anyway.

To use MDI, simply click the Multiple Document Interface check box in the Windows settings of the REALbasic Build dialog box (see Figure 18-3). Conversely, to use SDI, leave the Multiple Document Interface check box unchecked.

The final adjustment you must make before building your completed Windows application is changing the Caption setting in Figure 18-3. The Caption setting displays a title in your application's main window. The Caption field usually matches the Name field but without the customary .exe. This is also the text that appears in the taskbar when a user minimizes your application.

With all the settings in the Build dialog box complete, it's time to make the final application. Click the Build button or press Return, and REALbasic churns out a Windows-compatible application for you in seconds.

You need to test this Windows version by using it with a Windows operating system. REALbasic can't do that for you. REALbasic is a programming environment that runs on the Macintosh, so whenever you test your application in the REALbasic environment, you are seeing your application as a Macintosh application. This gives you an idea of what your application will look like in Windows, but it is not a test of your Windows code. If you have only a Macintosh on hand, PC emulators, such as the popular VirtualPC from Connectix, do the job admirably.

Part V
The Part of Tens

The 5th Wave   By Rich Tennant

"What do you mean you're updating our Web page?"

In this part . . .

Whether you need some help or would like to know a few pointers for making the most of your REALbasic skills, these chapters can help. The final part of the book gives you ten quick tips that the pros use for improving the REALbasic experience and ten important suggestions for evading trouble.

Chapter 19

Ten Tips for REAL Pros

*R*EALbasic is a great environment for creating applications quickly and easily, but you can make it even easier. After you use REALbasic for a while, you're bound to stumble across a variety of tricks that can save you lots of time. This chapter works to reduce the amount of time that passes before you discover some great tips. Some you might have figured out on your own after trial and error; others are hidden features. Either way, they work to accomplish one goal — saving you time. Follow these ten tips and you can drastically expedite your REALbasic programming endeavors.

Use Keyboard Shortcuts

One sure-fire way to speed up your REALbasic programming is to use the many available keyboard shortcuts. If you expand any of the menus in REALbasic, you see keyboard shortcuts for many options. Table 19-1 lists some of the most important ones.

Table 19-1	Common Keyboard Shortcuts
Shortcut	*Use It To*
⌘-S	Save
⌘-O	Open
⌘-Q	Quit
⌘-Shift-M	Build an application
⌘-Option-M	Create a method
⌘-Option-P	Create a property
⌘-1	Display the *Language Reference*
⌘-0	Display the Project window

Use these shortcuts whenever possible. The more you stay at the keyboard rather than reaching for the mouse, the more time you'll save.

Even cooler than the standard keyboard shortcuts are the hidden ones. Table 19-2 displays some of the secret keyboard tricks of the REALbasic Pros.

Table 19-2	Hidden Keyboard Shortcuts
Shortcut	*Use It To*
Option-Tab	Toggle between the Window Editor and Code Editor
⌘-Shift-/	Escape if your application freezes during testing
⌘-Z	Multiple undos take you back in time; REALbasic has no limits
Help key	Display the *Language Reference*

Duplicate Items in a Project

There may come a time when you want to make a copy of a window or a class in a project. You can't do so directly in the Project window, but the task is still simple.

Drag the window or class that you want to duplicate from the Project window to the desktop. In the Project window, rename the object you want to duplicate. Finally, drag the copy from the desktop back into the Project window.

Use Hidden Copy and Cut Features

The copy, paste, and cut features are great timesavers, but they're only the tip of the iceberg. REALbasic has hidden copy and cut features that enhance your Clipboard use tremendously.

To access the hidden features, press and hold the Shift key while choosing the Edit menu. The Copy and Cut menu items change to read Copy and Append and Cut and Append, respectively, as shown in Figure 19-1.

Figure 19-1:
Press the Shift key to see hidden Clipboard features.

The Copy and Append item copies the currently selected text and attaches it to the end of any text that already exists on the Clipboard. The Cut and Append menu item cuts the selected text and appends it to any text already on the Clipboard. This trick is useful for combining code from several different locations in your project.

Don't Forget Language Reference Tricks

The *Language Reference* that accompanies REALbasic is an invaluable tool. You'll find yourself using it nearly every time you sit down with REALbasic. To open the *Language Reference,* press ⌘-1 or the Help key. After the *Reference* is open, press ⌘-/ to expand the window to the full size of the screen.

You can search for entries in the *Language Reference* in one of two ways. First, place your mouse cursor in the Search field and type your search word. As you type the word, REALbasic attempts to auto-complete your typing. If it guesses correctly, you may press Tab to accept the guess. After you have finished entering the term, click Search or press Enter.

If you click somewhere outside the Search field but within the Language Reference window, you can begin typing the name of a REALbasic method or control. As you type, REALbasic attempts to guess what you are typing and automatically displays the information for its guess.

Disable Auto-Alignment

When you stretch and resize controls in the Window Editor, REALbasic always shows you when you are passing the edge of another control by displaying guidelines. At times, these guidelines can prevent you from easily positioning or resizing a control. If this happens, simply press the @cmd key while dragging to temporarily disable the auto-alignment feature of REALbasic. As soon as you let go of the ⌘ key, the feature reappears.

Use Drag-and-Drop

REALbasic supports all types of drag-and-drop features that can help you speed along your development. The most obvious drag-and-drop feature is in the *Language Reference.* The *Reference* has many code examples to demonstrate essential ideas of particular methods and control. You can drag these code samples directly into the Code Editor. The examples often make a good base from which to start programming.

The Project window also has important drag-and-drop features. You can add graphics files, sound files, custom classes, XCMDs, AppleScripts, databases, movie files, and REALbasic modules to you project by dragging them from the Finder directly to the Project window. The converse also holds true. You can drag any component of your project from the Project window to anywhere in the Finder. This is helpful for using components in other projects.

One peculiar drag-and-drop behavior of REALbasic is the capability to drag a window from the Project window to a PushButton in another window. When you do, the Code Editor immediately opens and REALbasic adds code to the `Action` Event of the PushButton likes this:

```
Sub Action()
Window1.Show
End Sub
```

Therefore, when a user presses this PushButton, Window1 appears.

To duplicate a control in a Window Editor, press and hold the Option key while dragging-and-dropping the control you want to duplicate.

Make Good Use of Text Clippings

One of Apple's greatest, yet perhaps the least mentioned, inventions is the text-clipping file. It's a file in the Finder that acts a little like a text file and a bit like a Clipboard. You can open a text clipping in the Finder by simply clicking it. It opens and has the appearance of a text file. The strange part is that it you don't need an application to view it. While you view it in the Finder, you can't alter it; it's read-only.

What's so great about a text clipping? It just begs you to drag and drop it places> Where? To places such as inside the REALbasic Code Editor. That's right! You may drag text clippings of source code directly into any event in the Code Editor. The *REALbasic For Dummies* CD has several code examples in text clipping format. Drag these from the CD on your desktop into any place you need them in your code, and you gain instant functionality without a single keystroke.

The reverse is also true. You can drag text from the REALbasic Code Editor to the Finder to create a text clipping of the code. This is extremely useful for storing commonly used code examples or when you want to transfer code from one project to another. To perform this action, select any text you want, and drag that selection to the Finder.

Let Auto-Complete Help

REALbasic has some handy auto-completion features that any poor speller or forgetful person will be certain to love. If you're neither, auto-completion can still help you.

As you merrily type away in the Code Editor, REALbasic is secretly watching every letter you type, but there's no reason to be paranoid. As you type, REALbasic attempts to guess what you're typing and displays its guess in light gray lettering. If it guesses correctly before you've typed the entire command, press the Tab key and the entire command appears before your eyes. You can usually get a match within two or three keys for most commands. REALbasic even watches for the names of properties, methods, or classes you've created and tries to auto-complete them.

Starting with REALbasic 3.0, auto-complete also shows you all possibilities in a miniature popup menu. Press the arrow keys to navigate this menu and press Enter when you reach your desired selection.

Select Multiple Items

When you create interfaces with REALbasic, it's sometimes useful to be able to move more than one control at a time. To do so, press Shift while clicking each control you want to move. As you select each one, a ring appears around the control.

If you need to deselect one of the controls in your selection, simply Shift-click the control you want to deselect. Deselecting all controls in this manner resets the Properties window, displaying the properties of the window itself. This can be a timesaver. It also helps if all the controls are obscuring the window, such that you can't select the window to change its properties.

Reuse Code

The last tip of this chapter isn't fancy. Rather, it's a feature of REALbasic that you might overlook. When you create methods in a module, they're global, which means anything in your project can access the included methods. This is a blessing in disguise. Because the methods are so readily accessible, you can export the module and drag it into any other project. The new project can make use of the new functions immediately.

Why reinvent the wheel each time you sit down to program? It makes much more sense, for example, to create a simple module that contains any methods you use a lot. The same holds true for classes. *Reuse* is the name of the game here. The more you reuse code, the less work you'll have to do. And when you work less, you play more! (I knew that would get your attention.)

For example, to export a module from your project, choose File⇨Export Module after selecting the Module in the Project window. The Export menu item changes depending on which component you have selected in the Project window. Select a window and the Export menu item changes to File⇨Export Window. To add the component to a new project, choose File⇨Import.

Chapter 20

Ten REAL Pitfalls and How to Avoid Them

● ●

In This Chapter

▶ Infinite loops

▶ Nil objects

▶ Your project losing its guts

▶ Flickering EditFields

▶ Automatic rebuilds

▶ Going back in time

▶ Generic application icons

▶ Disabled menus

▶ Flickering graphics

▶ Unreported bugs

● ●

*P*rogramming can be a fun and exciting skill, but not when you run into troubles. Computers are complicated creatures — and getting them to behave can be difficult. When you get stuck on a problem, computer programming begins to feel a lot more like work and a lot less like fun.

This chapter tries to help you through your darkest programming days by listing common problems you might run across while using REALbasic, along with their solutions. As you become proficient with REALbasic, you'll undoubtedly be able to add to this list.

Infinite Loops

Consider what happens if you enter the following code into the Action event of a PushButton:

```
Sub Action()
  Dim i as Integer
  i=5
  Do
    i=i+1
  Loop Until i=5
  MsgBox Str(i)
End Sub()
```

The code starts by defining and assigning a value of 5 to an integer (i). Next, a Do-Until loop starts, incrementing the i variable each time through the loop. The first time through the loop, i is equal to 6. This means the condition of i=5 at the end of the loop is not satisfied, nor will it ever be. The loop repeats forever. This kind of phenomenon is called an endless, or *infinite,* loop.

Infinite loops are nothing new to programming. Almost every programming language has some feature for repeating tasks. Infinite loops have been such a common malady that Apple Computer, Inc. even uses it in their address:

```
1 Infinite Loop
Cupertino, CA 95014
```

As you can see, you're in good company if you manage to get yourself stuck in an infinite loop.

When you test code that has an infinite loop, your computer will appear to freeze and displays the watch cursor, to indicate that it is performing a task. To escape from the loop, press ⌘-Shift-. (that's a period on the end, by the way). The REALbasic environment comes to the foreground and you can choose Debug⇨Kill to halt the execution of your program.

Sometimes, you'll unearth an infinite loop only after testing your code. With your handy ⌘-Shift-. escape route, though, you can easily break out of the loop and make some adjustments to prevent the loop from taking over your program. For example, to update the preceding code example, change it to something like this:

```
Sub Action()
  Dim i as Integer
  i=1
  Do
    i=i+1
  Loop Until i=5
  MsgBox Str(i)
End Sub()
```

This time around, the i variable starts with a value of 1. After the loop executes four times, i equals 5 and the loop ends.

Nil Objects

One of the biggest no-nos of object-oriented programming with REALbasic is attempting to access or use an object that doesn't exist. Consider this example:

```
Sub Open()
Dim p as Picture
dim i as Integer

i=p.Width
End Sub
```

Add this code in the Open event of a window and watch your program come to a screeching halt when you try to test it. REALbasic presents you with a formidable error:

```
Unhandled NilObjectException raised
```

To translate this into something more English-like, substitute the following words:

- NilObject = "Object doesn't exist"
- Exception = error
- raised = occurred

Thus, your newly translated error message reads:

```
Unhandled "Object doesn't exist" error occurred
```

That's much better, isn't it? Still, there's the issue of that leading Unhandled term. Unhandled simply means that you haven't taken care of this error yet.

Now, why doesn't the object exist? Because no one ever created it. For example, to create a Picture object, you can use the NewPicture method:

```
p = NewPicture(320,240,32)
```

The updated code would then look like this:

```
Sub Open()
Dim p as Picture
dim i as Integer

p = NewPicture(320,240,32)
i=p.Width
End Sub
```

If you test this code, you'll see that the error no longer occurs. Sometimes, however, this code will still fail. If the call to `NewPicture` is unable to create a new Picture object (due to low memory conditions, for example), the preceding code will continue to produce the same `Unhandled NilObjectException` error.

To safeguard against using an object that doesn't exist, you can check to see whether it exists first. If an object doesn't exist, it's equal to Nil. To test if an object exists, use code like this:

```
if p<>Nil then
   // we have an object!
   // so, we can use it here...
end if
```

In case you forgot, <> means *not equal to*. By making sure the object is not equal to Nil before attempting to use it, you avoid using code that tries to use a nonexistent object. The completed solution follows:

```
Sub Open()
Dim p as Picture
dim i as Integer

p = NewPicture(320,240,32)
if p <> Nil then
    i=p.Width
end if
End Sub
```

One important time to check for Nil objects is when you are using FolderItems. When you use the `GetOpenFolderItem` or `SelectFolder` method, you permit the user to choose a file or folder from the standard Open dialog box.

Keep in mind, however, that the Open dialog box has a Cancel button. If the user chooses to dismiss the Open dialog box without choosing a file, the `SelectFolder` or `GetOpenFolderItem` method does not return a FolderItem object. The next thing you know, REALbasic is flashing the familiar `Unhandled NilObjectException` error message again. The remedy works the same as it did for the picture object earlier.

The following example displays the name of a folder in a MsgBox, if the user chooses one and doesn't press Cancel:

```
dim f as FolderItem
f = SelectFolder
if f <> Nil then
  MsgBox f.Name
end if
```

Get in the habit of checking for Nil objects. Doing so will help you avoid debugging hassles — and your program won't crash on a user.

Your Project Losing Its Guts

One of REALbasic's great hidden features is that it can keep track of the location of your project's components on your hard drive. Whenever you drag a PICT, AppleScript, or audio file into the Project window, REALbasic silently takes note of the location from whence it came. (Take that, Shakespeare!) When you open the project later, REALbasic can continue using the components. Usually, that is.

Unfortunately, you, like all humans, are a finicky creature, constantly changing your mind. Perhaps you are a neat freak and frequently organize your files. Or maybe you just switched to a new hard drive. Whatever the case, when you start moving files around, REALbasic's behind-the-scenes work of keeping track of your files can go a little haywire. Consequently, REALbasic may not be able to find the original items in your project. When this occurs, REALbasic is usually pretty good about asking you to show it the location of a particular item. If you have many components in your project, however, locating each missing part is tedious. To speed this process, simply delete each of the external components from the Project window, and then drag fresh copies from the Finder back into the Project window.

Before you begin deleting components from your project, make sure it's safe to do so. The following items are safe to delete and add again to your project:

- ✔ Picture files (such as PICT, JPEG, or TIFF)
- ✔ QuickTime movies
- ✔ Audio files
- ✔ AppleScripts
- ✔ XCMDs

Do *not* delete any of the following unless you are certain that you have exported a copy at some point in the past:

- ✔ Windows
- ✔ Menus
- ✔ Modules
- ✔ Classes

The main idea here is that if you originally added the component to the project by dragging it from the Finder into the Project window, you may need to import it again if REALbasic can't find it. The remaining components of the project are part of the project file itself, so REALbasic won't lose tracks of them.

Flickering EditFields

If you are new to programming, you may not fully appreciate some of the grunt work that REALbasic automatically does for you. For example, whenever you move a window around on the screen, REALbasic takes care of refreshing the screen for you. Because this refresh behavior is automatic, it can sometimes produce undesirable effects. For example, it's perfectly correct to add text to an EditField like this:

```
EditField1.Text = EditField1.Text + "abc"
```

One side effect, however, is that the EditField flashes or flickers when this code executes. You may not notice the effect from this one line of code, but if you perform this operation repeatedly, you'll definitely witness it. Why? When you change the Text property of an EditField, REALbasic automatically refreshes the display of the EditField, causing a brief flicker of light while redrawing it.

Luckily, the solution is simple. Instead of changing the Text property directly, set the location where you want to append the text, which is the end of the EditField's current text, in this example:

```
EditField1.SelStart = Len(EditField1.Text)
```

Then tack on the text with the following command:

```
EditField1.SelText = "More text"
```

When you add text to an EditField in this manner, the automatic refresh doesn't occur and your EditField becomes flicker-free.

Automatic Crash Recovery

While programming with REALbasic, you may one day crash during a test run. Remember that, as a programmer, you sometimes access low-level aspects of the operation of a computer. Also keep in mind that accessing this low level can sometimes leave your computer in a compromising position — ready to crash. Should you crash your machine while testing your code, REALbasic will attempt — with your approval — to recover the project file the next time you open it.

Going Back in Time

Nobody's perfect all the time, and REALbasic has a great feature to help you out when you aren't. Whenever you make a false move and enter the wrong code, move a control to a bad location, or resize a window to the wrong dimensions, you can easily go back in time to repair any mistakes you made.

To undo any mistakes, choose Edit⇨Undo or press ⌘-Z. REALbasic automatically updates your project as if you hadn't performed the last action at all. Even cooler, you can continue undoing actions to your heart's content. REALbasic has unlimited Undos. This means you can go back 5, 10, or even 100 steps backwards in time. Now, if only you could get REALbasic to accomplish the same feat for humans.

Generic Application Icons

After you have written and tested your code, the final step of software creation is to build an executable application. When you do so, you can assign a custom icon to the application by pasting an icon from the Clipboard into the icon box of the Build dialog box. If everything goes smoothly, an application with the appropriate icon should appear in the Finder. If everything doesn't go smoothly, an application with a generic icon appears in the Finder, as shown in Figure 20-1.

Figure 20-1:
Sometimes your new application's icon gets lost and reverts to a generic application icon.

The application should work properly. It just has the wrong icon. Furthermore, when you run the application, the icon that appears in the Application Switcher or Dock (depending on which version of the Mac OS you're using) is generic.

A few things can cause this behavior. First, be sure that you have given your application a creator code. A *creator code* is a 4-character alphanumeric sequence that uniquely identifies your application. Because this code identifies your own application, the Mac OS uses it to keep track of the custom icon that it should use with your application. If you manage to use the same creator code as that of an existing application, don't be surprised to see your application's icon suddenly morph into an icon of another application.

To add a creator code to your project, choose Edit⇨Project Settings. The Project Settings dialog box appears. In the Mac Creator field, enter the four-character creator code, shown in Figure 20-2.

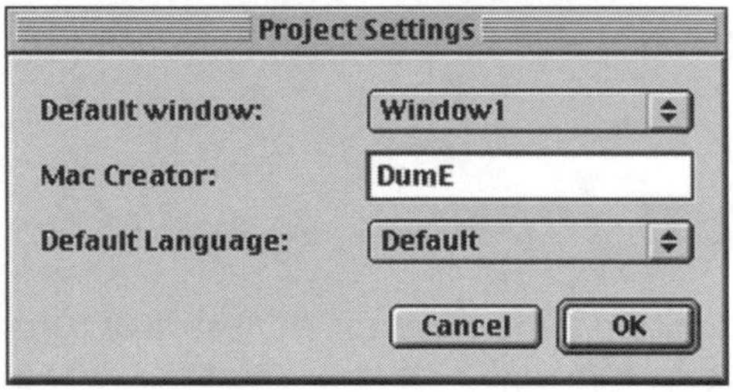

Figure 20-2:
Set your application's creator code here.

```
Project Settings
Default window:      Window1      ▲▼
Mac Creator:         DumE
Default Language:    Default      ▲▼
                     Cancel        OK
```

If you have an idea for a creator code and want to make sure another application isn't already using it, you can check Apple's site. You can search for any creator code combinations you can dream up:

```
developer.apple.com/dev/cftype/find.html
```

To ensure that your application has its own creator code, it's a good idea to register your application with Apple. Apple maintains a database of creator codes that identify every application in existence (at least for those who register). It takes only a few seconds to register, and then you have the peace of mind that your application will own its own creator code. Did I mention that registration is free? To register your creator code, go here:

```
developer.apple.com/dev/cftype/register.html
```

After you procure a unique creator code, you may still find that your newly built application does not properly display its custom icon. If this happens, your best bet is to rebuild the desktop database, which keeps track of file icon information. By forcing it to rebuild itself, you can be sure that it discovers your newly created application and its creator code.

To rebuild the desktop database, restart your Macintosh while pressing ⌘-Option. Continue to press this key combination for the duration of the startup process.

Disabled Menus

On occasion, you may find that a menu doesn't refresh and appear as you expect. Luckily, it's not difficult to cure this problem. Simply use the `EnableMenuItems` method whenever you want to force a menu refresh.

The most common menu refresh problems occur when you close a modal or movable modal dialog box. Sometimes the menu bar doesn't refresh, which can disable it. In this situation, call `EnableMenuItems` in the `Close` event of the window:

```
Sub Close()
   EnableMenuItems
End Sub
```

Flickering Canvas

Just as Editfields can flicker when you update them, Canvas controls can too. Programmers have long used a trick to minimize the flickering that can occur when creating computer graphics. Instead of the usual task of drawing directly to the Graphics object of a Canvas, it's faster to first draw to a Picture object and then transfer the picture to the Graphics object of the Canvas. Although two steps are involved instead of one, the process is faster and virtually eliminates the flickering Canvas effect.

To illustrate, draw a simple square in the `Paint` event of a Canvas:

```
Sub Paint(g as Graphics)
   g.Fillrect 0,0,me.Width,me.Height
End Sub
```

Although you'll be hard pressed to see the difference with only this small square, in more complex examples you'll instantly recognize the flicker.

The preferred method is to draw to a Picture object and then transfer (also known as *blit*) the graphics from the Picture object directly to the Canvas:

```
Sub Paint(g as Graphics)
   Dim myPicture as Picture
   myPicture = newpicture(100,100,32)
   myPicture.Graphics.FillRect 0,0,100,100
   g.DrawPicture myPicture,0,0
End Sub
```

Because you can't see the Picture object as you draw to it, programmers often say they are *drawing offscreen*. By drawing offscreen first and blitting the result to a Canvas, you can safely say goodbye to flicker.

Unreported Bugs

At some point in your REALbasic journey, you may run across what you think is a bug in REALbasic. REAL Software encourages you to report bugs to them. They even went to the trouble of creating an application for reporting bugs to them. It's called REALBugs.

REALBugs is on the *REALbasic For Dummies* CD and at the REALbasic homepage:

```
www.realbasic.com
```

On occasion, REAL Software provides free updates with feature enhancements and bug fixes. These features and fixes are the result of users like you reporting problems to REAL Software. By submitting bug reports, you help REAL Software provide you with the best possible product. Because REAL Software updates REALbugs from time to time, be sure to check their Web site periodically for the latest version.

Appendix

About the CD

On the CD-ROM:

- ✔ REALbasic 3.0, the award-winning development environment
- ✔ Valentina, a great database demo for use with REALbasic
- ✔ Loads of useful plugins and code from leading REALbasic developers
- ✔ Code examples covering all aspects of REALbasic development to help you create useful and fun applications quickly

System Requirements

Make sure that your computer meets the minimum system requirements listed in the following. If your computer doesn't match up to most of these requirements, you may have problems using the contents of the CD.

- ✔ A Mac OS computer with a 68040 or faster processor.
- ✔ Mac OS system software 7.6.1 or later.
- ✔ At least 16 MB of total RAM installed on your computer. For best performance, we recommend at least 32MB of RAM.
- ✔ At least 50MB of hard drive space available to install all the software from this CD. (You need less space if you don't install every program.)
- ✔ QuickTime 3.0 or higher.
- ✔ A CD-ROM drive — double-speed (2x) or faster.
- ✔ A monitor capable of displaying at least 256 colors or grayscale.
- ✔ A modem with a speed of at least 14,400 bps.

If you need more information on the basics, check out *PCs For Dummies,* 7th Edition, by Dan Gookin; *Macs For Dummies,* 6th Edition, by David Pogue; *iMac For Dummies,* by David Pogue; *Windows 98 For Dummies, or Windows 95 For Dummies,* 2nd Edition, all by Andy Rathbone (all published by Hungry Minds, Inc.)

Using the CD

To install the items from the CD to your hard drive, follow these steps:

1. **Insert the CD into your computer's CD-ROM drive.**

   In a moment, an icon representing the CD you just inserted appears on your Mac desktop. Chances are, the icon looks like a CD-ROM.

2. **Double-click the CD icon to show the CD's contents.**

3. **Double-click the License Agreement icon.**

   This is the license that you are agreeing to by using the CD. You can close this window after you've looked over the agreement.

4. **Double-click the Read Me First icon.**

   The Read Me First text file contains information about the CD's programs and any last-minute instructions you may need to install them correctly.

5. **To install most programs, open the program folder and double-click the icon called Install or Installer.**

   Sometimes the installers are self-extracting archives, which means that the program files have been bundled into an archive, and this self-extractor unbundles the files and places them on your hard drive. This kind of program is often called an .sea. If you double-click anything with .sea in the title, it will run just like an installer.

6. **Some programs don't come with installers. For those, just drag the program's folder from the CD window and drop it onto your hard drive icon.**

After you have installed the programs you want, you can eject the CD. Carefully place it back in the plastic jacket of the book for safekeeping.

What You'll Find

Shareware programs are fully functional, free, trial versions of copyrighted programs. If you like particular programs, register with their authors for a nominal fee and receive licenses, enhanced versions, and technical support. *Freeware programs* are free, copyrighted games, applications, and utilities. You can copy them to as many computers as you like — free — but they have no technical support. GNU software is governed by its own license, which is included inside the folder of the GNU software. There are no restrictions on distribution of this software. See the GNU license for more details. *Trial, demo,* or *evaluation versions* are usually limited either by time or functionality (such as being unable to save projects).

REALbasic category

REALbasic 3.0, from REAL Software

For Mac OS. Trial version. In case you don't have a connection to the information superhighway, the CD includes a 30-day trial version of REALbasic 3.0.

With the 30-day trial version of REALbasic, you can program using the Classic Mac OS environment as well as the spiffy new Mac OS X. Projects created with REALbasic can produce applications for Classic and Carbon Macintosh environments as well as Windows 95, 98, NT, and 2000. Applications created with the trial version of REALbasic display a warning dialog box each time they are executed and shut down in five minutes.

Tasty Bytes category

Sample files from the book, by the author

For Mac. These files contain all the sample code from the book, as well as accessory files for creating fun and useful applications. You can browse these files directly from the CD, or you can copy them to your hard drive and use them as the basis for your own projects. To find the files on the CD, open the Tasty Bytes folder. To copy the files to your hard drive, just drag the Tasty Bytes folder to your hard drive.

Source code snippets, by the author

For Mac. Handy source code examples to accompany the sample code in the book. The short pieces of code demonstrate methods for accomplishing various common tasks. They are stored in Text Clipping format. To use the code in your REALbasic project, open the Code Editor to the desired location and drag the Text Clipping into the REALbasic Code Editor. You may also open Text Clipping in the Finder and choose Edit⇨Copy to paste the code example to the clipboard. Later, you can insert it into your REALbasic project by choosing Edit⇨Paste.

Useful Tools category

Valentina, from Paradigma Software c/o Proactive International

For Mac and Windows. Demo. If you manage to outgrow the built-in REALbasic database format, Valentina offers a compelling upgrade. Created with cross-platform access, speed, and interoperability with REALbasic in mind, Valentina makes a fine addition to any developer's arsenal.

ToolBox-Methods R1, by Doug Holton

For Mac (adaptable to Windows). Tutorial. A code tutorial in electronic book format about the many uses of the REALbasic `Declare` command. It shows simple and useful examples to help you get a grip on the fundamentals of using the `Declare` statement.

WASTEfield Plugin PPC, by Doug Holton

For Mac. Freeware. A custom control plugin implementing the popular TextEdit replacement written by Marco Piovanelli. You can use it to supplement or even replace the standard REALbasic EditField control. With the WASTEfield plugin, you can embed audio and graphics in an EditField-like control and perform numerous text manipulations with ease.

FileIcon Plugin, by Doug Holton

For Mac. Freeware. This plugin allows you to retrieve the icon from any file on your hard drive and display it in a REALbasic Canvas.

AppleScript Plugin, by Doug Holton

For Mac. Freeware. A unique plugin that gives you the capability to run or record AppleScripts on the fly from within your REALbasic projects.

Window Splitter, Shapes, Style Grid, Custom Grid, and Grid Control Plugins, from Einhugur Software

For Mac. Demo. A set of fantastic controls for anyone's REALbasic toolbox. These plugins provide cool visual controls for spicing up your interface.

MADPlug, from Essence Software

For Mac. Freeware. MADPlug is a plugin for REALbasic that allows developers to play SoundTracker format music files. It makes use of the PlayerPro MADLibrary, written by Antoine Rosset. MADPlug supports the playback of MAD, MOD, S3M, XM, IT, OCTA, MTM, and MED format music files. The use of tracker format music is good for performance-critical applications such as games.

QD3DViewer, from Essence Software

For Mac. Freeware. QD3DViewer is a plugin for REALbasic that allows developers to provide previewing and manipulation of 3DMF files in their applications.

Nubz SMTPSocket, from Nubz Development

For Mac. Freeware. Need to send email from within a REALbasic project? Give the Nubz SMTPSocket a try!

Speech Recognition, from Nubz Development

For Mac. Freeware. Classes and a plugin for adding interesting speech recognition capabilities to your own applications.

TT's FolderItem Extension, by Thomas Tempelmann

For Mac. Freeware. Use this plugin to launch applications in the background and open documents with any application.

RB Plugin Plunger, by Thomas Tempelmann

For Mac. Freeware. RB Plugin Plunger is an application that looks inside any REALbasic plugin to reveal its methods, properties, and other vital information. This is an invaluable tool for instantly recalling how any plugin works.

Plugin Starter, by Thomas Tempelmann

For Mac and Microsoft Windows. Freeware. If you are itching to try your hand at creating REALbasic plugins, Thomas Tempelmann's Plugin Starter is an excellent place to begin. It lays out all the code in a well-documented manner and enables you to build plugins for Classic Macintosh, Carbon, and Windows applications.

hairlines@last, from ZegSoft

For Mac. Demo. The hairlines@last plugin gives users of REALbasic 2.1.2 the opportunity to add high-resolution printing to their projects. New printing features in REALbasic 3.0 make this plugin unnecessary for REALbasic 3.0 users.

SPBAudioLib, by Benjamin Schneider

For Mac. Freeware. 49 REALbasic methods for recording audio on the Macintosh.

If You Have Problems of the CD Kind

I tried my best to compile programs that work on most computers with the minimum system requirements. Alas, your computer may differ, and some programs may not work properly for some reason.

The two likeliest problems are that you don't have enough memory (RAM) for the programs you want to use, or you have other programs running that are affecting the installation or running of a program. If you get error messages such as `Not enough memory` or `Setup cannot continue`, try one or more of these methods and then try using the software again:

- **Turn off any antivirus software that you have on your computer.** Installers sometimes mimic virus activity and may make your computer incorrectly believe that a virus is infecting it.

- **Close all running programs.** The more programs you're running, the less memory is available to other programs. Installers also typically update files and programs; if you keep other programs running, installation may not work properly.

✔ **Have your local computer store add more RAM to your computer.** This is, admittedly, a drastic and somewhat expensive step. However, if you have a Mac OS computer with a PowerPC chip, adding more memory can really help the speed of your computer and enable more programs to run at the same time.

If you still have trouble installing the items from the CD, please call the Hungry Minds Customer Service phone number: 800-762-2974 (outside the U.S., call 317-572-3993).

Index

Notes

Notes

Notes

Hungry Minds, Inc.
End-User License Agreement

READ THIS. You should carefully read these terms and conditions before opening the software packet(s) included with this book ("Book"). This is a license agreement ("Agreement") between you and Hungry Minds, Inc. ("HMI"). By opening the accompanying software packet(s), you acknowledge that you have read and accept the following terms and conditions. If you do not agree and do not want to be bound by such terms and conditions, promptly return the Book and the unopened software packet(s) to the place you obtained them for a full refund.

1. **License Grant.** HMI grants to you (either an individual or entity) a nonexclusive license to use one copy of the enclosed software program(s) (collectively, the "Software") solely for your own personal or business purposes on a single computer (whether a standard computer or a workstation component of a multi-user network). The Software is in use on a computer when it is loaded into temporary memory (RAM) or installed into permanent memory (hard disk, CD-ROM, or other storage device). HMI reserves all rights not expressly granted herein.

2. **Ownership.** HMI is the owner of all right, title, and interest, including copyright, in and to the compilation of the Software recorded on the disk(s) or CD-ROM ("Software Media"). Copyright to the individual programs recorded on the Software Media is owned by the author or other authorized copyright owner of each program. Ownership of the Software and all proprietary rights relating thereto remain with HMI and its licensers.

3. **Restrictions On Use and Transfer.**

    (a) You may only (i) make one copy of the Software for backup or archival purposes, or (ii) transfer the Software to a single hard disk, provided that you keep the original for backup or archival purposes. You may not (i) rent or lease the Software, (ii) copy or reproduce the Software through a LAN or other network system or through any computer subscriber system or bulletin-board system, or (iii) modify, adapt, or create derivative works based on the Software.

    (b) You may not reverse engineer, decompile, or disassemble the Software. You may transfer the Software and user documentation on a permanent basis, provided that the transferee agrees to accept the terms and conditions of this Agreement and you retain no copies. If the Software is an update or has been updated, any transfer must include the most recent update and all prior versions.

4. **Restrictions on Use of Individual Programs.** You must follow the individual requirements and restrictions detailed for each individual program in the "About the CD" appendix of this Book. These limitations are also contained in the individual license agreements recorded on the Software Media. These limitations may include a requirement that after using the program for a specified period of time, the user must pay a registration fee or discontinue use. By opening the Software packet(s), you will be agreeing to abide by the licenses and restrictions for these individual programs that are detailed in the "About the CD" appendix and on the Software Media. None of the material on this Software Media or listed in this Book may ever be redistributed, in original or modified form, for commercial purposes.

5. **Limited Warranty.**

   (a) HMI warrants that the Software and Software Media are free from defects in materials and workmanship under normal use for a period of sixty (60) days from the date of purchase of this Book. If HMI receives notification within the warranty period of defects in materials or workmanship, HMI will replace the defective Software Media.

   (b) **HMI AND THE AUTHOR OF THE BOOK DISCLAIM ALL OTHER WARRANTIES, EXPRESS OR IMPLIED, INCLUDING WITHOUT LIMITATION IMPLIED WARRANTIES OF MERCHANTABILITY AND FITNESS FOR A PARTICULAR PURPOSE, WITH RESPECT TO THE SOFTWARE, THE PROGRAMS, THE SOURCE CODE CONTAINED THEREIN, AND/OR THE TECHNIQUES DESCRIBED IN THIS BOOK. HMI DOES NOT WARRANT THAT THE FUNCTIONS CONTAINED IN THE SOFTWARE WILL MEET YOUR REQUIREMENTS OR THAT THE OPERATION OF THE SOFTWARE WILL BE ERROR FREE.**

   (c) This limited warranty gives you specific legal rights, and you may have other rights that vary from jurisdiction to jurisdiction.

6. **Remedies.**

   (a) HMI's entire liability and your exclusive remedy for defects in materials and workmanship shall be limited to replacement of the Software Media, which may be returned to HMI with a copy of your receipt at the following address: Software Media Fulfillment Department, Attn.: REALbasic For Dummies, Hungry Minds, Inc., 10475 Crosspoint Blvd., Indianapolis, IN 46256, or call 1-800-762-2974. Please allow four to six weeks for delivery. This Limited Warranty is void if failure of the Software Media has resulted from accident, abuse, or misapplication. Any replacement Software Media will be warranted for the remainder of the original warranty period or thirty (30) days, whichever is longer.

   (b) In no event shall HMI or the author be liable for any damages whatsoever (including without limitation damages for loss of business profits, business interruption, loss of business information, or any other pecuniary loss) arising from the use of or inability to use the Book or the Software, even if HMI has been advised of the possibility of such damages.

   (c) Because some jurisdictions do not allow the exclusion or limitation of liability for consequential or incidental damages, the above limitation or exclusion may not apply to you.

7. **U.S. Government Restricted Rights.** Use, duplication, or disclosure of the Software for or on behalf of the United States of America, its agencies and/or instrumentalities (the "U.S. Government") is subject to restrictions as stated in paragraph (c)(1)(ii) of the Rights in Technical Data and Computer Software clause of DFARS 252.227-7013, or subparagraphs (c) (1) and (2) of the Commercial Computer Software - Restricted Rights clause at FAR 52.227-19, and in similar clauses in the NASA FAR supplement, as applicable.

8. **General.** This Agreement constitutes the entire understanding of the parties and revokes and supersedes all prior agreements, oral or written, between them and may not be modified or amended except in a writing signed by both parties hereto that specifically refers to this Agreement. This Agreement shall take precedence over any other documents that may be in conflict herewith. If any one or more provisions contained in this Agreement are held by any court or tribunal to be invalid, illegal, or otherwise unenforceable, each and every other provision shall remain in full force and effect.

Installation Instructions

The *REALbasic For Dummies* CD offers valuable information that you won't want to miss. To install the items from the CD to your hard drive, follow these steps.

1. **Insert the CD into your computer's CD-ROM drive.**

   In a moment, an icon representing the CD you just inserted appears on your Mac desktop. Chances are, the icon looks like a CD-ROM.

2. **Double-click the CD icon to show the CD's contents.**

3. **Double-click the License Agreement icon.**

   This is the license that you are agreeing to by using the CD. You can close this window after you've looked over the agreement.

4. **Double-click the Read Me First icon.**

   The Read Me First text file contains information about the CD's programs and any last-minute instructions you may need to install them correctly.

5. **To install most programs, open the program folder and double-click the icon called Install or Installer.**

   Sometimes the installers are self-extracting archives, which means that the program files have been bundled into an archive, and this self-extractor unbundles the files and places them on your hard drive. This kind of program is often called an .sea. If you double-click anything with .sea in the title, it will run just like an installer.

6. **Some programs don't come with installers. For those, just drag the program's folder from the CD window and drop it onto your hard drive icon.**

After you have installed the programs you want, you can eject the CD. Carefully place it back in the plastic jacket of the book for safekeeping.

For more information, see the "About the CD" appendix.

FOR DUMMIES
BOOK REGISTRATION

Register
This Book
and Win!

We want to hear from you!

Visit **dummies.com** to register this book and tell us how you liked it!

✔ Get entered in our monthly prize giveaway.

✔ Give us feedback about this book — tell us what you like best, what you like least, or maybe what you'd like to ask the author and us to change!

✔ Let us know any other *For Dummies* topics that interest you.

Your feedback helps us determine what books to publish, tells us what coverage to add as we revise our books, and lets us know whether we're meeting your needs as a *For Dummies* reader. You're our most valuable resource, and what you have to say is important to us!

Not on the Web yet? It's easy to get started with *Dummies 101: The Internet For Windows 98* or *The Internet For Dummies* at local retailers everywhere.

Or let us know what you think by sending us a letter at the following address:

For Dummies Book Registration
Dummies Press
10475 Crosspoint Blvd.
Indianapolis, IN 46256

...FOR DUMMIES™

BESTSELLING
BOOK SERIES